CALIFORNIA TRAILS
NORTH COAST REGION

Printed in the United States of America

Cover photos
Clockwise from bottom left: South Shore Drive, South Shore Drive, Mount Shasta Loop

Rear cover photos
From left: Grizzly Peak Trail, New Pine Creek to Fort Bidwell Trail

CALIFORNIA TRAILS
NORTH COAST REGION

PETER MASSEY
JEANNE WILSON
ANGELA TITUS

ADLER
PUBLISHING

Acknowledgements

Many people and organizations have made significant contributions to the research and production of this book.

Cover Design Concept: **Rudy Ramos**
Text Design and Maps: **Deborah Rust Design**
Layout: **Bob Schram**
Copyediting and Proofreading: **Sallie Greenwood, Alice Levine**

We would like to thank Scott J. Lawson, director, and staff of the Plumas
County Museum; Deborah Tibbetts, district archaeologist at Lassen National
Forest; Bev Way, Bill Tierney, Jami Nield, Nancy Gardner, and Gerald R. Gates
of Modoc National Forest.

Staff at many offices of the National Forest Service also provided us with
valuable assistance.

Publisher's Note: Every effort has been taken to ensure that the information in
this book is accurate at press time. Please visit our website to advise us of any
changes or corrections you find. We also welcome recommendations for new
4WD trails or other suggestions to improve the information in this book.

Adler Publishing Company, Inc.
1601 Pacific Coast Highway, Suite 290
Hermosa Beach, CA 90254
Phone: 800-660-5107
Fax: 310-698-0709
4WDbooks.com

ADLER
PUBLISHING

Contents

Before You Go

Why a 4WD Does It Better

The design and engineering of 4WD vehicles provide them with many advantages over normal cars when you head off the paved road:
- improved distribution of power to all four wheels;
- a transmission transfer case, which provides low-range gear selection for greater pulling power and for crawling over difficult terrain;
- high ground clearance;
- less overhang of the vehicle's body past the wheels, which provides better front- and rear-clearance when crossing gullies and ridges;
- large-lug, wide-tread tires;
- rugged construction (including under-body skid plates on many models).

If you plan to do off-highway touring, all of these considerations are important whether you are evaluating the capabilities of your current 4WD or are looking to buy one; each is considered in detail in this chapter.

To explore the most difficult trails described in this book, you will need a 4WD vehicle that is well rated in each of the above features. If you own a 2WD sport utility vehicle, a lighter car-type SUV, or a pickup truck, your ability to explore the more difficult trails will depend on conditions and your level of experience.

A word of caution: Whatever type of 4WD vehicle you drive, understand that it is not invincible or indestructible. Nor can it go everywhere. A 4WD has a much higher center of gravity and weighs more than a car, and so has its own consequent limitations.

Experience is the only way to learn what your vehicle can and cannot do. Therefore, if you are inexperienced, we strongly recommend that you start with trails that have lower difficulty ratings. As you develop an understanding of your vehicle and of your own taste for adventure, you can safely tackle the more challenging trails.

One way to beef up your knowledge quickly, while avoiding the costly and sometimes dangerous lessons learned from on-the-road mistakes, is to undertake a 4WD course taught by a professional. Look in the Yellow Pages for courses in your area.

Using This Book

Route Planning

The regional map on pages xx and xx provide a convenient overview of the trails in that portion of the state northern and western part of California. Each 4WD trail is shown, as are major highways and towns, helping you plan various routes by connecting a series of 4WD trails and paved roads.

As you plan your overall route, you will probably want to utilize as many 4WD trails as possible. However, check the difficulty rating and time required for each trail before finalizing your plans. You don't want to be stuck 50 miles from the highway—at sunset and without camping gear, since your trip was supposed to be over hours ago—when you discover that your vehicle can't handle a certain difficult passage.

Difficulty Ratings

We utilize a point system to rate the difficulty of each trail. Any such system is subjective, and your experience of the trails will vary depending on your skill and the road conditions at the time. Indeed, any amount of rain may make the trails much more difficult, if not completely impassable.

We have rated the 4WD trails on a scale of 1 to 10—1 being passable for a normal passenger vehicle in good conditions and 10 requiring a heavily modified vehicle and an experienced driver who expects to encounter vehicle damage. Because this book is designed for owners of unmodified 4WD vehicles—who we assume do not want to damage their vehicles—most of the trails are rated 5 or lower. A few trails are included that rate as high as 7, while those rated 8 to 10 are beyond the scope of this book.

This is not to say that the moderate-rated trails are easy. We strongly recommend that inexperienced drivers not tackle trails rated at 4 or higher until they have undertaken a number of the lower-rated ones, so that they can gauge their skill level and prepare for the difficulty of the higher-rated trails.

In assessing the trails, we have always assumed good road conditions (dry road surface, good visibility, and so on). The factors influencing our ratings are as follows:

■ obstacles such as rocks, mud, ruts, sand, slickrock, and stream crossings;
■ the stability of the road surface;
■ the width of the road and the vehicle clearance between trees or rocks;
■ the steepness of the road;
■ the margin for driver error (for example, a very high, open shelf road would be rated more difficult even if it was not very steep and had a stable surface).

The following is a guide to the ratings.

Rating 1: The trail is graded dirt but suitable for a normal passenger vehicle. It usually has gentle grades, is fairly wide, and has very shallow water crossings (if any).

Rating 2: High-clearance vehicles are preferred but not necessary. These trails are dirt roads, but they may have rocks, grades, water crossings, or ruts that make clearance a concern in a normal passenger vehicle. The trails are fairly wide, making passing possible at almost any point along the trail. Mud is not a concern under normal weather conditions.

Rating 3: High-clearance 4WDs are preferred, but any high-clearance vehicle is acceptable. Expect a rough road surface; mud and sand are possible but will be easily passable. You may encounter rocks up to 6 inches in diameter, a loose road surface, and shelf roads, though these will be wide enough for passing or will have adequate pull-offs.

Rating 4: High-clearance 4WDs are recommended, though most stock SUVs are acceptable. Expect a rough road surface with rocks larger than 6 inches, but there will be a reasonable driving line available. Patches of mud are possible but can be readily negotiated; sand may be deep and require lower tire pressures. There may be stream crossings up to 12 inches deep, substantial sections of single-lane shelf road, moderate grades, and sections of moderately loose road surface.

Rating 5: High-clearance 4WDs are required. These trails have either a rough, rutted surface, rocks up to 9 inches, mud and deep sand that may be impassable for inexperienced drivers, or stream crossings up to 18 inches deep. Certain sections may be steep enough to cause traction problems, and you may encounter very narrow shelf roads with steep drop-offs and tight clearance between rocks or trees.

Rating 6: These trails are for experienced four-wheel drivers only. They are potentially dangerous, with large rocks, ruts, or terraces that may need to be negotiated. They may also have stream crossings at least 18 inches deep, involve rapid currents, unstable stream bottoms, or difficult access; steep slopes, loose surfaces, and narrow clearances; or very narrow sections of shelf road with steep drop-offs and possibly challenging road surfaces.

Rating 7: Skilled, experienced four-wheel drivers only. These trails include very challenging sections with extremely steep grades, loose surfaces, large rocks, deep ruts, and/or tight clearances. Mud or sand may necessitate winching.

Rating 8 and above: Stock vehicles are likely to be damaged and the trail may be impassable. Highly skilled, experienced four-wheel drivers only.

Scenic Ratings

If rating the degree of difficulty is subjective, rating scenic beauty is guaranteed to lead to arguments. Northern California contains a spectacular variety of scenery—from coastal cliffs and redwood forests to the towering mountain peaks and ranges. Despite the subjectivity of attempting a comparative rating of diverse scenery, we have tried to provide a guide to the relative scenic quality of the various trails. The ratings are based on a scale of 1 to 10, with 10 being the most attractive.

Remoteness Ratings

Many trails in Northern California are in remote mountain country; sometimes the trails are seldom traveled, and the likelihood is low that another vehicle will appear within a reasonable time to assist you if you get stuck or break down. We have included a ranking for remoteness of +0 through +2. Prepare carefully before tackling the higher-rated, more remote trails (see Special Preparations for Remote Travel, page 11-12). For trails with a high remoteness rating, consider traveling with a second vehicle.

Estimated Driving Times

In calculating driving times, we have not allowed for stops. Your actual driving time may be considerably longer depending on the number and duration of the stops you make. Add more time if you prefer to drive more slowly than good conditions allow.

Current Road Information

All the 4WD trails described in this book may become impassable in poor weather conditions. Storms can alter roads, remove tracks, and create impassable washes. Most of the trails described, even easy 2WD trails, can quickly become impassable even to 4WD vehicles after only a small amount of rain. For each trail, we have provided a phone number for obtaining current information about conditions.

Abbreviations

The route directions for the 4WD trails use a series of abbreviations as follows:

SO	CONTINUE STRAIGHT ON
TL	TURN LEFT
TR	TURN RIGHT
BL	BEAR LEFT
BR	BEAR RIGHT
UT	U-TURN

Using Route Directions

For every trail, we describe and pinpoint (by odometer reading) nearly every significant feature along the route—such as intersections, streams, washes, gates, cattle guards, and so on—and provide directions from

these landmarks. Odometer readings will vary from vehicle to vehicle, so you should allow for slight variations. Be aware that trails can change quickly. A new trail may be cut around a washout, a faint trail can be graded by the county, or a well-used trail may fall into disuse. All these factors will affect the accuracy of the given directions.

If you diverge from the route, zero your trip meter upon your return and continue along the route, making the necessary adjustment to the point-to-point odometer readings. In the directions, we regularly reset the odometer readings—at significant landmarks or popular lookouts and spur trails—so that you won't have to recalculate for too long.

Most of the trails can be started from either end, and the route directions include both directions of travel; reverse directions are printed in green below the main directions. When traveling in reverse, read from the bottom of the table and work up.

Route directions include cross-references whenever two 4WD trails included in this book connect; these cross-references allow for an easy change of route or destination.

Each trail includes periodic latitude and longitude readings to facilitate the use of a global positioning system (GPS) receiver. These readings may also assist you in finding your location on the maps. The GPS coordinates are given in the format dd°mm.mm'. To save time when loading coordinates into your GPS receiver, you may wish to include only one decimal place, since in Northern California, the first decimal place equals about 150 yards and the second only about 15 yards.

Map References

We recommend that you supplement the information in this book with more-detailed maps. For each trail, we list the sheet maps and road atlases that provide the best detail for the area. Typically, the following references are given:

- Bureau of Land Management Maps
- U.S. Forest Service Maps
- *California Road & Recreation Atlas,* 2nd

ed. (Medford, Oregon: Benchmark Maps, 1998)—Scale 1:300,000

■ *Northern California Atlas & Gazetteer,* 5th ed. (Yarmouth, Maine: DeLorme Mapping, 2000)—Scale 1:150,000

■ Maptech-Terrain Navigator Topo Maps—Scale 1:100,000 and 1:24,000

■ *Trails Illustrated* Topo Maps; National Geographic Maps—Various scales, but all contain good detail.

We recommend the *Trails Illustrated* series of maps as the best for navigating these trails. They are reliable, easy to read, and printed on nearly indestructible plastic paper. However, this series covers only a few of the 4WD trails described in this book.

The DeLorme *Northern California Atlas & Gazetteer* is useful and has the advantage of providing you with maps of the entire state at a reasonable price. Although its 4WD trail information doesn't go beyond what we provide, it is useful if you wish to explore the hundreds of side roads.

U.S. Forest Service maps lack the topographic detail of the other sheet maps and, in our experience, are occasionally out of date. They have the advantage of covering a broad area and are useful in identifying land use and travel restrictions. These maps are most useful for the longer trails.

In our opinion, the best single option by far is the Terrain Navigator series of maps published on CD-ROM by Maptech. These CD-ROMs contain an amazing level of detail because they include the entire set of 1,941 U.S. Geological Survey topographical maps of California at the 1:24,000 scale and all 71 maps at the 1:100,000 scale. These maps offer many advantages over normal maps:

■ GPS coordinates for any location can be found and loaded into your GPS receiver. Conversely, if you have your GPS coordinates, your location on the map can be pinpointed instantly.

■ Towns, rivers, passes, mountains, and many other sites are indexed by name so that they can be located quickly.

■ 4WD trails can be marked and profiled for elevation changes and distances from point to point.

■ Customized maps can be printed out.

Maptech uses 14 CD-ROMs to cover the entire state of California; they can be purchased individually or as part of a two-state package at a heavily discounted price. The CD-ROMs can be used with a laptop computer and a GPS receiver in your vehicle to monitor your location on the map and navigate directly from the display.

All these maps should be available through good map stores. The Maptech CD-ROMs are available directly from the company (toll free at 800-627-7236, or on the internet at www.maptech.com).

Backcountry Driving Rules and Permits

Four-wheel driving involves special driving techniques and road rules. This section is an introduction for 4WD beginners.

4WD Road Rules

To help ensure that these trails remain open and available for all four-wheel drivers to enjoy, it is important to minimize your impact on the environment and not be a safety risk to yourself or anyone else. Remember that the 4WD clubs in California fight a constant battle with the government and various lobby groups to retain the access that currently exists.

The fundamental rule when traversing the 4WD trails described in this book is to use common sense. In addition, special road rules for 4WD trails apply:

■ Vehicles traveling uphill have the right of way.

■ If you are moving more slowly than the vehicle behind you, pull over to let the other vehicle by.

■ Park out of the way in a safe place. Blocking a track may restrict access for emergency vehicles as well as for other recreationalists. Set the parking brake—don't rely on leaving the transmission in park. Manual transmissions should be left in the lowest gear.

Tread Lightly!

Remember the rules of the Tread Lightly! program:

■ Be informed. Obtain maps, regulations, and other information from the forest service or from other public land agencies. Learn the rules and follow them.

■ Resist the urge to pioneer a new road or trail or to cut across a switchback. Stay on constructed tracks and avoid running over young trees, shrubs, and grasses, damaging or killing them. Don't drive across alpine tundra; this fragile environment can take years to recover.

■ Stay off soft, wet roads and 4WD trails readily torn up by vehicles. Repairing the damage is expensive, and quite often authorities find it easier to close the road rather than repair it.

■ Travel around meadows, steep hillsides, stream banks, and lake shores that are easily scarred by churning wheels.

■ Stay away from wild animals that are rearing young or suffering from a food shortage. Do not camp close to the water sources of domestic or wild animals.

■ Obey gate closures and regulatory signs.

■ Preserve America's heritage by not disturbing old mining camps, ghost towns, or other historical features. Leave historic sites, Native American rock art, ruins, and artifacts in place and untouched.

■ Carry out all your trash and even that of others.

■ Stay out of designated wilderness areas. They are closed to all vehicles. It is your responsibility to know where the boundaries are.

■ Get permission to cross private land. Leave livestock alone. Respect landowners' rights.

Report violations of these rules to help keep these 4WD trails open and to ensure that others will have the opportunity to visit these backcountry sites. Many groups are actively seeking to close these public lands to vehicles, thereby denying access to those who are unable, or perhaps merely unwilling, to hike long distances. This magnificent countryside is owned by, and should be available to, all Americans.

Special Preparations for Remote Travel

When traveling in remote areas, you should take some special precautions to ensure that you don't end up in a life-threatening situation:

■ When planning a trip into remote areas, always inform someone as to where you are going, your route, and when you expect to return. Stick to your plan.

■ Be sure your vehicle is in good condition with a sound battery, good hoses, spare tire, spare fan belts, necessary tools, and reserve gasoline and oil. Other spare parts and extra radiator water are also valuable. If traveling in pairs, share the common spares and carry a greater variety.

■ Keep an eye on the sky. Flash floods can occur in a wash any time you see thunderheads—even when it's not raining a drop where you are.

■ Test trails on foot before driving through washes and sandy areas. One minute of walking may save hours of hard work getting your vehicle unstuck.

■ If your vehicle breaks down, stay near it. Your emergency supplies are there. Your car has many other items useful in an emergency. Raise your hood and trunk lid to denote "help needed." Remember, a vehicle can be seen for miles, but a person on foot is very difficult to spot from a distance.

■ Leave a disabled vehicle only if you are positive of the route and the distance to help. Leave a note for rescuers that gives the time you left and the direction you are taking.

■ If you must walk, rest for at least 10 minutes out of each hour. If you are not normally physically active, rest up to 30 minutes out of each hour. Find shade, sit down, and prop up your feet. Adjust your shoes and socks, but do not remove your shoes—you may not be able to get them back on swollen feet.

■ If you have water, drink it. Do not ration it.

■ If water is limited, keep your mouth

closed. Do not talk, eat, smoke, drink alcohol, or take salt.

■ If you are stalled or lost, set signal fires. Set smoky fires in the daytime and bright ones at night. Three fires in a triangle denote "help needed."

■ A roadway is a sign of civilization. If you find a road, stay on it.

■ When hiking in remote areas, equip each person, especially children, with a police-type whistle. It makes a distinctive noise with little effort. Three blasts denote "help needed."

■ Avoid unnecessary contact with wildlife. Put your hands or feet only where your eyes can see. Some mice in California carry the deadly Hanta virus, a pulmonary syndrome fatal in 60 to 70 percent of human cases. Fortunately the disease is very rare—by February 2006, only 43 cases had been reported in California and 438 nationwide—but caution is still advised. Other rodents may transmit bubonic plague. the same epidemic that killed one-third of Europe's population in the 1300s. Be especially wary near sick animals and keep pets, especially cats, away from wildlife and their fleas. Another creature to watch for is the western black-legged tick, the carrier of Lyme disease. Wearing clothing that covers legs and arms, tucking pants into boots, and using insect repellent are good ways to avoid fleas and ticks.

Obtaining Permits

Backcountry permits, which usually cost a fee, are required for certain activities on public lands in California, whether the area is a national park, state park, national monument, Indian reservation, or BLM land.

Restrictions may require a permit for overnight stays, which can include backpacking and 4WD or bicycle camping. Permits may also be required for day use by vehicles, horses, hikers, or bikes in some areas.

When possible, we include information about fees and permit requirements and where permits may be obtained, but these regulations change constantly. If in doubt, check with the most likely governing agency.

Assessing Your Vehicle's Off-Road Ability

Many issues come into play when evaluating your 4WD vehicle, although most of the 4WDs on the market are suitable for even the roughest trails described in this book. Engine power will be adequate in even the least-powerful modern vehicle. However, some vehicles are less suited to off-highway driving than others, and some of the newest, carlike sport utility vehicles simply are not designed for off-highway touring. The following information should allow you to identify the good, the bad, and the ugly.

Differing 4WD Systems

All 4WD systems have one thing in common: The engine provides power to all four wheels rather than to only two, as is typical in most standard cars. However, there are a number of differences in the way power is applied to the wheels.

The other feature that distinguishes nearly all 4WDs from normal passenger vehicles is that the gearboxes have high and low ratios that effectively double the number of gears. The high range is comparable to the range on a passenger car. The low range provides lower speed and more power, which is useful when towing heavy loads, driving up steep hills, or crawling over rocks. When driving downhill, the 4WD's low range increases engine braking.

Various makes and models of SUVs offer different drive systems, but these differences center on two issues: the way power is applied to the other wheels if one or more wheels slip, and the ability to select between 2WD and 4WD.

Normal driving requires that all four wheels be able to turn at different speeds; this allows the vehicle to turn without scrubbing its tires. In a 2WD vehicle, the front wheels (or rear wheels in a front-wheel-drive vehicle) are not powered by the engine and thus are free to turn individually at any speed. The rear wheels, powered by the engine, are only able to turn at different speeds because of the differential, which applies power to the faster-turning wheel.

This standard method of applying traction has certain weaknesses. First, when power is applied to only one set of wheels, the other set cannot help the vehicle gain traction. Second, when one powered wheel loses traction, it spins, but the other powered wheel doesn't turn. This happens because the differential applies all the engine power to the faster-turning wheel and no power to the other wheels, which still have traction. All 4WD systems are designed to overcome these two weaknesses. However, different 4WDs address this common objective in different ways.

Full-Time 4WD. For a vehicle to remain in 4WD all the time without scrubbing the tires, all the wheels must be able to rotate at different speeds. A full-time 4WD system allows this to happen by using three differentials. One is located between the rear wheels, as in a normal passenger car, to allow the rear wheels to rotate at different speeds. The second is located between the front wheels in exactly the same way. The third differential is located between the front and rear wheels to allow different rotational speeds between the front and rear sets of wheels. In nearly all vehicles with full-time 4WD, the center differential operates only in high range. In low range, it is completely locked. This is not a disadvantage because when using low range the additional traction is normally desired and the deterioration of steering response will be less noticeable due to the vehicle traveling at a slower speed.

Part-Time 4WD. A part-time 4WD system does not have the center differential located between the front and rear wheels. Consequently, the front and rear drive shafts are both driven at the same speed and with the same power at all times when in 4WD. This system provides improved traction because when one or both of the front or rear wheels slips, the engine continues to provide power to the other set. However, because such a system doesn't allow a difference in speed between the front and rear sets of wheels, the tires scrub when turning, placing additional strain on the whole drive system. Therefore, such a system can be used only in slippery conditions; otherwise, the ability to steer the vehicle will deteriorate and the tires will quickly wear out.

Some vehicles, such as Jeeps with Selectrac and Mitsubishi Monteros with Active Trac 4WD, offer both full-time and part-time 4WD in high range.

Manual Systems to Switch Between 2WD and 4WD. There are three manual systems for switching between 2WD and 4WD. The most basic requires stopping and getting out of the vehicle to lock the front hubs manually before selecting 4WD. The second requires you to stop, but you change to 4WD by merely throwing a lever inside the vehicle (the hubs lock automatically). The third allows shifting between 2WD and 4WD high range while the vehicle is moving. Any 4WD that does not offer the option of driving in 2WD must have a full-time 4WD system.

Automated Switching Between 2WD and 4WD. Advances in technology are leading to greater automation in the selection of two- or four-wheel drive. When operating in high range, these high-tech systems use sensors to monitor the rotation of each wheel. When any slippage is detected, the vehicle switches the proportion of power from the wheel(s) that is slipping to the wheels that retain grip. The proportion of power supplied to each wheel is therefore infinitely variable as opposed to the original systems where the vehicle was either in two-wheel drive or four-wheel drive.

In recent years, this process has been spurred on by many of the manufacturers of luxury vehicles entering the SUV market— Mercedes, BMW, Cadillac, Lincoln, and Lexus have joined Range Rover in this segment.

Manufacturers of these higher-priced vehicles have led the way in introducing sophisticated computer-controlled 4WD systems. Although each of the manufacturers has its own approach to this issue, all the systems automatically vary the allocation of power between the wheels within milliseconds of the sensors' detecting wheel slippage.

Limiting Wheel Slippage

All 4WDs employ various systems to limit wheel slippage and transfer power to the wheels that still have traction. These systems may completely lock the differentials, or they may allow limited slippage before transferring power back to the wheels that retain traction.

Lockers completely eliminate the operation of one or more differentials. A locker on the center differential switches between full-time and part-time 4WD. Lockers on the front or rear differentials ensure that power remains equally applied to each set of wheels regardless of whether both have traction. Lockers may be controlled manually, by a switch or a lever in the vehicle, or they may be automatic.

The Toyota Land Cruiser offers the option of having manual lockers on all three differentials, while other brands such as the Mitsubishi Montero offer manual lockers on the center and rear differential. Manual lockers are the most controllable and effective devices for ensuring that power is provided to the wheels with traction. However, because they allow absolutely no slippage, they must be used only on slippery surfaces.

An alternative method for getting power to the wheels that have traction is to allow limited wheel slippage. Systems that work this way may be called limited-slip differentials, posi-traction systems, or in the center differential, viscous couplings. The advantage of these systems is that the limited difference they allow in rotational speed between wheels enables such systems to be used when driving on a dry surface. All full-time 4WD systems allow limited slippage in the center differential.

For off-highway use, a manually locking differential is the best of the above systems, but it is the most expensive. Limited-slip differentials are the cheapest but also the least satisfactory, as they require one wheel to be slipping at 2 to 3 mph before power is transferred to the other wheel. For the center differential, the best system combines a locking differential and, to enable full-time use, a viscous coupling.

Tires

The tires that came with your 4WD vehicle may be satisfactory, but many 4WDs are fitted with passenger-car tires. These are unlikely to be the best choice because they are less rugged and more likely to puncture on rocky trails. They are particularly prone to sidewall damage as well. Passenger vehicle tires also have a less aggressive tread pattern than specialized 4WD tires, thus providing less traction in mud.

For information on purchasing tires better suited to off-highway conditions, see Special 4WD Equipmen, pages 20-23.

Clearance

Road clearances vary considerably among different 4WD vehicles—from less than 7 inches to more than 10 inches. Special vehicles may have far greater clearance. For instance, the Hummer has a 16-inch ground clearance. High ground clearance is particularly advantageous on the rockier or more rutted 4WD trails in this book.

When evaluating the ground clearance of your vehicle, you need to take into account the clearance of the bodywork between the wheels on each side of the vehicle. This is particularly relevant for crawling over larger rocks. Vehicles with sidesteps have significantly lower clearance than those without.

Another factor affecting clearance is the approach and departure angles of your vehicle—that is, the maximum angle the ground can slope without the front of the vehicle hitting the ridge on approach or the rear of the vehicle hitting on departure. Mounting a winch or tow hitch to your vehicle is likely to reduce your angle of approach or departure.

If you do a lot of driving on rocky trails, you will inevitably hit the bottom of the vehicle sooner or later. When this happens, you will be far less likely to damage vulnerable areas such as the oil pan and gas tank if your vehicle is fitted with skid plates. Most manufacturers offer skid plates as an option. They are worth every penny.

Maneuverability

When you tackle tight switchbacks, you will quickly appreciate that maneuverability is an important criterion when assessing 4WD vehicles. Where a full-size vehicle may be forced to go back and forth a number of times to get around a sharp turn, a small 4WD might go straight around. This is not only easier, it's safer.

If you have a full-size vehicle, all is not lost. We have traveled many of the trails in this book in a Suburban. That is not to say that some of these trails wouldn't have been easier to negotiate in a smaller vehicle! We have noted in the route descriptions if a trail is not suitable for larger vehicles.

In Summary

Using the criteria above, you can evaluate how well your 4WD will handle off-road touring, and if you haven't yet purchased your vehicle, you can use these criteria to help select one. Choosing the best 4WD system is, at least partly, subjective. It is also a matter of your budget. However, for the type of off-highway driving covered in this book, we make the following recommendations:

■ Select a 4WD system that offers low range and, at a minimum, has some form of limited slip differential on the rear axle.

■ Use light truck, all-terrain tires as the standard tires on your vehicle. For sand and slickrock, these will be the ideal choice. If conditions are likely to be muddy, or traction will be improved by a tread pattern that will give more bite, consider an additional set of mud tires.

■ For maximum clearance, select a vehicle with 16-inch wheels or at least choose the tallest tires that your vehicle can accommodate. Note that if you install tires with a diameter greater than standard, the odometer will undercalculate the distance you have traveled. Your engine braking and gear ratios will also be affected.

■ If you are going to try the rockier 4WD trails, don't install a sidestep or low-hanging front bar. If you have the option, have underbody skid plates mounted.

■ Remember that many of the obstacles you encounter on backcountry trails are more difficult to navigate in a full-size vehicle than in a compact 4WD.

Four-Wheel Driving Techniques

Safe four-wheel driving requires that you observe certain golden rules:

■ Size up the situation in advance.

■ Be careful and take your time.

■ Maintain smooth, steady power and momentum.

■ Engage 4WD and low-range gears before you get into a tight situation.

■ Steer toward high spots, trying to put the wheel over large rocks.

■ Straddle ruts.

■ Use gears and not just the brakes to hold the vehicle when driving downhill. On very steep slopes, chock the wheels if you park your vehicle.

■ Watch for logging and mining trucks and smaller recreational vehicles, such as all-terrain vehicles (ATVs).

■ Wear your seat belt and secure all luggage, especially heavy items such as tool boxes or coolers. Heavy items should be secured by ratchet tie-down straps rather than elastic-type straps, which are not strong enough to hold heavy items if the vehicle rolls.

California's 4WD trails have a number of common obstacles, and the following provides an introduction to the techniques required to surmount them.

Rocks. Tire selection is important in negotiating rocks. Select a multiple-ply, tough sidewall, light-truck tire with a large-lug tread.

As you approach a rocky stretch, get into 4WD low range to give yourself maximum slow-speed control. Speed is rarely necessary, since traction on a rocky surface is usually good. Plan ahead and select the line you wish to take. If a rock appears to be larger than the clearance of your vehicle, don't try to straddle it. Check to see that it is not higher than the frame of your vehicle once you get a wheel over it. Put a wheel up on the rock and slowly climb it, then gently drop over the other side using the brake to ensure a smooth landing. Bouncing the car over rocks increases the likelihood of damage, as the body's clearance is reduced by the suspension compressing. Running boards also significantly reduce your clearance in this respect.

It is often helpful to use a "spotter" outside the vehicle to assist you with the best wheel placement.

Steep Uphill Grades. Consider walking the trail to ensure that the steep hill before you is passable, especially if it is clear that backtracking is going to be a problem.

Select 4WD low range to ensure that you have adequate power to pull up the hill. If the wheels begin to lose traction, turn the steering wheel gently from side to side to give the wheels a chance to regain traction.

If you lose momentum, but the car is not in danger of sliding, use the foot brake, switch off the ignition, leave the vehicle in gear (if manual transmission) or park (if automatic), engage the parking brake, and get out to examine the situation. See if you can remove any obstacles, and figure out the line you need to take. Reversing a couple of yards and starting again may allow you to get better traction and momentum.

If halfway up, you decide a stretch of road is impassably steep, back down the trail. Trying to turn the vehicle around on a steep hill is extremely dangerous; you will very likely cause it to roll over.

Steep Downhill Grades. Again, consider walking the trail to ensure that a steep downhill is passable, especially if it is clear that backtracking uphill is going to be a problem.

Select 4WD low range and use first gear to maximize braking assistance from the engine. If the surface is loose and you are losing traction, change up to second or third gear. Do not use the brakes if you can avoid it, but don't let the vehicle's speed get out of control. Feather (lightly pump) the brakes if you slip under braking. For vehicles fitted with Anti-Lock Braking Systems, apply even pressure if you start to slip; the ABS helps keep vehicles on line.

Travel very slowly over rock ledges or ruts. Attempt to tackle these diagonally, letting one wheel down at a time.

If the back of the vehicle begins to slide around, gently apply the throttle and correct the steering. If the rear of the vehicle starts to slide sideways, do not apply the brakes.

Sand. As with most off-highway situations, your tires are the key to your ability to cross sand. It is difficult to tell how well a particular tire will handle in sand just by looking at it, so be guided by the manufacturer and your dealer.

The key to driving in soft sand is floatation, which is achieved by a combination of low tire pressure and momentum. Before crossing a stretch of sand, reduce your tire pressure to between 15 and 20 pounds. If necessary, you can safely go to as low as 12 pounds. As you cross, maintain momentum so that your vehicle rides on the top of the soft sand without digging in or stalling. This may require plenty of engine power. Avoid using the brakes if possible; removing your foot from the accelerator alone is normally enough to slow or stop. Using the brakes digs the vehicle deep in the sand.

Pump the tires back up as soon as you are out of the sand to avoid damage to the tires and the rims. Pumping back up requires a high-quality air compressor. Even then, it is a slow process.

Slickrock. When you encounter slickrock, first assess the correct direction of the trail. It is easy to lose sight of the trail on slickrock, as there are seldom any developed edges. Often the way is marked with small rock cairns, which are simply rocks stacked high enough to make a landmark.

All-terrain tires with tighter tread are more suited to slickrock than the more open, luggier type tires. As with rocks, a multiple-ply sidewall is important. In dry conditions, slickrock offers pavement-type grip. In rain or snow, you will soon learn how it got its name. Even the best tires may not get an adequate grip. Walk steep sections first; if you are slipping on foot, chances are your vehicle will slip too.

Slickrock is characterized by ledges and long

sections of "pavement." Follow the guidelines for travel over rocks. Refrain from speeding over flat-looking sections, as you may hit an unexpected crevice or water pocket, and vehicles bend easier than slickrock! Turns and ledges can be tight, and vehicles with smaller overhangs and better maneuverability are at a distinct advantage—hence the popularity of the compacts in the slickrock mecca of Moab, Utah.

On the steepest sections, engage low range and pick a straight line up or down the slope. Do not attempt to traverse a steep slope sideways.

Mud. Muddy trails are easily damaged, so they should be avoided if possible. But if you must traverse a section of mud, your success will depend heavily on whether you have open-lugged mud tires or chains. Thick mud fills the tighter tread on normal tires, leaving the tire with no more grip than if it were bald. If the muddy stretch is only a few yards long, the momentum of your vehicle may allow you to get through regardless.

If the muddy track is very steep, uphill or downhill, or off camber, do not attempt it. Your vehicle is likely to skid in such conditions, and you may roll or slip off the edge of the road. Also, check to see that the mud has a reasonably firm base. Tackling deep mud is definitely not recommended unless you have a vehicle-mounted winch—and even then, be cautious—because the winch may not get you out. Finally, check to see that no ruts are too deep for the ground clearance of your vehicle.

When you decide you can get through and have selected the best route, use the following techniques to cross through the mud:

■ Avoid making detours off existing tracks to minimize environmental damage.

■ Select 4WD low range and a suitable gear; momentum is the key to success, so use a high enough gear to build up sufficient speed.

■ Avoid accelerating heavily, so as to minimize wheel spinning and to provide maximum traction.

■ Follow existing wheel ruts, unless they are too deep for the clearance of your vehicle.

■ To correct slides, turn the steering wheel in the direction that the rear wheels are skidding, but don't be too aggressive or you'll overcorrect and lose control again.

■ If the vehicle comes to a stop, don't continue to accelerate, as you will only spin your wheels and dig yourself into a rut. Try backing out and having another go.

■ Be prepared to turn back before reaching the point of no return.

Stream Crossings. By crossing a stream that is too deep, drivers risk far more than water flowing in and ruining the interior of their vehicles. Water sucked into the engine's air intake will seriously damage the engine. Likewise, water that seeps into the air vent on the transmission or differential will mix with the lubricant and may lead to serious problems in due course.

Even worse, if the water is deep or fast flowing, it could easily carry your vehicle downstream, endangering the lives of everyone in the vehicle.

Some 4WD manuals tell you what fording depth the vehicle can negotiate safely. If your vehicle's owner's manual does not include this information, your local dealer may be able to assist. If you don't know, then avoid crossing through water that is more than a foot or so deep.

The first rule for crossing a stream is to know what you are getting into. You need to ascertain how deep the water is, whether there are any large rocks or holes, if the bottom is solid enough to avoid bogging down the vehicle, and whether the entry and exit points are negotiable. This may take some time and involve getting wet, but you take a great risk by crossing a stream without first properly assessing the situation.

The secret to water crossings is to keep moving, but not too fast. If you go too fast, you may drown the electrics, causing the vehicle to stall midstream. In shallow water (where the surface of the water is below the bumper), your primary concern is to safely negotiate the bottom of the stream, avoiding any rock damage and maintaining momentum if there is a danger of getting stuck or of slipping on the exit.

In deeper water (between 18 and 30 inches), the objective is to create a small bow wave in front of the moving vehicle. This requires a speed that is approximately walking pace. The bow wave reduces the depth of the water around the engine compartment. If the water's surface reaches your tailpipe, select a gear that will maintain moderate engine revs to avoid water backing up into the exhaust; and do not change gears midstream.

Crossing water deeper than 25 to 30 inches requires more extensive preparation of the vehicle and should be attempted only by experienced drivers.

Snow. The trails in this book that receive heavy snowfall are closed in winter. Therefore, the snow conditions that you are most likely to encounter are an occasional snowdrift that has not yet melted or fresh snow from an unexpected storm. Getting through such conditions depends on the depth of the snow, its consistency, the stability of the underlying surface, and your vehicle.

If the snow is no deeper than about 9 inches and there is solid ground beneath it, crossing the snow should not be a problem. In deeper snow that seems solid enough to support your vehicle, be extremely cautious: If you break through a drift, you are likely to be stuck, and if conditions are bad, you may have a long wait.

The tires you use for off-highway driving, with a wide tread pattern, are probably suitable for these snow conditions. Nonetheless, it is wise to carry chains (preferably for all four wheels), and if you have a vehicle-mounted winch, even better.

Vehicle Recovery Methods

If you do enough four-wheel driving, you are sure to get stuck sooner or later. The following techniques will help you get back on the go. The most suitable method will depend on the equipment available and the situation you are in—whether you are stuck in sand, mud, or snow, or are high-centered or unable to negotiate a hill.

Towing. Use a nylon yank strap of the type discussed in the Special 4WD Equipment section below. This type of strap will stretch 15 to 25 percent, and the elasticity will assist in extracting the vehicle.

Attach the strap only to a frame-mounted tow point. Ensure that the driver of the stuck vehicle is ready, take up all but about 6 feet of slack, then move the towing vehicle away at a moderate speed (in most circumstances this means using 4WD low range in second gear) so that the elasticity of the strap is employed in the way it is meant to be. Don't take off like a bat out of hell or you risk breaking the strap or damaging a vehicle.

Never join two yank straps together with a shackle. If one strap breaks, the shackle will become a lethal missile aimed at one of the vehicles (and anyone inside). For the same reason, never attach a yank strap to the tow ball on either vehicle.

Jacking. Jacking the vehicle allows you to pack rocks, dirt, or logs under the wheel or to use your shovel to remove an obstacle. However, the standard vehicle jack is unlikely to be of as much assistance as a high-lift jack. We highly recommend purchasing a good high-lift jack as a basic accessory if you decide that you are going to do a lot of serious, off-highway four-wheel driving. Remember a high-lift jack is of limited use if your vehicle does not have an appropriate jacking point. Some brush bars have two built-in forward jacking points.

Tire Chains. Tire chains can be of assistance in both mud and snow. Cable-type chains provide much less grip than link-type chains. There are also dedicated mud chains with larger, heavier links than on normal snow chains. It is best to have chains fitted to all four wheels.

Once you are bogged down is not the best time to try to fit the chains; if at all possible, try to predict their need and have them on the tires before trouble arises. An easy way to affix chains is to place two small cubes of wood under the center of the stretched-out chain. When you drive your tires up on the blocks of wood, it is easier to stretch the chains over the tires because the pressure is off.

Winching. Most recreational four-wheel drivers do not have a winch. But if you get serious about four-wheel driving, this is probably the first major accessory you should consider buying.

Under normal circumstances, a winch would be warranted only for the more difficult 4WD trails in this book. Having a winch is certainly comforting when you see a difficult section of road ahead and have to decide whether to risk it or turn back. Also, major obstacles can appear when you least expect them, even on trails that are otherwise easy.

Owning a winch is not a panacea to all your recovery problems. Winching depends on the availability of a good anchor point, and electric winches may not work if they are submerged in a stream. Despite these constraints, no accessory is more useful than a high-quality, powerful winch when you get into a difficult situation.

If you acquire a winch, learn to use it properly; take the time to study your owner's manual. Incorrect operation can be extremely dangerous and may cause damage to the winch or to your anchor points, which are usually trees.

Navigation by the Global Positioning System (GPS)

Although this book is designed so that each trail can be navigated simply by following the detailed directions provided, nothing makes navigation easier than a GPS receiver.

The global positioning system (GPS) consists of a network of 24 satellites, nearly 13,000 miles in space, in six different orbital paths. The satellites are constantly moving at about 8,500 miles per hour, making two complete orbits around the earth every 24 hours.

Each satellite is constantly transmitting data, including its identification number, its operational health, and the date and time. It also transmits its location and the location of every other satellite in the network.

By comparing the time the signal was transmitted to the time it is received, a GPS receiver calculates how far away each satellite is. With a sufficient number of signals, the receiver can then triangulate its location. With three or more satellites, the receiver can determine latitude and longitude coordinates. With four or more, it can calculate el-

evation. By constantly making these calculations, it can determine speed and direction. To facilitate these calculations, the time data broadcast by GPS is accurate to within 40 billionths of a second.

The U.S. military uses the system to provide positions accurate to within half an inch. When the system was first established, civilian receivers were deliberately fed slightly erroneous information in order to effectively deny military applications to hostile countries or terrorists—a practice called selective availability (SA). However on May 1, 2000, in response to the growing importance of the system for civilian applications, the U.S. government stopped intentionally downgrading GPS data. The military gave its support to this change once new technology made it possible to selectively degrade the system within any defined geographical area on demand. This new feature of the system has made it safe to have higher-quality signals available for civilian use. Now, instead of the civilian-use signal having a margin of error being between 20 and 70 yards, it is only about one-tenth of that.

A GPS receiver offers the four-wheeler numerous benefits:

■ You can track to any point for which you know the longitude and latitude coordinates with no chance of heading in the wrong direction or getting lost. Most receivers provide an extremely easy-to-understand graphic display to keep you on track.

■ It works in all weather conditions.

■ It automatically records your route for easy backtracking.

■ You can record and name any location, so that you can relocate it with ease. This may include your campsite, a fishing spot, or even a silver mine you discover!

■ It displays your position, allowing you to pinpoint your location on a map.

■ By interfacing the GPS receiver directly to a portable computer, you can monitor and record your location as you travel (using the appropriate map software) or print the route you took.

However, remember that GPS units can fail, batteries can go flat, and tree cover and tight canyons can block the signals. Never rely entirely on GPS for navigation. Always carry a compass for backup.

Special 4WD Equipment

Tires

When 4WD touring, you will likely encounter a wide variety of terrain: rocks, mud, talus, slickrock, sand, gravel, dirt, and bitumen. The immense variety of tires on the market includes many specifically targeted at one or another of these types of terrain, as well as tires designed to adequately handle a range of terrain.

Every four-wheel driver seems to have a preference when it comes to tire selection, but most people undertaking the 4WD trails in this book will need tires that can handle all of the above types of terrain adequately.

The first requirement is to select rugged, light-truck tires rather than passenger-vehicle tires. Check the size data on the sidewall: it should have "LT" rather than "P" before the number.

Among light-truck tires, you must choose between tires that are designated "all-terrain" and more-aggressive, wider-tread mud tires. Either type will be adequate, especially on rocks, gravel, talus, or dirt. Although mud tires have an advantage in muddy conditions and soft snow, all-terrain tires perform better on slickrock, in sand, and particularly on ice and paved roads.

When selecting tires, remember that they affect not just traction but also cornering ability, braking distances, fuel consumption, and noise levels. It pays to get good advice before making your decision.

Global Positioning System Receivers

GPS receivers have come down in price considerably in the past few years and are rapidly becoming indispensable navigational tools. Many higher-priced cars now offer integrated GPS receivers, and within the next few years, receivers will become available on most models.

Battery-powered, hand-held units that meet the needs of off-highway driving currently range from less than $100 to a little over $300 and continue to come down in price. Some high-end units feature maps that are incorporated in the display, either from a built-in database or from interchangeable memory cards. Currently, only a few of these maps include 4WD trails.

If you are considering purchasing a GPS unit, keep the following in mind:

- Price. The very cheapest units are likely outdated and very limited in their display features. Expect to pay from $125 to $300.
- The display. Compare the graphic display of one unit with another. Some are much easier to decipher or offer more alternative displays.
- The controls. GPS receivers have many functions, and they need to have good, simple controls.
- Vehicle mounting. To be useful, the unit needs to be placed where it can be read easily by both the driver and the navigator. Check that the unit can be conveniently located in your vehicle. Different units have different shapes and different mounting systems.
- Map data. More and more units have map data built in. Some have the ability to download maps from a computer. Such maps are normally sold on a CD-ROM. GPS units have a finite storage capacity and having the ability to download maps covering a narrower geographical region means that the amount of data relating to that specific region can be greater.
- The number of routes and the number of sites (or "waypoints") per route that can be stored in memory. For off-highway use, it is important to be able to store plenty of waypoints so that you do not have to load coordinates into the machine as frequently. Having plenty of memory also ensures that you can automatically store your present location without fear that the memory is full.
- Waypoint storage. The better units store up to 500 waypoints and 20 reversible routes of up to 30 waypoints each. Also consider the number of characters a GPS receiver allows you to use to name waypoints. When you try to recall a waypoint, you may have difficulty recognizing names restricted

to only a few characters.

■ Automatic route storing. Most units automatically store your route as you go along and enable you to display it in reverse to make backtracking easy.

After you have selected a unit, a number of optional extras are also worth considering:

■ A cigarette lighter electrical adapter. Despite GPS units becoming more power efficient, protracted in-vehicle use still makes this accessory a necessity.

■ A vehicle-mounted antenna, which will improve reception under difficult conditions. (The GPS unit can only "see" through the windows of your vehicle; it cannot monitor satellites through a metal roof.) Having a vehicle-mounted antenna also means that you do not have to consider reception when locating the receiver in your vehicle.

■ An in-car mounting system. If you are going to do a lot of touring using the GPS, consider attaching a bracket on the dash rather than relying on a Velcro mount.

■ A computer-link cable and digital maps. Data from your GPS receiver can be downloaded to your PC; maps and waypoints can be downloaded from your PC; or if you have a laptop computer, you can monitor your route as you go along, using one of a number of inexpensive map software products on the market.

Yank Straps

Yank straps are industrial-strength versions of the flimsy tow straps carried by the local discount store. They are 20 to 30 feet long and 2 to 3 inches wide, made of heavy nylon, rated to at least 20,000 pounds, and have looped ends.

Do not use tow straps with metal hooks in the ends (the hooks can become missiles in the event the strap breaks free). Likewise, never join two yank straps together using a shackle.

CB Radios

If you are stuck, injured, or just want to know the conditions up ahead, a citizen's band (CB) radio can be invaluable.

CB radios are relatively inexpensive and do not require an FCC license. Their range is limited, especially in very hilly country, as their transmission patterns basically follow lines of sight. Range can be improved using single sideband (SSB) transmission, an option on more expensive units. Range is even better on vehicle-mounted units that have been professionally fitted to ensure that the antenna and cabling are matched appropriately.

Winches

There are three main options when it comes to winches: manual winches, removable electric winches, and vehicle-mounted electric winches.

If you have a full-size 4WD vehicle—which can weigh in excess of 7,000 pounds when loaded—a manual winch is of limited use without a lot of effort and considerable time. However, a manual winch is a very handy and inexpensive accessory if you have a small 4WD. Typically, manual winches are rated to pull about 5,500 pounds.

Electric winches can be mounted to your vehicle's trailer hitch to enable them to be removed, relocated to the front of your vehicle (if you have a hitch installed), or moved to another vehicle. Although this is a very useful feature, a winch is heavy, so relocating one can be a two-person job. Consider that 5,000-pound-rated winches weigh only about 55 pounds, while 12,000-pound-rated models weigh around 140 pounds. Therefore, the larger models are best permanently front-mounted. Unfortunately, this position limits their ability to winch the vehicle backward.

When choosing among electric winches, be aware that they are rated for their maximum capacity on the first wind of the cable around the drum. As layers of cable wind onto the drum, they increase its diameter and thus decrease the maximum load the winch can handle. This decrease is significant: A winch rated to pull 8,000 pounds on a bare drum may only handle 6,500 pounds on the second layer, 5,750 pounds on the third layer, and 5,000 pounds on the fourth. Electric winches also draw a high level of current and may necessitate upgrading the battery in your 4WD or adding a second battery.

There is a wide range of mounting options—from a simple, body-mounted frame that holds the winch to heavy-duty winch bars that replace the original bumper and incorporate brush bars and mounts for auxiliary lights.

If you buy a winch, either electric or manual, you will also need quite a range of additional equipment so that you can operate it correctly:

- at least one choker chain with hooks on each end,
- winch extension straps or cables,
- shackles,
- a receiver shackle,
- a snatch block,
- a tree protector,
- gloves.

Grill/Brush Bars and Winch Bars

Brush bars protect the front of the vehicle from scratches and minor bumps; they also provide a solid mount for auxiliary lights and often high-lift jacking points. The level of protection they provide depends on how solid they are and whether they are securely mounted onto the frame of the vehicle. Lighter models attach in front of the standard bumper, but the more substantial units replace the bumper. Prices range from about $150 to $450.

Winch bars replace the bumper and usually integrate a solid brush bar with a heavy-duty winch mount. Some have the brush bar as an optional extra to the winch bar component. Manufacturers such as Warn, ARB, and TJM offer a wide range of integrated winch bars. These are significantly more expensive, starting at about $650.

Remember that installing heavy equipment on the front of the vehicle may necessitate increasing the front suspension rating to cope with the additional weight.

Portable Air Compressors

Most portable air compressors on the market are flimsy models that plug into the cigarette lighter and are sold at the local discount store. These are of very limited use for four-wheel driving. They are very slow to inflate the large tires of a 4WD vehicle; for instance, to reinflate from 15 to 35 pounds typically takes about 10 minutes for each tire. They are also unlikely to be rated for continuous use, which means that they will overheat and cut off before completing the job. If you're lucky, they will start up again when they have cooled down, but this means that you are unlikely to reinflate your tires in less than an hour.

The easiest way to identify a useful air compressor is by the price—good ones cost $200 or more. Many of the quality units feature a Thomas-brand pump and are built to last. Another good unit is sold by ARB. All these pumps draw between 15 and 20 amps and thus should not be plugged into the cigarette lighter socket but attached to the vehicle's battery with clips. The ARB unit can be permanently mounted under the hood. Quick-Air makes a range of units including a 10-amp compressor that can be plugged into the cigarette lighter socket and performs well.

Auxiliary Driving Lights

There is a vast array of auxiliary lights on the market today, and selecting the best lights for your purpose can be a confusing process.

Auxiliary lights greatly improve visibility in adverse weather conditions. Driving lights provide a strong, moderately wide beam to supplement headlamp high beams, giving improved lighting in the distance and to the sides of the main beam. Fog lamps throw a wide-dispersion, flat beam; and spots provide a high-power, narrow beam to improve lighting range directly in front of the vehicle. Rear-mounted auxiliary lights provide greatly improved visibility for backing up.

For off-highway use, you will need quality lights with strong mounting brackets. Some high-powered off-highway lights are not approved by the U.S. Department of Transportation for use on public roads.

Roof Racks

Roof racks can be excellent for storing gear, as well as providing easy access for certain weatherproof items. However, they raise the center of gravity on the vehicle, which can substantially alter the rollover angle. A roof rack is best used for lightweight objects that are well strapped down. Heavy recovery gear and other bulky items should be packed low in the vehicle's interior to lower the center of gravity and stabilize the vehicle.

A roof rack should allow for safe and secure packing of items and be sturdy enough to withstand knocks.

Packing Checklist

Before embarking on any 4WD adventure, whether a lazy Sunday drive on an easy trail or a challenging climb over rugged terrain, be prepared. The following checklist will help you gather the items you need.

Essential
- ❏ Rain gear
- ❏ Small shovel or multipurpose ax, pick, shovel, and sledgehammer
- ❏ Heavy-duty yank strap
- ❏ Spare tire that matches the other tires on the vehicle
- ❏ Working jack and base plate for soft ground
- ❏ Maps
- ❏ Emergency medical kit, including sun protection and insect repellent
- ❏ Bottled water
- ❏ Blankets or space blankets
- ❏ Parka, gloves, and boots
- ❏ Spare vehicle key
- ❏ Jumper leads
- ❏ Heavy-duty flashlight
- ❏ Multipurpose tool, such as a Leatherman
- ❏ Emergency food—high-energy bars or similar

Worth Considering
- ❏ Global Positioning System (GPS) receiver
- ❏ Cell phone
- ❏ A set of light-truck, off-highway tires and matching spare
- ❏ High-lift jack
- ❏ Additional tool kit
- ❏ CB radio
- ❏ Portable air compressor
- ❏ Tire gauge
- ❏ Duct and electrical tape
- ❏ Tire-sealing kit
- ❏ Tire chains
- ❏ Chainsaw or Wyoming saw (or similar)
- ❏ Binoculars
- ❏ Firearms
- ❏ Whistle
- ❏ Flares
- ❏ Vehicle fire extinguisher
- ❏ Gasoline, engine oil, and other vehicle fluids
- ❏ Portable hand winch
- ❏ Electric cooler

If Your Credit Cards Aren't Maxed Out
- ❏ Electric, vehicle-mounted winch and associated recovery straps, shackles, and snatch blocks
- ❏ Vehicle-mounted off-road or driving lights
- ❏ Locking differential(s)

Trails in the North Coast Region

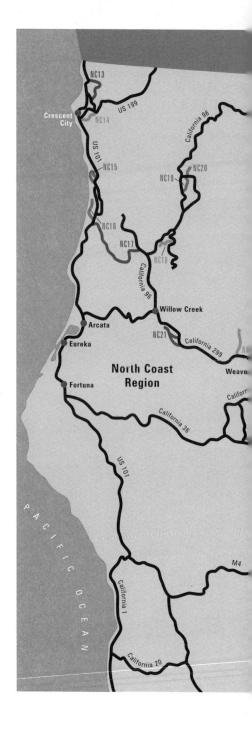

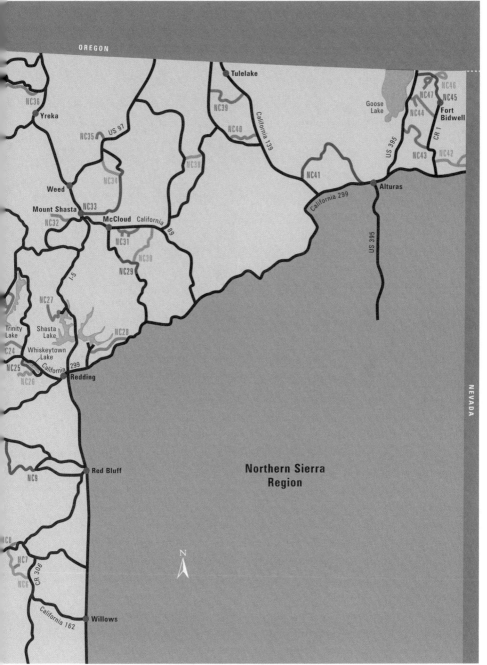

OREGON

Tulelake

NC36

Yreka

US 97

NC35

NC39

California 139

NC40

Goose
Lake

NC46
NC47 NC45
NC44

Fort
Bidwell

CR 1

US 395

NC43 NC42

NC38

NC34

Weed

Mount Shasta NC33

NC32

McCloud California

89

NC41

California 299

Alturas

NC31

NC30

NC29

I-5

NC27

Trinity
Lake

Shasta
Lake

Whiskeytown
Lake

C24

NC25

California 299

NC26

Redding

NC28

US 395

NC9

Red Bluff

**Northern Sierra
Region**

NEVADA

C8

NC7

CR 306

NC6

California 162

Willows

N

MAP CONTINUES ON PAGE 27

Trails in the North Coast Region

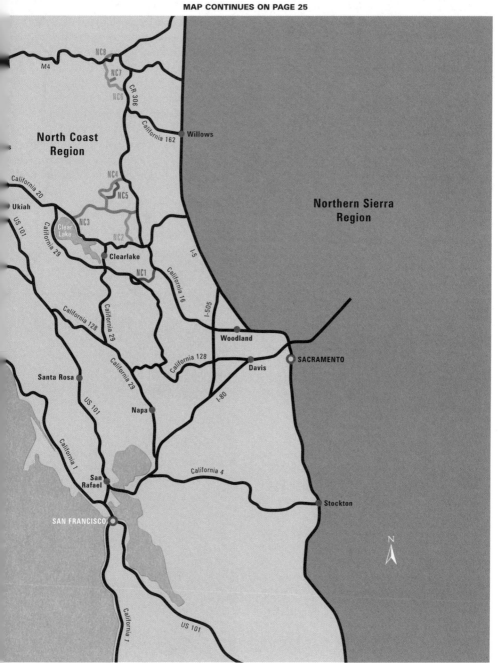

North Coast Region

Northern Sierra Region

NC8

M4

NC7

NC6

CR 306

California 162

Willows

NC4

NC5

Ukiah

US 101

California 20

NC3

Clear Lake

California 29

Clearlake

NC2

NC1

I-5

California 16

California 128

California 29

I-505

Woodland

California 128

Davis

SACRAMENTO

Santa Rosa

US 101

California 29

I-80

Napa

California 1

San Rafael

California 4

SAN FRANCISCO

Stockton

California 1

US 101

N

Rayhouse Road

STARTING POINT California 16, 9 miles south of the intersection with California 20
FINISHING POINT Morgan Valley Road, 12.5 miles southeast of the intersection of California 53 and California 29
TOTAL MILEAGE 13.1 miles
UNPAVED MILEAGE 13.1 miles
DRIVING TIME 1.5 hours
ELEVATION RANGE 600–2,500 feet
USUALLY OPEN Year-round
BEST TIME TO TRAVEL Dry weather
DIFFICULTY RATING 3
SCENIC RATING 8
REMOTENESS RATING +0

Special Attractions
■ Picnic area beside Cache Creek in Cache Creek Canyon Regional Park.
■ Varied scenery, from ridge tops to canyons.
■ Canoe put-in on Cache Creek and access to hiking and mountain bike trails.

History
Cache Creek, at the start of this trail, was named by explorer and fur trapper Ewing Young. In 1832, Young camped just downstream in Cañada de Capay, also know as the Capay Valley, and cached goods nearby, remembering the river as Cache Creek. Kaipai, as local Patwin Indians knew the cañada or valley, means "stream." The confluence of Cache and Bear Creeks, 2 miles upstream from the start of the described trail, was once the location of a Patwin village named Tebti, meaning "confluence." The picnic area at the start of the trail was once the site of Lopa, another Patwin village.

The settlement of Rumsey, in the upper reaches of Cañada de Capay, was named for Captain D. C. Rumsey, who settled here in 1892. The town was the end of the line for a railroad that was intended to connect Vacaville and Clear Lake. The ambitious railroad up the spectacular steep-sided Cache Creek Canyon never progressed north of Rumsey.

Rumsey had an earthquake of unknown magnitude sometime after the quake that devasted San Francisco in 1906. The earthquake caused a landslide that blocked the confluence of Crack and Cache Creeks, some 10 miles upstream from the start of this trail. Water backed up beginning at the lower end of Kennedy Flats, where the river narrows at the foot of Baldy Mountain. It didn't take long for people in Rumsey to notice that Cache Creek had all but dried up.

High water in Cache Creek can close the trail

The trail from Blue Ridge toward Davis Creek Reservoir

Fearing the worst, most of the community took to the surrounding hills, while a daring party headed up the canyon to determine the cause. They found that the landslide was impounding Cache Creek's water up to 4 miles behind the dam. When the water finally broke through, the flood caused immense damage to Rumsey, but the hardy townsfolk rebuilt.

Description

This trail crosses the southern end of Blue Ridge and travels through BLM and private lands. It begins at a picnic area in Cache Creek Canyon Regional Park and immediately dips down to ford through wide Cache Creek. Do not attempt to cross if the creek is in flood. A pleasant creekside camping area is a short distance north along California 16. As the trail climbs onto Blue Ridge, a couple of different trails for hikers and mountain bikers branch off from the main route.

The easy going trail climbs up a wide shelf road with ample passing places. On top of Blue Ridge, one track leads back down toward Cal-

ifornia 16 and another travels past Fiske Lake and continues along the ridge tops. The trail starts to descend steeply toward Davis Creek Reservoir, an extremely pretty reed-fringed lake surrounded by hills; it is privately owned, and no fishing, boating, or swimming is allowed. This narrow and rough shelf road is what gives the trail its difficulty rating of 3. Some remains of the Reed Mine, including some old cabins and mine workings, can be seen beside the road. These are on private property and should not be disturbed.

The road, designated Rayhouse Road in Yolo County, improves as you enter Lake County, where it is called Reiff Road. Reiff Road is graded and wide, and leads to private properties off Morgan Valley Road.

Current Road Information

Bureau of Land Management
Ukiah Field Office
2550 North State Street
Ukiah, CA 95482
(707) 468-4000

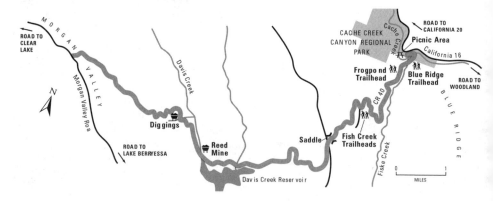

Map References

BLM Healdsburg
USGS 1:24,000 Glascock Mt., Knoxville,
 Jericho Valley, Wilson Valley
 1:100,000 Healdsburg
Maptech CD-ROM: North Coast/Mendocino
Northern California Atlas & Gazetteer, p. 84
California Road & Recreation Atlas, p. 64

Route Directions

▼ 0.0   From California 16, 9 miles south of
 the intersection with California 20, zero
 trip meter and turn southwest onto CR
 40. The road leads off through the
 Cache Creek Canyon Regional Park picnic area—lower site. The picnic area
 is on the right. The trail immediately
 swings around and descends toward
 Cache Creek.
4.6 ▲ Trail ends at T-intersection with
 California 16 at the Cache Creek
 Canyon Regional Park picnic area—
 lower site. Turn right for Woodland;
 turn left for California 20.
   GPS: N38°54.52' W122°18.64'

▼ 0.1   SO Seasonal closure gate; then cattle
 guard.
4.5 ▲ SO Cattle guard; then seasonal closure gate.
▼ 0.2   SO Cross over Cache Creek on concrete ford.
4.4 ▲ SO Cross over Cache Creek on concrete ford.
▼ 0.3   SO Blue Ridge Trail for hikers through gate
 on left; then cattle guard.
4.3 ▲ SO Cattle guard; then Blue Ridge Trail for

hikers through gate on right.
▼ 0.5   SO Cross over Fiske Creek on bridge. Start
 of shelf road.
4.1 ▲ SO End of shelf road. Cross over Fiske
 Creek on bridge.
▼ 0.7   SO Frogpond Trail, a 5-mile loop for hikers,
 equestrians, and mountain bikers, on
 right.
3.9 ▲ SO Frogpond Trail, a 5-mile loop for hikers,
 equestrians, and mountain bikers, on
 left.
   GPS: N38°54.22' W122°18.58'

▼ 2.5   SO Fish Creek Trail for hikers, equestrians,
 and mountain bikers on left.
2.1 ▲ SO Fish Creek Trail for hikers, equestrians,
 and mountain bikers on right.
   GPS: N38°53.53' W122°19.03'

▼ 2.6   SO Track on right.
2.0 ▲ SO Track on left.
▼ 2.9   SO Alternative Fish Creek Trail for hikers,
 equestrians, and mountain bikers on
 left goes to Fiske Creek Road; then
 track on right.
1.7 ▲ SO Track on left; then alternative Fish
 Creek Trail for hikers, equestrians, and
 mountain bikers on right goes to Fiske
 Creek Road.
   GPS: N38°53.42' W122°19.19'

▼ 3.1   BL Track on right.
1.5 ▲ BR Track on left.
▼ 4.6   SO 4-way intersection on saddle. Track on
 right goes to Buck Island. Track on left

goes to Fiske Lake and Blue Ridge Trail. Zero trip meter.

▲ .0 ▲ Continue to the north.

GPS: N38°52.68' W122°19.60'

Walker Ridge Road

▼ 0.0 Continue to the south.

3.5 s ▲ SO 4-way intersection on saddle. Track on left goes to Buck Island. Track on right goes to Fiske Lake and Blue Ridge Trail. Zero trip meter.

▼ 0.3 SO Cross through wash.
3.2 ▲ SO Cross through wash.

▼ 2.7 SO End of shelf road. Davis Creek Reservoir on left.
3.8 ▲ SO Leave Davis Creek Reservoir. Start of shelf road.

▼ 3.1 SO Cross over spillway; then pass along dam.
3.4 ▲ SO Pass along dam; then cross over spillway.

GPS: N38°51.84' W122°21.15'

▼ 4.2 SO Cross over Davis Creek. Remains of the Reed Mine on left and right.
4.3 ▲ SO Remains of the Reed Mine on left and right. Cross over Davis Creek; then Davis Creek Reservoir on right.

GPS: N38°51.80' W122°22.14'

▼ 5.2 SO Cross over creek.
3.3 ▲ SO Cross over creek.

▼ 5.4 SO Track on left into diggings.
3.1 ▲ SO Track on right into diggings.

GPS: N38°52.31' W122°22.92'

▼ 6.2 SO Closure gate; then track on left.
2.3 ▲ SO Track on right; then closure gate.

▼ 6.3 SO Track on right and track on left.
2.2 ▲ SO Track on right and track on left.

▼ 6.4 SO Track on left.
2.1 ▲ SO Track on right.

▼ 8.5 Trail ends at T-intersection with paved Morgan Valley Road. Turn right for Clear Lake; turn left for Lake Berryessa.
0.0 ▲ Trail commences on Morgan Valley Road, 12.5 miles southeast of the intersection of California 53 and California 29 at Lower Lake. Zero trip meter and turn northeast on graded dirt Reiff Road.

GPS: N38°52.55' W122°25.40'

STARTING POINT North Coast #3: Bartlett Springs Road, 2.8 miles from the eastern end
FINISHING POINT California 20, 5.9 miles west of the intersection with California 16
TOTAL MILEAGE 14 miles
UNPAVED MILEAGE 14 miles
DRIVING TIME 1.5 hours
ELEVATION RANGE 1,900–3,400 feet
USUALLY OPEN Year-round
BEST TIME TO TRAVEL Dry weather
DIFFICULTY RATING 1
SCENIC RATING 8
REMOTENESS RATING +0

Special Attractions

■ Winding ridge top trail.
■ Views of Indian Valley Reservoir.

History

Walker Ridge Road overlooks Indian Valley Reservoir in Little Indian Valley, formerly a favorite camping and hunting grounds for the Patwin tribe. The $9 million reservoir was established in 1975 when a dam was constructed across a narrow section of the North Fork of Cache Creek. The reservoir's convoluted shoreline stretches nearly 40 miles, creating a surface area of nearly 4,000 acres when the reservoir is full. Although it is in Lake County, the reservoir provides water for Yolo County to the southeast.

Walker Ridge Road ends immediately west of Wilbur, a mining community that dates back to the 1860s when Ezekial Wilbur and Edwin T. Howell began prospecting for copper on the banks of the West Fork of Sulphur Creek. Their mining venture failed, but the hot springs in the creek paid off. Howell opted out of the failed mine, while Wilbur turned his attention to the springs and established Wilbur Springs Hotel in 1865. The resort immediately became a favorite stage stop. A Victorian-style hotel was added in 1915, and it continues to be a popular retreat.

The Manzanita Gold Mine, just upstream from the hot springs, was established in the late 1880s and became one of the most productive gold mines in Colusa County. Eventually the Manzanita produced mercury. Many other mines appeared along the West Fork of Sulphur Creek. The Empire, Wide Awake, Central, and Elgin Mines all had their day in this picturesque canyon.

NORTH COAST #2: WALKER RIDGE ROAD

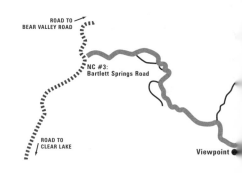

Description

Walker Ridge Road connects North Coast #3: Bartlett Springs Road with California 20. It runs across an open ridge top and offers excellent views in all directions. The trail is an easy, graded road, and passenger vehicles should generally be able to reach the start of the trail by traveling the first 2.8 miles of the 2-rated Bartlett Springs Road. From the ridge top, Indian Valley Reservoir can be seen in the valley to the west.

The vegetation on the ridge is mainly chap-

Indian Valley Reservoir

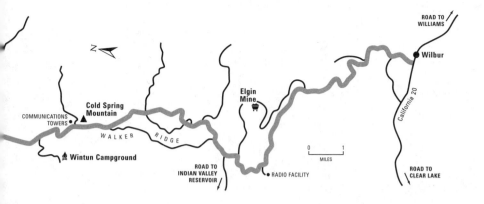

arral. The road originally served mines along the way, some of which are still active. Its primary use nowadays is as an access road for hunters.

Current Road Information

Bureau of Land Management
Ukiah Field Office
2550 North State Street
Ukiah, CA 95482
(707) 468-4000

Map References

BLM   Lakeport
USGS 1:24,000 Leesville, Wilbur Springs
      1:100,000 Lakeport
Maptech CD-ROM: North Coast/Mendocino
Northern California Atlas & Gazetteer, p. 76

Route Directions

▼ 0.0   From a 4-way intersection on North
         Coast #3: Bartlett Springs Road, 2.8
         miles from the eastern end, zero trip
         meter and turn southeast on graded
         dirt road, following the BLM sign for
         Indian Valley Dam.
4.9 ▲   Trail ends at a 4-way intersection with
         North Coast #3: Bartlett Springs Road.
         Turn left to follow this trail to Nice and
         Clear Lake; turn right to exit to
         Leesville and Williams.
         GPS: N39°09.51′ W122°28.73′

▼ 0.8   SO Track on right.
4.1 ▲   SO Track on left.

▼ 0.9   SO Track on left.
4.0 ▲   SO Track on right.
▼ 1.4   BL Two tracks on right.
3.5 ▲   BR Two tracks on left.
▼ 1.5   SO Track on right.
3.4 ▲   SO Track on left.
▼ 1.9   SO Track on right.
3.0 ▲   SO Track on left.
▼ 2.8   SO Track on left.
2.1 ▲   SO Track on right.
▼ 3.2   SO Track on left.
1.7 ▲   SO Track on right.
▼ 3.8   SO Turnout on right with views of Indian
         Valley Reservoir.
1.1 ▲   SO Turnout on left with views of Indian
         Valley Reservoir.
         GPS: N39°07.19′ W122°29.93′

▼ 4.0   SO Track on left.
0.9 ▲   SO Track on right.
▼ 4.9   SO Graded road on right goes to Wintun
         Campground. Zero trip meter.
0.0 ▲   Continue to the northwest.
         GPS: N39°06.36′ W122°29.59′

▼ 0.0   Continue to the southeast.
4.0 ▲   SO Graded road on left goes to Wintun
         Campground. Zero trip meter.
▼ 0.8   SO Cold Spring Mountain. Track on left
         goes past communications towers.
3.2 ▲   SO Cold Spring Mountain. Track on right
         goes past communications towers.
         GPS: N39°05.90′ W122°29.27′

▼ 1.3   SO Track on right.
2.7 ▲   SO Track on left.

Cold Spring Mountain, the highest point along the ridge

▼ 2.1   SO   Track on left and track on right.
1.9 ▲   SO   Track on right and track on left.
▼ 2.6   SO   Track on right.
1.4 ▲   SO   Track on left.
▼ 3.0   SO   Two tracks on right and track on left.
1.0 ▲   SO   Two tracks on left and track on right.
▼ 3.1   SO   Track on left.
0.9 ▲   SO   Track on right.
▼ 3.3   SO   Track on left.
0.7 ▲   SO   Track on right.
▼ 3.7   SO   Track on right.
0.3 ▲   SO   Track on left.
▼ 4.0   BL   Graded road on right goes to Blue Oak
              and Indian Valley Dam. Also track on
              right. Zero trip meter.
0.0 ▲   Continue to the northeast.
              GPS: N39°03.78' W122°29.36'

▼ 0.0   Continue to the southeast.
5.1 ▲   BR   Graded road on left goes to Blue Oak

and Indian Valley Dam. Also second
track on left. Zero trip meter.
▼ 0.3   SO   Track on left.
4.8 ▲   SO   Track on right.
▼ 1.1   SO   Track on right to radio facility; then
              track on left.
4.0 ▲   SO   Track on right; then track on left to
              radio facility.
▼ 2.2   SO   Track on left.
2.9 ▲   SO   Track on right.
▼ 2.6   SO   Graded road on left to Elgin Mine—
              private property.
2.5 ▲   SO   Graded road on right to Elgin Mine—
              private property.
              GPS: N39°02.75' W122°27.95'

▼ 3.1   SO   Track on left.
2.0 ▲   SO   Track on right.
▼ 3.3   SO   Track on right.
1.8 ▲   SO   Track on left.

▼ 4.1	SO	Track on left.
1.0 ▲	SO	Track on right.
▼ 4.7	SO	Track on right.
0.4 ▲	SO	Track on left.
▼ 5.1		Track on left; then trail ends at T-intersection with California 20 near Wilbur. Turn right for Clear Lake; turn left for Williams.
0.0 ▲		Trail commences on California 20, 5.9 miles west of the intersection with California 16. Zero trip meter and turn north on graded dirt road, following sign for Walker Ridge Road.

GPS: N39°01.39′ W122°27.15′

NORTH COAST #3

Bartlett Springs Road

STARTING POINT Bear Valley Road, 11 miles south of Lodoga

FINISHING POINT California 20, at the southern end of Nice on the northern shores of Clear Lake

TOTAL MILEAGE 33.7 miles

UNPAVED MILEAGE 33.5 miles

DRIVING TIME 2.5 hours

ELEVATION RANGE 1,400–3,900 feet

USUALLY OPEN April to December

BEST TIME TO TRAVEL April to December

DIFFICULTY RATING 2

SCENIC RATING 9

REMOTENESS RATING +1

Special Attractions

- Clear Lake—California's largest natural lake entirely within the state.
- Fishing at Indian Valley Reservoir.
- Long winding trail that travels through canyons and ridge tops in Mendocino National Forest.

History

Bartlett Springs Road follows a stagecoach route that connected Leesville, a settlement now abandoned in Bear Valley, with a number of mountain resorts to the west. The road crosses Bartlett Mountain to end at an old

mineral water bottling plant beside Clear Lake.

Kentuckian Greene Bartlett drove cattle to California in the 1850s and eventually settled in Napa County in the early 1860s. Bartlett's health was poor, so he took his doctor's advice and moved to higher elevations in the vicinity of the North Fork of Cache Creek; he discovered Bartlett Springs in 1870 and established a resort. Word spread about its healthful waters and within three years, the resort boasted a large hotel and some 40 cabins. In its fourth year, Bartlett Springs had nearly 80 cabins, and a steady stream of stagecoaches plied the bumpy wagon road to its doors. The springs' mineral waters were bottled at a plant on Clear Lake.

A community developed at the resort to cater to the ever-increasing numbers of guests. By the turn of the twentieth century, stores, a post office, and other business were well established. Unfortunately, a disastrous fire in 1934 brought an end to the resort. By 1935, the post office had closed and only a few people remained in the valley.

Stages passed through the community of Barkerville before stopping at the well-known Hough Springs Resort. Built in the early 1880s, the resort's hotel and cabins were a welcome sight to the passengers after the rough and dusty wagon ride. From here, stages proceeded up the North Fork of the Cache Creek Valley, past Allen Springs, to the more developed Bartlett Springs Resort.

Description

Bartlett Springs Road is a pleasant drive through a variety of scenery in Mendocino National Forest. The trail begins in the wide Bear Valley and travels west past Indian Valley Reservoir. Many side trails lead down to the shore of the reservoir, but there are no developed facilities at its north end. After crossing the North Fork of Cache Creek, the trail enters BLM land and passes a large, well-used informal camping area. The route follows the North Fork of Cache Creek in its narrow canyon for some distance, and the road is narrow and rough enough that a high-clearance vehicle is recommended.

Bartlett Mineral Springs, established in 1870, is now abandoned

North Coast #4: Pacific Ridge Trail joins this trail at Hough Springs. Bartlett Springs Road continues along a wider graded dirt road toward Clear Lake. There is some private property along this county-maintained road, and there are few camping opportunities. Be sure to remain on marked trails to avoid straying onto private property. Watch out for coyotes, deer, and bobcats on the open ridge top, and raptors soaring in the air currents above. The trail descends toward Clear Lake to finish on California 20 at the southern edge of Nice. The final part of the trail provides views over Clear Lake to the distant Mayacmas Mountains.

Current Road Information
Bureau of Land Management
Ukiah Field Office
2550 North State Street
Ukiah, CA 95482
(707) 468-4000

Mendocino National Forest
Upper Lake Ranger District
10025 Elk Mountain Road
Upper Lake, CA 95485
(707) 275-2361

Map References
BLM Lakeport
USFS Mendocino National Forest
USGS 1:24,000 Leesville, Hough Springs, Bartlett Springs, Bartlett Mt., Lucerne
1:100,000 Lakeport
Maptech CD-ROM: North Coast/Mendocino
Northern California Atlas & Gazetteer,
pp. 76, 75
California Road & Recreation Atlas, p. 63

Route Directions

▼ 0.0   From Bear Valley Road, 11 miles south of Lodoga, zero trip meter and turn

UKIAH

Mendocino County was made up of three Mexican land grants, the Yokayo, del Norte (also known as Garcia grant), and the Sanel, or Felix, grants. In 1845, Mexican Governor Pío Pico gave the Yokayo, in the Russian River Valley, to Cayetano Juarez, a militia captain and native Californian. The city of Ukiah takes its name from the phonetic pronunciation of Yokayo, which is Pomo for "deep valley."

State Street, Ukiah, circa 1930

In 1856, Samuel Lowry built a log cabin on the site, now 60 miles north of Santa Rosa on US 101. The first post office was established in 1858, and once Ukiah had a sufficient population, the town became the Mendocino County seat. Until then, the county, one of the original 27, had been administered from Sonoma.

Harrison Standley, the first postmaster, built a hotel in 1858, and the *Mendocino Herald* began publication in 1860. Property prices surged in 1889 when a railroad reached the town. A fire burned much of the Ukiah in 1917, then a town of nearly 2,000 people. The Parducci Winery opened in 1931 and was for many years the northernmost winery in the state. Ukiah, amid great redwoods, thrived in the late 1940s and early 1950s as a logging town. Now the area has numerous wineries, such as Fetzer, vineyards, pear orchards, and wood product plants. Ukiah's population has topped 15,000.

The Grace Hudson Museum and Sun House, once the home of artist Grace Hudson and her physician husband and amateur anthropologist, John Hudson, has a large collection of artifacts, Grace Hudson's paintings, Pomo Indian baskets, and historic photos. The house, built in 1911, is of redwood and is a classic of the California Craftsman style.

US 101, a principal north-south highway, brings hundreds of tourists to the region to enjoy nearby Lake Mendocino and the Cow Mountain Recreation Area.

NORTH COAST #3: BARTLETT SPRINGS ROAD

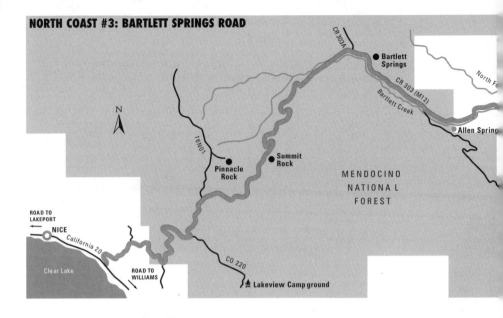

<table>
<tr><td></td><td></td><td>southwest on paved road, following the sign to Indian Valley Reservoir and Bartlett Springs.</td></tr>
<tr><td>2.8 ▲</td><td></td><td>Trail ends at T-intersection with paved Bear Valley Road. Turn left for Lodoga and Williams; turn right for California 20.
GPS: N39°09.87' W122°26.38'</td></tr>
</table>

0.1 ▼	SO	Cross over Bear Creek. Road turns to graded dirt.
2.7 ▲	SO	Cross over Bear Creek. Road is now paved.
0.3 ▼	SO	Cross over Mill Creek on bridge.
2.5 ▲	SO	Cross over Mill Creek on bridge.
0.5 ▼	SO	Cross over creek.
2.3 ▲	SO	Cross over creek.
1.7 ▼	SO	Cross over creek.
1.1 ▲	SO	Cross over creek.
2.8 ▼	SO	4-way intersection. Graded road on left is North Coast #2: Walker Ridge Road. Graded road on right. Zero trip meter.
0.0 ▲		Continue to the northeast. GPS: N39°09.51' W122°28.73'

0.0 ▼		Continue to the west.
7.3 ▲	SO	4-way intersection. Graded road on right is North Coast #2: Walker Ridge Road. Graded road on left. Zero trip meter.
1.9 ▼	SO	Cross through Kilpepper Creek.

5.4 ▲	SO	Cross through Kilpepper Creek. GPS: N39°10.01' W122°30.41'
2.1 ▼	SO	Cross over creek on bridge.
5.2 ▲	SO	Cross over creek on bridge.
2.9 ▼	SO	Hiking trail on left; then cross over creek on bridge.
4.4 ▲	SO	Cross over creek on bridge; then hiking trail on right.
3.0 ▼	SO	Track on right; then track on left. Indian Valley Reservoir on left.
4.3 ▲	SO	Track on right; then track on left. Leaving Indian Valley Reservoir.
3.3 ▼	SO	Start to cross dam.
4.0 ▲	SO	Leave dam. GPS: N39°10.05' W122°32.03'

3.5 ▼	SO	Leave dam.
3.8 ▲	SO	Start to cross dam.
4.0 ▼	SO	Track on left. Many tracks on left lead down to the lakeshore for the next 3.3 miles.
3.3 ▲	SO	Track on right.
4.3 ▼	SO	Two tracks on right.
3.0 ▲	SO	Two tracks on left.
4.6 ▼	SO	Cross over creek.
2.7 ▲	SO	Cross over creek.
4.7 ▼	SO	Track on right.
2.6 ▲	SO	Track on left. GPS: N39°09.52' W122°32.89'

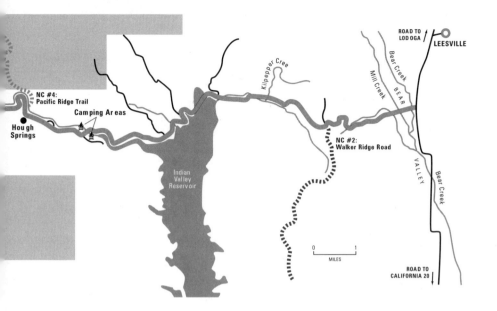

		▼ 0.9 SO Track on right.
▼ 5.0 SO Track on right; then cross over creek.		0.8 ▲ SO Track on left.
2.3 ▲ SO Cross over creek; then track on left.		▼ 0.9 SO Track on right.
▼ 5.6 SO Track on right.		0.7 ▲ SO Track on left.
1.7 ▲ SO Track on left.		▼ 1.6 SO Hough Springs on left—little remains.
▼ 6.7 SO Track on right.		0.1 ▲ SO Hough Springs on right—little remains.
0.6 ▲ SO Track on left.		▼ 1.7 SO Track on left. Track on right is North

▼ 7.3   SO   Track on right; then cross over North Fork Cache Creek on bridge. Camping areas on the right and left after bridge. End of tracks on left. Zero trip meter on far side of bridge.

0.0 ▲   Continue to the northeast. Track on left at far end of bridge. Many tracks on right lead down to lakeshore for next 3.3 miles.

       GPS: N39°09.40′ W122°35.12′

▼ 0.0   Continue to the southwest.

1.7 ▲   SO   Camping areas on the left and right. Zero trip meter and cross over North Fork Cache Creek on bridge.

▼ 0.1   SO   Track on left into camping area and track on right.

1.6 ▲   BL   Track on right into camping area and track on left.

▼ 0.5   SO   Track on right.
1.2 ▲   SO   Track on left.
▼ 0.8   SO   Track on right.
0.9 ▲   SO   Track on left.

▼ 1.7   SO   Track on left. Track on right is North Coast #4: Pacific Ridge Trail, which drops down to cross through North Fork Cache Creek. Intersection is unmarked. Zero trip meter.

0.0 s   Continue to the southeast.

       GPS: N39°09.92′ W122°36.75′

▼ 0.0   Continue to the northwest.

7.2 s   SO   Track on right. Track on left is North Coast #4: Pacific Ridge Trail, which immediately drops down to cross through North Fork Cache Creek. Intersection is unmarked. Zero trip meter.

▼ 0.1   SO   Track on left.
7.1 s   SO   Track on right.
▼ 0.8   SO   Track on right.
6.4 s   SO   Track on left.
▼ 0.9   SO   Track on right.
6.3 s   SO   Track on left.
▼ 2.7   SO   Cross over Bartlett Creek on bridge.
4.5 s   SO   Cross over Bartlett Creek on bridge.

       GPS: N39°09.92′ W122°38.67′

▼ 4.0　SO　Track on left.
3.2 s　SO　Track on right.
▼ 4.8　SO　Track on left.
2.4 s　SO　Track on right.
▼ 6.8　SO　Passing through Bartlett Mineral
　　　　　　Springs property.
0.4 s　SO　Passing through Bartlett Mineral
　　　　　　Springs property.
　　　　　　GPS: N39°11.01′ W122°42.17′

▼ 7.2　SO　Track on right is CR 303A (17N04) to
　　　　　　Twin Valley. Zero trip meter and follow
　　　　　　the sign to Bartlett Flat.
0.0 s　　　Continue to the east.
　　　　　　GPS: N39°11.07′ W122°42.48′

▼ 0.0　　　Continue to the west on CR 303 (M12).
7.9 s　SO　Track on left is CR 303A (17N04) to
　　　　　　Twin Valley. Zero trip meter and follow
　　　　　　the sign to Bartlett Springs.
▼ 0.6　SO　Cross over creek on bridge.
7.3 s　SO　Cross over creek on bridge.
▼ 4.7　BR　Two tracks on left.
3.2 s　BL　Two tracks on right.
▼ 5.1　SO　Pinnacle Rock on right and Summit
　　　　　　Rock on left.
2.8 s　SO　Pinnacle Rock on left and Summit Rock
　　　　　　on right.
　　　　　　GPS: N39°09.01′ W122°44.74′

▼ 6.2　SO　Track on left.
1.7 s　SO　Track on right.
▼ 7.3　SO　Track on right.
0.6 s　SO　Track on left.
▼ 7.9　SO　Track on right is16N01 to Pinnacle
　　　　　　Rock. Zero trip meter and follow the
　　　　　　sign to California 20.
0.0 s　　　Continue to the north.
　　　　　　GPS: N39°08.08′ W122°46.54′

▼ 0.0　　　Continue to the south.
5.8 s　SO　Track on left is 16N01 to Pinnacle
　　　　　　Rock. Zero trip meter and follow the
　　　　　　sign to Bartlett Springs.
▼ 0.8　SO　Track on left.
5.0 s　SO　Track on right.
▼ 1.1　BR　Track on left is CO 220 to Lakeview
　　　　　　USFS Campground. Remain on CO 303.
4.7 s　BL　Track on right is CO 220 to Lakeview

USFS Campground. Remain on CO
303.
　　　　　　GPS: N39°07.33′ W122°46.81′

▼ 3.2　SO　Track on left.
2.6 s　SO　Track on right.
▼ 3.7　SO　Leaving Mendocino National Forest.
2.1 s　SO　Entering Mendocino National Forest.
▼ 4.7　BL　Track on right and Fife Road on right.
1.1 s　BR　Fife Road on left and track on left.
▼ 5.7　SO　Road becomes paved.
0.1 s　SO　Road turns to graded dirt.
▼ 5.8　　　Trail ends at T-intersection with
　　　　　　California 20 on the northern shore of
　　　　　　Clear Lake. Turn left for Williams; turn
　　　　　　right for Lakeport.
0.0 s　　　Trail commences on California 20 on
　　　　　　the north shore of Clear Lake at the
　　　　　　southern end of Nice. Zero trip meter
　　　　　　and turn north on paved road, follow-
　　　　　　ing the sign for Bartlett Springs and
　　　　　　Hough Springs. There is a sign for
　　　　　　Bartlett Mineral Springs at the inter-
　　　　　　section
　　　　　　GPS: N39°06.75′ W122°49.14′

NORTH COAST #4

Pacific Ridge Trail

STARTING POINT Lodoga-Stonyford Road, 2
miles west of Lodoga and 6 miles south
of Stonyford
FINISHING POINT North Coast #3: Bartlett
Springs Road at Hough Springs
TOTAL MILEAGE 20.4 miles
UNPAVED MILEAGE 20.4 miles
DRIVING TIME 2 hours
ELEVATION RANGE 1,300–3,600 feet
USUALLY OPEN Year-round
BEST TIME TO TRAVEL Dry weather
DIFFICULTY RATING 2
SCENIC RATING 9
REMOTENESS RATING +0

Special Attractions

■ Access to a network of 4WD trails in the
Stonyford OHV Area.

Little Stony Creek's fall color

- Exceptional views from long sections of shelf road.
- Can be combined with North Coast #5: Lovelady Ridge Trail to make a challenging loop.

History

This trail begins at the settlement of Lodoga in Indian Valley, and makes its way across Pacific Ridge before dropping down to the North Fork of Cache Creek. The Patwin Indians, a subtribe of the Wintun, occupied this region prior to the arrival of settlers in the mid-nineteenth century. The Patwin, whose name means a single person or man in their language, lived on the western side of the lower Sacramento Valley. Their diet consisted mainly of acorns, pine nuts, wild grapes, and venison as well as salmon and steelhead, which spawned in the Sacramento River across the flat of Colusa Basin. The Patwin caught fish in weirs and then dried and pulverized them to make an easy-to-carry meal for later consumption.

Bahka, a group of Patwin villages, was located in Indian Valley near the site of Lodoga. Another village called Tsuhel-mem was also located in the aptly named valley.

Hough Springs, on the banks of the North Fork of Cache Creek, was a popular mountain resort in the early 1880s. The resort had an attractive hotel, separate cottages, and camping areas to entice visitors to its tranquil setting and cool summer temperatures.

Description

This trail follows Little Stony Creek before climbing up and over Pacific Ridge. It is rated a 2 for difficulty, mainly due to rough sections of shelf road along Pacific Ridge and a couple of shallow creek crossings that should not be difficult for high-clearance 2WD vehicles but will be impassable for low-slung vehicles. Like all creek crossings, high waters change conditions, and even those with high-clearance 4WDs should think twice before crossing in those conditions.

The first part of the trail, along pretty Little Stony Creek, passes through the

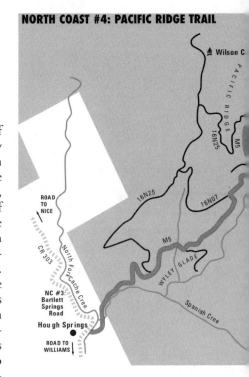

Stonyford OHV Area, which has a USFS campground and a day-use staging area. Many small trails lead off into the OHV area; some are only suitable for ATVs and motorbikes, but there are plenty of challenging and interesting runs for high-clearance 4WDs. Many of them are steep and climb high onto the ridge tops above Little Stony Creek. One of these trails, the 7-rated North Coast #5: Lovelady Ridge Trail, can be combined with the first part of this trail to make a more challenging loop.

Much of the middle part of the trail is a shelf road that winds above the creek. The trail then joins the better-graded forest road M5 and travels over Pacific Ridge. A long descent takes you to the final part of the trail and the rough crossing over the North Fork of Cache Creek at Hough Springs. The trail ends at the intersection with North Coast #3: Bartlett Springs Road.

Current Road Information

Bureau of Land Management
Ukiah Field Office
2550 North State Street

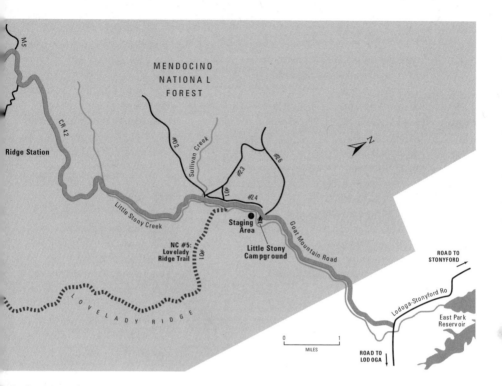

Ukiah, CA 95482
(707) 468-4000

Mendocino National Forest
Grindstone Ranger District
325 North Humboldt Avenue
Willows, CA 95988
(530) 934-3316

Map References
BLM   Lakeport
USFS   Mendocino National Forest
USGS   1:24,000   Gilmore Peak, Fouts
Springs, Hough Springs, Bartlett Springs
       1:100,000 Lakeport
Maptech CD-ROM: North Coast/Mendocino
Northern California Atlas & Gazetteer,
       pp. 76, 75
California Road & Recreation Atlas, p. 63
Other: Stonyford OHV Area Guide
       (incomplete)

Route Directions

▼ 0.0   From Lodoga–Stonyford Road, 2 miles
             west of Lodoga and 6 miles south of

Stonyford, zero trip meter and turn
south on graded dirt Goat Mountain
Road, following the sign for Goat
Mountain.

4.3 ▲   Trail ends at T-intersection with
             Lodoga–Stonyford Road. Turn right for
             Lodoga; turn left for Stonyford.
             GPS: N39°18.30′ W122°31.55′

▼ 1.2   SO   Entering Mendocino National Forest.
3.1 ▲   SO   Leaving Mendocino National Forest.
▼ 3.2   SO   Cattle guard.
1.1 ▲   SO   Cattle guard.
▼ 3.5   SO   Little Stony USFS Campground on left.
             Track on right is #26 for 4WDs, ATVs,
             and motorbikes—rated blue.
0.8 ▲   SO   Track on left is #26 for 4WDs, ATVs,
             and motorbikes—rated blue. Little
             Stony USFS Campground on right.
             GPS: N39°17.23′ W122°34.58′

▼ 3.7   SO   Day-use staging area on left. Track on
             right is #24 for ATVs and motorbikes
             only—rated green.
0.6 ▲   SO   Day-use staging area on right. Track on
             left is #24 for ATVs and motorbikes

only—rated green.

▼ 4.3   SO   Track on left is North Coast #5: Lovelady Ridge Trail (#01) for 4WDs, ATVs, and motorbikes—rated blue. Track on right is also #01, but is for ATVs and motorbikes only—rated black. Zero trip meter. Start of shelf road along creek.

0.0 ▲   Continue to the north. End of shelf road.
             GPS: N39°16.77' W122°35.13'

▼ 0.0   Continue to the south.

7.4 ▲   SO   Track on right is North Coast #5: Lovelady Ridge Trail (#01) for 4WDs, ATVs, and motorbikes—rated blue. Track on left is also #01, but is for ATVs and motorbikes only—rated black. Zero trip meter.

▼ 0.4   SO   Track on right is #24 for ATVs and motorbikes only—rated green; second track on right is #02 for motorbikes only—rated black. Cross over Sullivan

Creek on bridge.

7.0 ▲   SO   Cross over Sullivan Creek on bridge; then track on left is #02 for motorbikes only—rated black. Second track on left is #24 for ATVs and motorbikes only—rated green.
             GPS: N39°16.56' W122°35.43'

▼ 0.5   SO   Track on right is #02 for motorbikes only—rated black.

6.9 ▲   SO   Track on left is #02 for motorbikes only—rated black.

▼ 2.8   SO   Cross over Little Stony Creek on bridge; then track on right.

4.7 ▲   SO   Track on left; then cross over Little Stony Creek on bridge.
             GPS: N39°15.21' W122°36.50'

▼ 4.9   SO   Track on left. End of shelf road.

2.5 ▲   SO   Track on right. Start of shelf road.

▼ 5.4   SO   Track on right.

2.0 ▲   SO   Track on left.

Hillside above Wyley Glade

▼ 6.8 BR Track on left. Follow sign for Goat Mountain.
0.6 ▲ BL Track on right.
GPS: N39°14.76′ W122°39.09′

▼ 7.4 TL T-intersection with M5. Zero trip meter and follow the sign for Pacific Ridge.
0.0 ▲ Continue to the northeast on CR 42.
GPS: N39°14.89′ W122°39.67′

▼ 0.0 Continue to the south.
2.8 ▲ TR M5 continues straight ahead. Zero trip meter and follow the sign for Stonyford.

▼ 0.2 SO Track on left; then track on right.
2.6 ▲ SO Track on left; then track on right.
▼ 1.7 SO Track on right is 16N25 to Wilson Camp.
1.1 ▲ SO Track on left is 16N25 to Wilson Camp.
GPS: N39°13.62′ W122°38.99′

▼ 2.4 SO Track on left is 16N02 to Pacific Ridge Station. Follow the sign to Hough Springs.
0.4 ▲ SO Track on right is 16N02 to Pacific Ridge Station. Follow the sign to Cedar Camp.
GPS: N39°13.35′ W122°38.38′

▼ 2.7 SO Track on right.
0.1 ▲ SO Track on left.
▼ 2.8 TR Track straight ahead is North Coast #5: Lovelady Ridge Trail (16N06), signposted to Kanaka Glade. Zero trip meter and follow the sign for Hough Springs.
0.0 ▲ Continue to the northwest, remaining on M5.
GPS: N39°13.40′ W122°37.99′

▼ 0.0 Continue to the west, heading downhill and remaining on M5.
5.9 ▲ TL Track straight ahead is North Coast #5: Lovelady Ridge Trail (16N06), signposted to Kanaka Glade. Zero trip meter and follow the sign for Goat Mountain.
▼ 0.9 TL Track ahead is 16N07 to Wilson Camp. Follow the sign to Hough Springs. Road is now marked 16N44 as well as M5.
5.0 ▲ TR T-intersection. Track on left is 16N07

to Wilson Camp. Remain on M5
GPS: N39°12.80′ W122°37.80′

▼ 2.5 SO Track on left to Wyley Glade.
3.4 ▲ BL Track on right to Wyley Glade.
GPS: N39°11.80′ W122°37.27′

▼ 2.6 SO Cattle guard; then cross over creek.
3.3 ▲ SO Cross over creek; then cattle guard.
▼ 3.4 SO Track on right is 16N25. Continue straight ahead, joining 16N25 and following the sign for Hough Springs.
2.5 ▲ SO Track on left is 16N25. Continue straight ahead on 16N44, following the sign to Pacific Ridge.
GPS: N39°11.28′ W122°37.19′

▼ 3.5 SO Track on left.
2.4 ▲ SO Track on right.
▼ 5.2 SO Exiting Mendocino National Forest.
0.7 ▲ SO Entering Mendocino National Forest.
GPS: N39°10.25′ W122°37.03′

▼ 5.3 SO Track on right; then cross through Spanish Creek.
0.6 ▲ BR Cross through Spanish Creek; then track on left.
▼ 5.7 SO Start to cross through North Fork Cache Creek.
0.2 ▲ SO Exit North Fork Cache Creek.
▼ 5.8 BR Bear right and exit creek.
0.1 ▲ BL Bear left and start to cross through North Fork Cache Creek.
▼ 5.9 Trail ends at T-intersection with North Coast #3: Bartlett Springs Road (CR 303) at Hough Springs. Turn right to follow this trail to Nice; turn left to follow this trail to Leesville and on to Williams.
0.0 ▲ Trail begins on North Coast #3: Bartlett Springs Road (CR 303) at Hough Springs, 11.8 miles west of the eastern end in Bear Valley and 20.9 miles east of Nice. Zero trip meter and turn east onto unmarked trail that descends toward North Fork Cache Creek. The formed trail is well used and rough.
GPS: N39°09.92′ W122°36.75′

Lovelady Ridge Trail

STARTING POINT North Coast #4: Pacific Ridge Trail, 5.9 miles from the southern end
FINISHING POINT North Coast #4: Pacific Ridge Trail, 4.3 miles from the northern end
TOTAL MILEAGE 8.8 miles
UNPAVED MILEAGE 8.8 miles
DRIVING TIME 1 hour
ELEVATION RANGE 1,600–3,800 feet
USUALLY OPEN Year-round
BEST TIME TO TRAVEL Dry weather
DIFFICULTY RATING 7
SCENIC RATING 9
REMOTENESS RATING +0

Special Attractions

- Very steep, challenging trail for stock high-clearance 4WDs.
- Excellent views from the open ridge top.
- Access to a network of trails within the Stonyford OHV Area.

History

Lovelady Ridge is named for a pioneer family who settled at the base of the hill in the late 1860s. Joshua West Lovelady, an Alabama native, married Nancy McGaha of Tennessee in February 1851. Together, they made their way west as members of the ill-fated Fancher party in the spring of 1857. The couple's seven-month overland wagon trip almost ended in tragedy before reaching California. Captain Alexander Fancher, a Tennessean, organized a 40-wagon emigrant train in northwestern Arkansas. The group followed a southern route to California, and their trip across the Plains and over the Rockies into what was then Utah Territory was relatively uneventful. However, this all changed on September 11, 1857 when the party was attacked by Mormons and Indians at Mountain Meadows, in present-day southwestern Utah. More than 100 members of the party lost their lives in the massacre; the only survivors were a few children. Fortunately, the Lovelady family had left the wagon train two days before the bloody massacre.

Joshua and Nancy Lovelady lived in Nevada County for 10 years before moving to Colusa County. The 11-member Lovelady family eventually acquired a ranch of more than 300 acres at the southern end of Indian Valley. Joshua died 1886 and Nancy died in 1910.

Description

This challenging and extremely steep trail is an enjoyable run for experienced drivers of stock, high-clearance 4WDs. The trail, one of many within the Stonyford OHV Area, travels along Pacific Ridge, then Lovelady Ridge, and finally drops sharply to Little Stony Creek and North Coast #4: Pacific Ridge Trail. The trail's difficulty comes from the steepness of some sections that reach an angle of 30 degrees in places. The surface is mainly smooth, but some loose, low-traction sections combined with the steep grade make for a challenging run. Low-range 4WD is definitely required.

The trail leaves North Coast #4: Pacific Ridge Trail and travels a short distance along Pacific Ridge to Pacific Point. The trail is easy-going at this point—high-clearance 2WDs can generally reach Pacific Point. However, they should go no farther. Views from Pacific Point are spectacular, with Indian Valley Reservoir to the east and the ridges of the Coast Ranges to the north and south.

For the next few miles the trail undulates along Lovelady Ridge. You are mainly heading downhill in the forward direction, but there are a few steep climbs in either direction. One particularly steep section (downhill in the forward direction) has an alternate route rated 8 because of the uneven and extremely low-traction surface. Avoiding the alternate route keeps the trail's difficulty to a 7. The final mile drops steeply off the end of the ridge to cross through Little Stony Creek, finally finishing back on North Coast #4: Pacific Ridge Trail.

Trails in the OHV area are closed if there is 2 inches of moisture in a 24-hour period. This trail is definitely one to avoid in wet weather because the surface becomes greasy

Ascending the Pacific Ridge

NORTH COAST #5: LOVELDAY RIDGE TRAIL

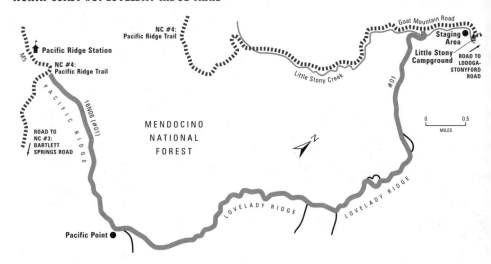

and extremely dangerous. Note that the Stonyford OHV Area map shows the northern end of this trail as suitable for ATVs and motorbikes only. This is incorrect—the trail is clearly marked on the ground as suitable for vehicles, and it is more than ample width.

Current Road Information
Mendocino National Forest
Grindstone Ranger District
825 North Humboldt Avenue
Willows, CA 95988
(530) 934-3316

Map References
BLM   Lakeport
USFS   Mendocino National Forest
USGS   1:24,000   Bartlett Springs, Hough
     Springs, Gilmore Peak
     1:100,000 Lakeport
Maptech CD-ROM: North Coast/Mendocino
Northern California Atlas & Gazetteer, p. 76
California Road & Recreation Atlas, p. 63
     (route not shown)
Other: Stonyford OHV Area Guide

Route Directions

▼ 0.0   From North Coast #4: Pacific Ridge Trail, 5.9 miles from the southern end, zero trip meter and proceed southeast

on 16N06, following the sign to Kanaka Ridge and Pacific Point. Road is also marked as #01 for 4WDs, ATVs, and motorbikes—rated blue.

2.4 ▲   Trail ends back on North Coast #4: Pacific Ridge Trail. Turn right to return to Lodoga–Stonyford Road; turn left to follow Pacific Ridge Trail to North Coast #3: Bartlett Springs Road.
     GPS: N39°13.40' W122°37.99'

▼ 2.4 BL Trail forks at unmarked intersection. Zero trip meter. Pacific Point is the rise on the right.
0.0 ▲   Continue to the south.
     GPS: N39°12.93' W122°35.78'

▼ 0.0   Continue to the north.
4.6 ▲ SO Track on left at unmarked intersection. Zero trip meter. Pacific Point is the rise on the left.
▼ 0.6 SO Track on left.
4.0 ▲ SO Track on right.
▼ 2.2 SO Track on right.
2.4 ▲ SO Track on left.
▼ 2.3 SO Track on right.
2.3 ▲ SO Track on left.
     GPS: N39°14.39' W122°34.81'

▼ 2.4 SO Track on right.
2.2 ▲ SO Track on left.

Challenging descent along Lovelady Ridge

▼ 2.6　SO　Track on right.
2.0 ▲　SO　Track on left.
▼ 2.8　BL　Track on right.
1.8 ▲　BR　Track on left.
　　　GPS: N39°14.66' W122°34.37'

▼ 3.0　SO　Two tracks on right.
1.6 ▲　SO　Two tracks on left.
▼ 3.2　SO　Track on right.
1.4 ▲　SO　Track on left.
▼ 3.9　SO　Track on left is a cut-across. Remain
　　　　on main trail.
0.7 ▲　SO　Cut-across rejoins.
▼ 4.0　SO　Cut-across rejoins.
0.6 ▲　BL　Track on right is a cut-across. Remain
　　　　on main trail.
　　　GPS: N39°15.39' W122°33.97'

▼ 4.4　SO　Track on right.
0.2 ▲　SO　Track on left.
▼ 4.6　TR　Track straight ahead is a steeper, alter-
　　　　nate 8-rated route. Zero trip meter and
　　　　turn right onto well-used track.
0.0 ▲　　　Continue to the southeast.
　　　GPS: N39°15.85' W122°33.99'

▼ 0.0　　　Continue to the north.
1.8 ▲　TL　Alternate route rejoins.
▼ 0.2　SO　Alternate route rejoins.
1.6 ▲　BL　Track on right is a steeper, alternate 8-
　　　　rated route.
▼ 1.7　SO　Cross through Little Stony Creek.
0.1 ▲　SO　Cross through Little Stony Creek.
▼ 1.8　　　Trail ends at T-intersection with North
　　　　Coast #4: Pacific Ridge Trail. Turn
　　　　right to exit to Lodoga–Stonyford
　　　　Road; turn left to travel this trail to
　　　　North Coast #3: Bartlett Springs Road.
0.0 ▲　　　From North Coast #4: Pacific Ridge
　　　　Trail, 4.3 miles from the northeastern
　　　　end, zero trip meter and turn east on
　　　　formed dirt trail marked Lovelady Ridge
　　　　Trail (#01) for 4WDs, ATVs, and
　　　　motorbikes—rated blue. Trail #01 con-
　　　　tinues on the far side of the road, but
　　　　is for ATVs and motorbikes only—
　　　　rated black.
　　　GPS: N39°16.77' W122°35.13'

Log Spring Ridge Trail

STARTING POINT Round Valley Road (M4),
13.5 miles southwest of Paskenta
FINISHING POINT CR 306, 8 miles north of Elk
Creek
TOTAL MILEAGE 19.3 miles
UNPAVED MILEAGE 18.6 miles
DRIVING TIME 2 hours
ELEVATION RANGE 800–4,500 feet
USUALLY OPEN April to December
BEST TIME TO TRAVEL Dry weather
DIFFICULTY RATING 1
SCENIC RATING 9
REMOTENESS RATING +0

Special Attractions

■ Optional 3-rated side trail to Buck Point
overlook.
■ Panoramic views of Rocky Ridge and the
Coast Ranges.
■ Access to a network of back roads and
4WD trails.

Description

Log Spring Ridge Trail, called Hull Road on
some maps, follows a chaparral-covered ridge
along the west side of the Sacramento Valley
and overlooks Mendocino National Forest in
the Coast Ranges and Rocky Ridge. The trail
is an easy one; generally suitable for passenger
vehicles in dry weather, but suitable only for
high-clearance 4WDs in wet weather. It accesses a network of backcountry roads and
4WD trails.

Most of the trail travels through an area
where motorized travel is restricted to num-
bered roads and trails. However, there are
plenty to choose from. One spur leads to
Buck Point, which overlooks Grindstone and
Grindstone Creek, as well as Rocky Ridge
and the Sacramento Valley. A more difficult
trail, 21N80, parallels much of the road and
offers an alternate route for high-clearance
4WDs that travels more along the actual
ridge top. The main trail ends by descending
to the valley toward Elk Creek.

Current Road Information

Mendocino National Forest
Grindstone Ranger District
825 North Humboldt Avenue
Willows, CA 95988
(530) 934-3316

Map References

BLM   Willows
USFS Mendocino National Forest
USGS 1:24,000 Hall Ridge, Alder
Springs, Chrome
1:100,000 Willows
Maptech CD-ROM: North Coast/Mendocino
Northern California Atlas & Gazetteer,
pp. 65, 66
California Road & Recreation Atlas, p. 58

Route Directions

▼ 0.0   From Round Valley Road (M4), at mile
          marker 14, 13.5 miles southwest of
          Paskenta, and 0.5 miles west of the

west end of North Coast #8: Nome
Cult Mountain House Trail, 12 miles
east of Log Springs USFS Work Station
zero trip meter and turn east on graded
dirt road 23N05. Intersection is
unmarked.

4.0 ▲   Trail ends at T-intersection with Round
          Valley Road (M4). Turn right for
          Paskenta.
          GPS: N39°49.62′ W122°40.56′

▼ 0.3 BL Paved road on right goes to Black Bear
          USFS Campground and Conklin
          Orchard.

3.7 ▲ BR Paved road on left goes to Black Bear
          USFS Campground and Conklin
          Orchard. Follow sign to Paskenta.
          GPS: N39°49.46′ W122°40.50′

▼ 1.2 SO Track on right and track on left.
2.8 ▲ SO Track on right and track on left.
▼ 1.6 SO Closed road on left is 23N05E to
          Houghton Place.

View from Buck Point

NORTH COAST #6: LOG SPRING RIDGE TRAIL

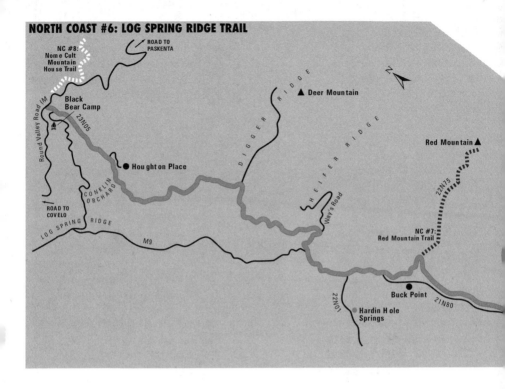

2.4 ▲	SO	Closed road on right is 23N05E to Houghton Place.
		GPS: N39°48.48' W122°40.51'

▼ 2.7	SO	Track on right.
1.3 ▲	SO	Track on left.
▼ 3.4	SO	Entering Glenn County. Track on right.
0.6 ▲	SO	Track on left. Entering Tehama County.
▼ 4.0	SO	Track on left to Freshwater Heliport. Zero trip meter.
0.0 ▲		Continue to the northwest.
		GPS: N39°47.29' W122°39.81'

▼ 0.0		Continue to the south.
3.6 ▲	SO	Track on right to Freshwater Heliport. Zero trip meter.
▼ 0.5	SO	Track on left to water point.
3.1 ▲	SO	Track on right to water point.
▼ 0.7	SO	Track on left through gate.
2.9 ▲	SO	Track on right through gate.
▼ 3.0	SO	Road on left is Way's Road.
0.6 ▲	BL	Road on right is Way's Road.
		GPS: N39°45.64' W122°39.36'

▼ 3.6	TL	T-intersection with graded road M9. Zero trip meter and follow the sign to

Doe Peak and Elk Creek.

0.0 ▲		Continue to the northeast.
		GPS: N39°45.54' W122°39.76'

▼ 0.0		Continue to the south.
2.4 ▲	TR	M9 continues straight ahead. Zero trip meter and turn right onto 23N05, following sign to Paskenta.
▼ 0.6	SO	Entering motor vehicle restricted travel area.
1.8 ▲	SO	Leaving motor vehicle restricted travel area.
▼ 0.9	BL	Graded road on right is 22N01 to Hardin Hole Springs.
1.5 ▲	SO	Graded road on left is 22N01 to Hardin Hole Springs.
		GPS: N39°44.96' W122°39.58'

▼ 1.6	SO	Track on right is 21N80; then cattle guard; then track on right is also 21N80, which goes 0.5 miles to Buck Point—rated 3.
0.8 ▲	SO	Track on left is 21N80, which goes 0.5 miles to Buck Point—rated 3; then cattle guard; then track on left is also 21N80.

▼ 2.4 TR Track on left; then track straight ahead is North Coast #7: Red Mountain Trail (22N75, shown on map as 22N04). Zero trip meter.

0.0 ▲ Continue to the west, remaining on M9. Immediately second track on right.

GPS: N39°44.29' W122°38.55'

▼ 0.0 Continue to the south, remaining on M9.

2.0 ▲ TL Track on right is North Coast #7: Red Mountain Trail (22N75, shown on map as 22N04). Zero trip meter.

▼ 0.6 SO Track on right. Ridge top trail crosses numerous times on left and right for the next 3.6 miles.

1.4 ▲ SO Track on left.

▼ 1.9 SO Track on right is 21N80. Tank on right.

0.1 ▲ SO Track on left is 21N80. Tank on left.

GPS: N39°42.87' W122°38.45'

Log Spring Ridge above the Sacramento Valley

▼ 2.0 SO Cattle guard; then track on right is 21N80. Second track on right at same intersection is 21N15 to Doe Peak and Manzanita Springs. Zero trip meter and follow the sign to Elk Creek.

0.0 ▲ Continue to the north, remaining on M9.
GPS: N39°42.75' W122°38.50'

▼ 0.0 Continue to the southeast, remaining on M9.

7.3 ▲ SO Track on left is 21N15 to Doe Peak and Manzanita Springs. Second track on left at same intersection is 21N80. Zero trip meter and follow the sign to Log Springs.

▼ 1.2 SO Track on right is 21N75.
6.1 ▲ SO Track on left is 21N75.

▼ 2.2 SO End of tracks crossing ridge tops.
5.1 ▲ SO Ridge top trail crosses numerous times on left and right for the next 3.6 miles.

▼ 2.4 SO Cattle guard.
4.9 ▲ SO Cattle guard.

▼ 2.6 SO Leaving Mendocino National Forest.
4.7 ▲ SO Entering Mendocino National Forest.
GPS: N39°43.10' W122°36.25'

▼ 6.1 SO Cattle guard.
1.2 ▲ SO Cattle guard.

▼ 6.3 SO Cattle guard. Leaving motor vehicle restricted travel area.
1.0 ▲ SO Cattle guard. Entering motor vehicle restricted travel area.

▼ 6.5 SO Track on right into private property.
0.8 ▲ BR Track on left into private property.
GPS: N39°41.90' W122°33.91'

▼ 6.6 SO Track on right into private property. Road becomes paved.
0.7 ▲ SO Track on left into private property. Road turns to graded dirt.

▼ 6.7 SO Cattle guard; then track on left.
0.6 ▲ BL Track on right; then cattle guard.

▼ 7.2 SO Cross over Watson Creek on bridge.
0.1 ▲ SO Cross over Watson Creek on bridge.

▼ 7.3 Cross over creek on bridge; then trail ends at T-intersection with CR 306. Turn left for Paskenta; turn right for Elk Creek.

0.0 ▲ Trail begins on CR 306, 3 miles north of intersection with California 162, 8 miles north of Elk Creek. Zero trip meter and turn west on paved road M9 (CR 313).
GPS: N39°41.94' W122°32.94'

Red Mountain Trail

STARTING POINT North Coast #6: Log Spring Ridge Trail, 10 miles south of the northern end
FINISHING POINT Red Mountain
TOTAL MILEAGE 2.4 miles (one-way)
UNPAVED MILEAGE 2.4 miles
DRIVING TIME 30 minutes (one-way)
ELEVATION RANGE 3,000–3,600 feet
USUALLY OPEN April to December
BEST TIME TO TRAVEL Dry weather
DIFFICULTY RATING 3
SCENIC RATING 9
REMOTENESS RATING +0

Special Attractions

■ Beautiful addition to North Coast #6: Log Spring Ridge Trail.
■ Panoramic views from Red Mountain.

History

The summit of Red Mountain rises 2,700 feet above the settlement of Chrome, named for chrome mines on the slopes below the peak. The mines, run by the Burrow family, operated until the middle of the twentieth century. Burrows Gap is one of the few passes in the 10-mile-long, north-south Rocky Ridge; it is clearly visible from the viewpoint on Red Mountain.

The striking lowlands below Red Mountain attracted many settlers, who typically raised sheep. William and Harriet Cushman set up ranch here in 1872. Harriet, from Connecticut, welcomed the move to warmer climes because her doctor feared her frail health would lead to tuberculosis. When she arrived after a long and dusty wagon ride from Sacramento she commented on the few shacks in the vicinity saying, "I could never live in a place like that." Much to her dismay, it was exactly where she was to live. Harriet and William planted orchards and raised sheep and goats. Harriet Cushman died in Orland in 1934 at age 95.

Description

This short spur branches off North Coast #6: Log Spring Ridge Trail near its midpoint and travels along a narrow shelf road to the old fire lookout site on Red Mountain. Communications equipment now stands on the mountain. The trail rates a 3 for difficulty because of the narrow shelf road and loose climb to the summit. From the top, 360-degree views include Black Butte Lake, Lassen Peak, and Rocky Ridge to the east; Mount Shasta to the north; and Stony Gorge Reservoir to the southeast. A small hiking trail leads off the ridge toward some mining remains.

Current Road Information

Mendocino National Forest
Grindstone Ranger District
825 North Humboldt Avenue
Willows, CA 95988
(530) 934-3316

Map References

BLM   Willows
USFS   Mendocino National Forest
USGS   1:24,000   Alder Springs, Chrome
     1:100,000   Willows
Maptech CD-ROM: North Coast/Mendocino
Northern California Atlas & Gazetteer,
    pp. 65, 66
California Road & Recreation Atlas, p. 58

Route Directions

▼ 0.0   From North Coast #6: Log Spring Ridge Trail, 10 miles south of the northern end at Round Valley Road

Red Mountain Trail

Black Diamond and Gray Eagle Mines.
End of shelf road.

▼ 2.3 Trail ends at communications towers
on Red Mountain.
GPS: N39°44.56' W122°36.52'

Gray Eagle Mine

Black Diamond Mine

COMMUNICATIONS TOWERS
Red Mountain▲
Gate

22N04

MENDOCINO
NATIONAL
FOREST

N

22N75

0   0.5
MILES

NC #6:
Log Spring Ridge Trail

M9

21N80

Buck Point

NORTH COAST #8

Nome Cult Mountain House Trail

STARTING POINT Round Valley Road (M4), 6.9 miles southwest of Paskenta
FINISHING POINT Round Valley Road (M4), 13.3 miles southwest of Paskenta
TOTAL MILEAGE 4 miles
UNPAVED MILEAGE 4 miles
DRIVING TIME 30 minutes
ELEVATION RANGE 1,000–3,000 feet
USUALLY OPEN April to December
BEST TIME TO TRAVEL Dry weather
DIFFICULTY RATING 4
SCENIC RATING 9
REMOTENESS RATING +0

Special Attractions
- Trail travels a section of the historic Nome Cult Trail.
- Excellent views of Rocky Ridge and the Sacramento Valley.
- Access to the hiking trail to Thomes Gorge.

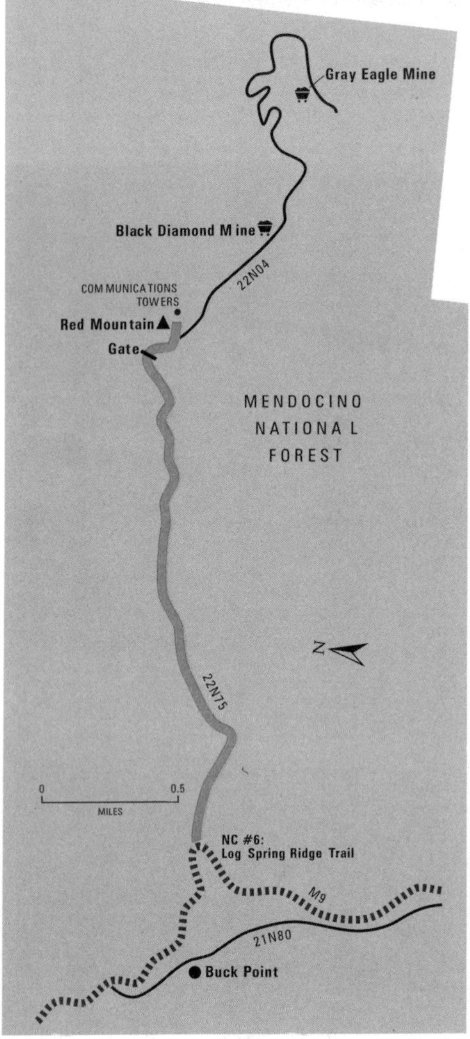

(M4), zero trip meter and turn east on dirt trail 22N75. Note that this road is shown on the forest service map as 22N04. Start of shelf road.
GPS: N39°44.29' W122°38.55'

▼ 0.4 SO Small track on right.
▼ 1.7 SO End of shelf road.
GPS: N39°44.53' W122°36.93'

▼ 2.1 SO Gate. Start of shelf road.
GPS: N39°44.61' W122°36.63'

▼ 2.2 SO Small track on right is 22N04 to the

History
After the arrival of settlers to this part of California, Indians were rounded up in 1854 and placed on the Nome Lackee Indian Reservation near Paskenta. Relocating the Nomlaki was as much a means to control them as it was to protect them from new settlers.

Another group of Indians, mainly Maidu, had been rounded up in Chico after five settlers' children were killed in Butte County. The settlers banded together to rid the northern Sacramento Valley of every Indian, and on September 4, 1863, 461 Indians left Chico under a cavalry escort to walk to the newly established Nome Cult Reservation in Round Valley. This 4WD trail follows part of their horrific 100-mile journey.

The ascent from the Sacramento Valley into the Coast Ranges marked the end for some of the Indians who had already walked more than 50 miles. They arrived at Mountain House on September 12, 1863, and camped for two days. About 150 Indians who were too old or sick to go on were left at Mountain House with four weeks provisions. The rest continued, forced to climb more than 6,000 feet before descending to Round Valley. Some mothers tried to kill their babies, fearing that, if they died, the children would be abandoned. Only 277 Indians completed the difficult journey to Round Valley.

Description

This short trail climbs the ridge and serves as a shortcut from the main forest road. Rated for 4WD vehicles only by the forest service, the trail is an easy to moderate run with a few rough spots for most high-clearance 4WDs. It switchbacks its way from oak-studded grasslands to chapparal-covered hillsides.

The Thomes Gorge Nomlaki Hiking Trail crosses the vehicle trail and heads north to the river gorge. There is limited parking at the trailhead. The hiking trail is rated difficult to very difficult, because of elevation changes along its 4.2-mile route.

Current Road Information

Bureau of Land Management
Redding Field Office
355 Hemsted Drive
Redding, CA 96002
(530) 224-2100

Mendocino National Forest
Grindstone Ranger District
825 North Humboldt Avenue
Willows, CA 95988
(530) 934-3316

Map References

BLM Willows
USFS Mendocino National Forest

Beginning of Nome Cult Mountain House Trail

USGS 1:24,000   Hall Ridge
        1:100,000   Willows
Maptech CD-ROM: North Coast/Mendocino
Northern California Atlas & Gazetteer, p. 65
California Road & Recreation Atlas, p. 58

Route Directions

▼ 0.0   From Paskenta, zero trip meter and turn south on Round Valley Road (M4). The road enters Mendocino National Forest after 6.3 miles. There is a marker for the original Nome Cult Trail at the national forest boundary. Mountain House, a site along the original Nome Cult Trail, was just north of the boundary. Continue 0.6 miles past the boundary to the start of the trail. Zero trip meter and turn west onto graded dirt road marked 23N35 (shown on the forest service map as 23N69). Road is marked for 4WDs only.

4.0 ▲   Trail ends back on Round Valley Road

Nome Cult Mountain House Trail

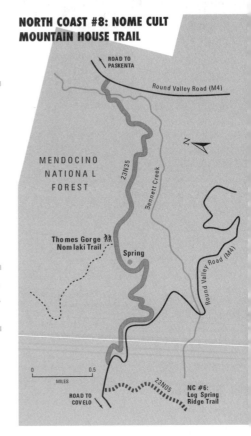

(M4). Turn left for Paskenta; turn right for Covelo.

GPS: N39°50.14′ W122°37.84′

▼ 0.2 SO Cross over Bennett Creek on bridge.
3.8 ▲ SO Cross over Bennett Creek on bridge.
▼ 1.8 SO Track on right.
2.2 ▲ SO Track on left.
▼ 1.9 SO Turnout on right; then Thomes Gorge Nomlaki Trail on right for hikers; then track on left through gate.
2.1 ▲ SO Track on right through gate; then Thomes Gorge Nomlaki Trail on left for hikers; then turnout on left.

GPS: N39°49.81′ W122°39.20′

▼ 2.2 SO Track on left to spring at Mud Flat Camp.
1.8 ▲ SO Track on right to spring at Mud Flat Camp.

GPS: N39°49.67′ W122°39.44′

▼ 2.8 SO Track on right.
1.2 ▲ SO Track on left.
▼ 4.0   Trail ends at T-intersection with paved Round Valley Road (M4). Turn left for Paskenta; turn right for Covelo.
0.0 ▲   Trail commences on paved Round

MAIDU

Maidu boy

Maidu woman

The Maidu were one of Northern California's largest tribes, numbering about 9,000 before European and American contact. Their territory was south of the Northern Paiute. The Maidu had no single leader or tribal identity. Instead, bands of up to 500 held stretches of territory that encompassed several villages. The bands were united into three geographic divisions, each speaking a slightly varied form of the Maidu language. The mountain group lived on the western side of the Sierra Nevada in the drainage area of North and Middle Forks of Feather River. The foothills group occupied a region to the west and south of the mountain group in the foothills of the Sierra Nevada and part of the Sacramento Valley. The valley group, who called themselves Nisenan, inhabited a large area of the Sacramento Valley, including the drainage basins of the American, Bear, and Yuba Rivers. The valley group was the most numerous of the three divisions.

Maidu territory had abundant resources and a generally pleasant climate. Oak groves provided ample acorns, and gathering them was an important time in tribal life, with whole villages participating in the harvest. Acorns had to be processed to remove tannin, a harmful toxin, before being eaten. The nuts were ground into powder in hollows chiseled into rocks, called nutting stones, which can still be found today.

They also collected other plants. Farming was unnecessary, although tobacco was sometimes grown in small plots. The Maidu also hunted small and large game. Several animals—grizzly bears, coyotes, and owls—were considered sacred and never killed.

Maidu houses were domed, wooden-framed structures, partially buried in the ground and covered with earth, which provided excellent insulation. They wore few clothes, and generally only young women wore more than a minimum.

Baskets were important to the Maidu. The twined, often conical containers were used for storage, carrying loads, dining, and even cooking. They dropped hot stones into large watertight baskets to heat acorn mush and water.

The Maidu followed the religious cult of Kuksu. The secret, selective religion held special rituals for the initiated. Members dressed in elaborate costumes and impersonated a variety of spirits during ceremonial dances.

Mourning ceremonies were important to all Maidu. They cremated individuals with their belongings, and if the death occurred in a home, the house was abandoned and burned, too. Mourning ceremonies were held annually to commemorate those who had died during the previous year. The Maidu believed that death liberated the soul and that the soul might enter an owl, a coyote, or a lizard and travel over the Milky Way to an idyllic afterlife, where constant feasting and games replaced work. A bad soul, however, would be reincarnated as a rock or a bush.

Maidu society was devastated by contact with Europeans and Americans. A malaria epidemic in 1833 killed an estimated 75 percent of the tribe, and the gold rush reduced them even more. In 1849, miners raided a Maidu village, raped the women, and killed the men who tried to stop them. When Maidu warriors retaliated by attacking a mining camp, the miners raided the village again, killing anyone they found. Such occurrences were not uncommon. By 1900, the Maidu population was about 1,000. Farmers and ranchers had carved up most of the Indians' land and tribal society was irrevocably changed. The remaining Maidu control Berry Creek and Enterprise Rancherias in Butte County and share the Susanville Rancheria and the Round Valley Indian Reservation with other tribes.

Valley Road (M4), 12.5 miles east of Log Springs USFS Work Station and 0.2 miles east of North Coast #6: Log Spring Ridge Trail. Zero trip meter and turn northeast on dirt road 23N35, marked for 4WDs only.
GPS: N39°49.63' W122°40.34'

Vestal and Pettyjohn Roads

STARTING POINT California 36, 12.5 miles east of Platina
FINISHING POINT Reeds Creek Road on Table Mountain, 17.5 miles west of Red Bluff
TOTAL MILEAGE 22.1 miles
UNPAVED MILEAGE 20.2 miles
DRIVING TIME 2 hours
ELEVATION RANGE 800–1,600 feet
USUALLY OPEN March to January
BEST TIME TO TRAVEL March to January
DIFFICULTY RATING 1
SCENIC RATING 8
REMOTENESS RATING +1

Special Attractions

- Wildlife viewing—deer, quail, and bobcat.
- Pretty winding road through the low rangeland east of Shasta-Trinity National Forests.

History

This trail begins about 30 miles east of Red Bluff on California 36 on the banks of Dry Creek, just east of Budden Canyon. Early ranchers like William Budden, a native of England, raised stock in the undulating foothills of the Coast Ranges. Budden emigrated to California at 20 years of age and lived at Beegum, just west of Budden Canyon, for most of 40 years. During his lifetime, he farmed at Dry Creek and also worked at Rosewood Ranch, to the east of Vestal Road. Vestal Road recalls the Vestals, a prominent family in Red Bluff's butcher industry.

Henry Wescott, from Oroville, operated a store along the old wagon road east of Red Bluff (now the route of California 36). In 1890, Joe Durrer, a Swiss, and his wife Elizabeth Schanick, a German, purchased the store and added an impressive cabin to house their young family. The site gained a post office, called Rosewood because of the wild roses that grew along Salt Creek. The 1894 gold strike at Harrison Gulch, west of Beegum, brought a surge of miners and merchants past the Rosewood trading post. A stage stop was established to provide food and accommodations for teamsters and a barn for their horses. Teamsters always carried rifles because breakdowns were inevitable on this lonely wagon road, and wildcats were prevalent in the region.

Fording Wells Creek near the beginning of the trail

The Midas Mine at Harrison Gulch produced several million dollars worth of gold over a 20-year period, beginning in 1894. The mine superintendent delivered gold bars to Red Bluff weekly; he drove a distinctive four-wheel, two-seater carriage pulled by especially fast and capable horses. Speed was essential because of the constant threat of bandits in this remote region. The superintendent would stop off at the Durrer's stage stop to change horses. He supposedly carried fake gold bars to hand over in case of a holdup.

Description

This backcountry drive passes through some quiet, pretty scenery between the Sacramento Valley and the eastern side of the Coast Ranges. The route passes through ranchlands along county roads, first Vestal Road and then Pettyjohn Road. Because it is entirely on private lands, there are no camping, hunting, or other recreational opportunities. However, you can expect to see deer, quail, and other wildlife along the way, even a bobcat if you are lucky.

The first half of the route is a narrow formed trail that winds through grasslands with occasional stands of oaks. The crossings of Wells Creek near the start of the trail normally have water. Drivers of low-clearance vehicles should assess the crossing before proceeding—the first is normally the deepest. Of course, if the creek is in flood or excessively deep, all vehicles should avoid the crossing.

Weemasoul Spring and Creek

The trail standard improves at the settlement of Cold Fork, and it follows a well-graded road to the end.

Current Road Information
Bureau of Land Management
Redding Field Office
355 Hemsted Drive
Redding, CA 96002
(530) 224-2100

Map References
BLM   Red Bluff
USFS Shasta-Trinity National Forests
      (incomplete)
USGS 1:24,000 Chickabally Mt., Cold
      Fork, Oxbow Bridge
      1:100,000 Red Bluff
Maptech CD-ROM: Shasta Lake/Redding
Northern California Atlas & Gazetteer,
      pp. 55, 56
California Road & Recreation Atlas, p. 58

Route Directions

▼ 0.0   From California 36, 0.2 miles west of
          Tehama County mile marker 9.5, 33
          miles west of Red Bluff and 12.5 miles
          east of Platina, zero trip meter and turn
          south on Vestal Road (CR 107) and
          cross cattle guard.
7.6 ▲   Cattle guard; then trail ends at T-intersection with California 36. Turn right
          for Red Bluff; turn left for Platina.
          GPS: N40°18.26' W122°42.98'

▼ 0.9   SO Ford through Wells Creek; then cattle
          guard.
6.7 ▲   SO Cattle guard; then ford through Wells
          Creek.
▼ 1.2   SO Ford through Wells Creek.
6.4 ▲   SO Ford through Wells Creek.
▼ 1.5   SO Ford through Wells Creek.
6.1 ▲   SO Ford through Wells Creek.
t 2.7   SO Cattle guard.
4.9 ▲   SO Cattle guard.
          GPS: N40°16.31' W122°42.48'

▼ 3.2   SO Cattle guard.
4.4 ▲   SO Cattle guard.

▼ 3.7   SO Corral on right at Wilson Flat.
3.9 ▲   SO Corral on left at Wilson Flat.
▼ 3.9   SO Cattle guard.
3.7 ▲   SO Cattle guard.
▼ 4.2   SO Unmarked graded road on right.
3.4 ▲   SO Unmarked graded road on left.
          GPS: N40°15.14' W122°42.67'

▼ 5.0   SO Track on right; then cattle guard.
2.6 ▲   SO Cattle guard; then track on left.
▼ 5.1   SO Cross through Salt Creek.
2.5 ▲   SO Cross through Salt Creek.
▼ 5.3   SO Cross through creek.
2.3 ▲   SO Cross through creek.
▼ 5.4   SO Cross through creek.
2.2 ▲   SO Cross through creek.
▼ 5.5   SO Cross through creek.
2.1 ▲   SO Cross through creek.
▼ 6.2   SO Cattle guard.
1.4 ▲   SO Cattle guard.
▼ 6.8   SO Cross through creek.
0.8 ▲   SO Cross through creek.
▼ 7.6   TR T-intersection. Vestal Road continues

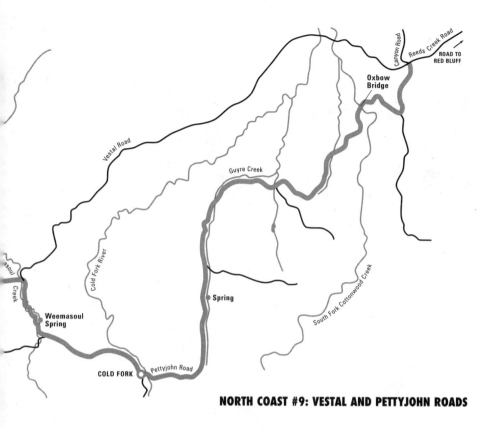

NORTH COAST #9: VESTAL AND PETTYJOHN ROADS

		to the left. Zero trip meter.	
.0 ▲		Continue to the west on Vestal Road.	
		GPS: N40°12.93' W122°41.11'	

▼ 0.0		Continue to the south.	
.6 ▲	TL	Graded road continues ahead. Zero t rip meter.	
▼ 0.4	SO	Cross through Weemasoul Creek; then cattle guard.	
.2 ▲	SO	Cattle guard; then cross through Weemasoul Creek.	
▼ 0.5	SO	Cross through creek.	
.1 ▲	SO	Cross through creek.	
▼ 0.6	SO	Cross through creek.	
.0 ▲	SO	Cross through creek.	
▼ 0.9	SO	Weemasoul Spring on left.	
.7 ▲	SO	Weemasoul Spring on right.	
		GPS: N40°12.29' W122°41.48'	

▼ 1.1	SO	Cross through creek.	
.5 ▲	SO	Cross through creek.	
▼ 1.2	BL	Track on right.	
.4 ▲	SO	Track on left.	

▼ 1.8	SO	Cross through creek twice.	
1.8 ▲	SO	Cross through creek twice.	
▼ 2.3	SO	Cattle guard.	
1.3 ▲	SO	Cattle guard.	
▼ 3.3	SO	Cattle guard.	
0.3 ▲	SO	Cattle guard.	
▼ 3.6	TL	Gate; then T-intersection with small paved road at Cold Fork. Zero trip meter and join the paved road.	
0.0 ▲		Continue to the north. Road is now graded dirt.	
		GPS: N40°10.38' W122°40.48'	

▼ 0.0		Continue to the east. Road is now paved Pettyjohn Road.	
5.9 ▲	TR	On a left-hand bend, zero trip meter and turn right onto a small dirt road and pass through a gate. Note that this intersection is unmarked, and appears to lead into private property.	
▼ 0.1	SO	Cross over Cold Fork River on bridge; then cattle guard.	
5.8 ▲	SO	Cattle guard; then cross over Cold Fork	

Trail along Wilson Flat

<table>
<tr><td></td><td></td><td>River on bridge.</td></tr>
<tr><td>▼ 0.2</td><td>SO</td><td>Road turns back to graded dirt.</td></tr>
<tr><td>5.7 ▲</td><td>SO</td><td>Road is now paved.</td></tr>
<tr><td>▼ 2.7</td><td>SO</td><td>Guyre Creek Spring on right.</td></tr>
<tr><td>3.2 ▲</td><td>SO</td><td>Guyre Creek Spring on left.</td></tr>
</table>

GPS: N40°10.66′ W122°38.30′

<table>
<tr><td>▼ 2.9</td><td>SO</td><td>Cattle guard.</td></tr>
<tr><td>3.0 ▲</td><td>SO</td><td>Cattle guard.</td></tr>
<tr><td>▼ 3.1</td><td>SO</td><td>Track on right to Van Horn Corral.</td></tr>
<tr><td>2.8 ▲</td><td>SO</td><td>Track on left to Van Horn Corral.</td></tr>
<tr><td>▼ 4.4</td><td>SO</td><td>Cattle guard; then cross through creek.</td></tr>
<tr><td>1.5 ▲</td><td>SO</td><td>Cross through creek; then cattle guard.</td></tr>
<tr><td>▼ 5.6</td><td>SO</td><td>Road becomes paved.</td></tr>
<tr><td>0.3 ▲</td><td>SO</td><td>Road turns to graded dirt.</td></tr>
<tr><td>▼ 5.8</td><td>SO</td><td>Cattle guard.</td></tr>
<tr><td>0.1 ▲</td><td>SO</td><td>Cattle guard.</td></tr>
<tr><td>▼ 5.9</td><td>SO</td><td>Cross over creek; then road on right through entrance way. Zero trip meter.</td></tr>
<tr><td>0.0 ▲</td><td></td><td>Continue to the west and cross over creek. Road is now paved.</td></tr>
</table>

GPS: N40°11.20′ W122°35.50′

<table>
<tr><td>▼ 0.0</td><td></td><td>Continue to the east. Road is now graded dirt.</td></tr>
<tr><td>5.0 ▲</td><td>SO</td><td>Road on left through entrance way. Zero trip meter.</td></tr>
<tr><td>▼ 1.3</td><td>SO</td><td>Cattle guard.</td></tr>
<tr><td>3.7 ▲</td><td>SO</td><td>Cattle guard.</td></tr>
<tr><td>▼ 1.7</td><td>SO</td><td>Cross through creek.</td></tr>
<tr><td>3.3 ▲</td><td>SO</td><td>Cross through creek.</td></tr>
<tr><td>▼ 2.1</td><td>SO</td><td>Road becomes paved.</td></tr>
<tr><td>2.9 ▲</td><td>SO</td><td>Road turns to graded dirt.</td></tr>
<tr><td>▼ 2.9</td><td>SO</td><td>Cross over South Fork Cottonwood Creek on Oxbow Bridge.</td></tr>
<tr><td>2.1 ▲</td><td>SO</td><td>Cross over South Fork Cottonwood Creek on Oxbow Bridge.</td></tr>
</table>

GPS: N40°11.16′ W122°33.00′

<table>
<tr><td>▼ 3.5</td><td>SO</td><td>Road turns to graded dirt.</td></tr>
<tr><td>1.5 ▲</td><td>SO</td><td>Road is now paved.</td></tr>
<tr><td>▼ 4.0</td><td>SO</td><td>Track on right.</td></tr>
<tr><td>1.0 ▲</td><td>SO</td><td>Track on left.</td></tr>
</table>

▼ 4.1	SO	Cattle guard.
.9 ▲	SO	Cattle guard.
▼ 5.0		Trail ends at 4-way intersection at Table Mountain. Turn right onto Reeds Creek Road for I-5 and Red Bluff. To reach Red Bluff, proceed east on Reeds Creek Road for 15 miles to Wilder Road (CR A7); then turn left at the T-intersection, remaining on CR A7, which turns into Walnut Street. Walnut Street intersects with Main Street in Red Bluff. It is 17.5 miles to Red Bluff from the end of the trail.
▮.0 ▲		To reach the start of the trail from Main Street in Red Bluff, turn southwest on Walnut Street, which leads off from the center of town. Remain on Walnut Street for 2.5 miles, which swings south and joins Wilder Road (CR A7). Turn right onto Reeds Creek Road and proceed 15 miles to the start of the trail. Trail begins at the 4-way intersection at Table Mountain. To the north is Canyon Road and to the west is Vestal Road. Zero trip meter and turn south on graded dirt Pettyjohn Road.

GPS: N40°11.13' W122°31.55'

Beegum Gorge Trail

STARTING POINT Intersection of California 36 and CR A16 in Platina

FINISHING POINT Campsite beside Beegum Creek

TOTAL MILEAGE 7.5 miles (one-way)

UNPAVED MILEAGE 7.5 miles

DRIVING TIME 1 hour (one-way)

ELEVATION RANGE 2,100–3,400 feet

USUALLY OPEN April to December

BEST TIME TO TRAVEL Dry weather

DIFFICULTY RATING 2

SCENIC RATING 9

REMOTENESS RATING +0

Special Attractions

■ Remains of the Chrome Mine.

■ Views into Beegum Gorge and camping along Beegum Creek.

History

Beegum Gorge is in the Harrison Gulch Mining District, a mining region active around the turn of the twentieth century. Platina, at the start of this trail, was originally known as Noble Station, a stage stop on the wagon road from Red Bluff to the nearby Midas Mine. The rich mine was discovered in 1894 and sparked a small gold rush lasting for the next two decades, until fires and floods doomed this remote find.

In the winter of 1966, a find of a different kind made headlines in this picturesque mountain region. The Hampton family, who lived west of Platina near Little Round Mountain, returned home after a two-day vacation to find the door of their house ripped off its hinges. They also found 18-inch-long footprints in the snow around the house. Tales of Bigfoot instantly resurfaced in the Platina community.

Description

Beegum Gorge Trail leads down a long shelf road that wraps around Beegum Gorge, to finish at a small, undeveloped USFS camping area along Beegum Creek. The first part of the road climbs the rise above Platinum Gulch through private property before entering BLM land. From here, the trail makes a steady descent along a shelf road, which has an adequate number of passing places. Lassen Peak can be seen through the gorge to the east. Beegum Peak, on the east side of the gorge, is made up of pocketed limestone that has some beehives.

After crossing Zachary Gulch, the trail passes the turn to a delightful camping area on the banks of Beegum Creek, with plenty of shade and a great swimming hole. The main trail continues for another 1.4 miles to a second, more open camping area beside the creek. A hiking trail to Seeliger Ranch leads out the back of the camping area. Although the trail is shown as continuing on forest maps, most drivers will prefer to stop at the creek. The trail becomes very brushy after the crossing and is mainly used by ATVs. The Chrome Mine is 0.2 miles past the creek crossing. A concrete slab, footings, and remains of a loading hopper can still be seen.

A trail, shown on forest maps as leading to the north, is well used but rated most difficult by the forest service because of extremely steep, loose-traction climbs up the ridge. The main trail should not be attempted in wet weather; the shelf road becomes treacherously greasy and dangerous when wet.

Current Road Information

Bureau of Land Management
Redding Field Office
355 Hemsted Drive
Redding, CA 96002
(530) 224-2100

Map References

BLM   Red Bluff
USFS   Shasta-Trinity National Forest

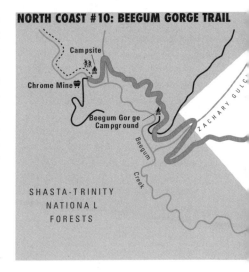

USGS 1:24,000   Beegum
        1:100,000 Red Bluff
Maptech CD-ROM: Shasta Lake/Redding
Northern California Atlas & Gazetteer, p. 55
California Road & Recreation Atlas, p. 51

Descending toward Beegum Gorge through Zachary Gulch

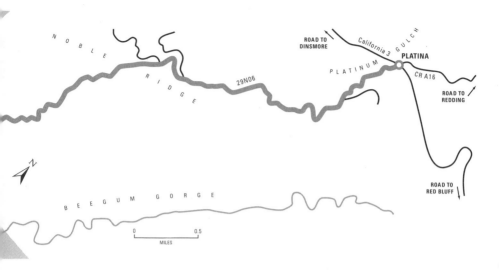

Route Directions

▼ 0.0   From the intersection of California 36 and CR A16 at Platina, 46 miles west of Red Bluff and 9 miles east of Wildwood, zero trip meter and turn south on dirt road 29N06, following the sign to Beegum Gorge Campground.
GPS: N40°21.68' W122°53.20'

▼ 0.7   SO   Track on left to communication towers.
GPS: N40°21.21' W122°53.31'

▼ 2.1   BR   Track on left.
▼ 2.2   SO   Track on right. Entering BLM land.
GPS: N40°20.53' W122°54.41'

▼ 2.5   SO   Track on right. Start of shelf road descent to Beegum Gorge.
▼ 5.2   BL   Turnout on right.
GPS: N40°18.69' W122°55.62'

▼ 5.7   BL   Cross over Zachary Gulch; then track on right.
GPS: N40°18.99' W122°55.71'

▼ 6.1   TR   Well-used track continues straight ahead for 0.2 miles to Beegum Gorge USFS Campground. Zero trip meter. End of shelf road.
GPS:N40°18.70' W122°55.91'

▼ 0.0   Continue to the north. Immediately track on right up hill.
▼ 1.1   SO   Cross over creek.
▼ 1.4   Trail ends at campsite on right beside creek. Trail bears left and fords through

Large wooden hopper at the Chrome Mine site at trail's end

Beegum Creek. A hiking trail to Seeliger Ranch leads out the back of the camping area. The trail continues over the creek, but it is brushy and mainly used by ATVs.

GPS: N40°18.66′ W122°56.67′

Knob Peak Trail

STARTING POINT California 36, 2.5 miles west of Platina
FINISHING POINT Knob Peak Fire Lookout
TOTAL MILEAGE 5.1 miles (one-way)
UNPAVED MILEAGE 4.6 miles
DRIVING TIME 30 minutes (one-way)
ELEVATION RANGE 2,800–4,800 feet
USUALLY OPEN May to December
BEST TIME TO TRAVEL Dry weather
DIFFICULTY RATING 1

SCENIC RATING 8
REMOTENESS RATING +0

Special Attractions
■ Excellent views from Knob Peak Fire Lookout.
■ Easy shelf road suitable for all vehicles in dry weather.

History
Knob Peak Fire Lookout (4,819 feet) is perched 1,700 feet above and 2 miles west of the Midas Mine, once a hive of activity in Harrison Gulch. This rich gold mining district was named after W. F. Harrison, who settled here in 1852. A number of prospectors, namely Messrs Benton, Fowler, and the Hurst brothers, struck gold here in the mid-1890s and started the Midas Mine, which eventually produced nearly $7 million worth of gold.

Several hundred miners arrived to establish the town of Knob, named for a nearby round hill. Saloons, hotels, trading posts, schools,

Eastern view from the lookout

staurants, a smelter, and more lined the streets f Knob by the turn of the twentieth century. Although far from Redding and Red Bluff, Knob enjoyed a vibrant social scene with regular plays, musical events, and the ever popular boxing matches. Stagecoaches plied the rough wagon road from Red Bluff to Knob daily. The population approached 2,000 at its peak shortly after the turn of the twentieth century.

In 1914, a fire destroyed the timber bracings in the mine, vital water pumps failed, and the shafts flooded. Attempts to get the mine running again failed and the town emptied. Little now remains in the Harrison Gulch Mining District except for foundations of the smelter and some tailings.

The Hayfork Wintun tribe, also known as Nor-el-muk, frequented the surrounding Trinity Mountains. The Nor-el-muk, meaning "southward uphill people," established permanent villages and used the region's abundant foods such as salmon, venison, and acorns. Their spiritual beliefs were closely linked to landscape features. Chanchelulla Peak, meaning "Black Rock" in their language, was the most revered feature in their ancestral territory. Chanchelulla Peak (6,380 feet) rises directly north of Knob Peak.

Description

Although Knob Peak Fire Lookout is only a short distance from California 36, it seems a world away. In dry weather, passenger vehicles can generally reach the lookout. The lookout stopped operating in the 1990s and was restored by the forest service in 2002. It is now available for overnight rentals. Please respect the privacy of people who may be renting the lookout. There is a closure gate 0.2 mile short of the tower. If the gate is closed, it is only a short hike to the top. Panoramic views from the lookout include Mount Shasta to the north, Lassen Peak to the east, the Trinity Alps Wilderness to the northwest, and the Yolla Bolly Middle Eel Wilderness to the south.

Current Road Information

Shasta-Trinity National Forest
Yolla Bolla Ranger District

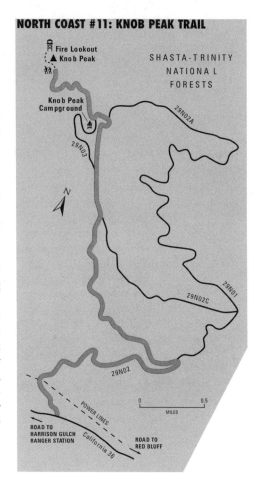

NORTH COAST #11: KNOB PEAK TRAIL

2555 State Highway 36
Platina, CA 96076
(530) 352-4211

Map References

BLM   Red Bluff
USFS   Shasta-Trinity National Forests
USGS   1:24,000   Beegum, Chanchelulla
            Peak
        1:100,000   Red Bluff
Maptech CD-ROM: Shasta Lake/Redding
Northern California Atlas & Gazetteer, p. 55
California Road & Recreation Atlas, p. 51

Route Directions

▼ 0.0   From California 36, 2.5 miles west of
            Platina and 1.8 miles east of the
            Harrison Gulch Ranger Station, zero
            trip meter and turn northwest onto

Knob Peak Fire Lookout prior to restoration

29N02. The turn is marked from the highway. Road is initially paved.
GPS: N40°22.07′ W122°55.86′

▼ 0.3 SO Track on left under power lines; then track on right is 29N02D. Road turns to graded dirt. Start of shelf road.
▼ 1.7 BL Track on right; then second track on right is 29N01. Remain on 29N02.
GPS: N40°22.72′ W122°55.16′

▼ 3.4 SO Track on right is 29N02C.
▼ 3.7 BR Track on right is 29N02B; then track on left is 29N03. Bear right, remaining on 29N02. Zero trip meter.
GPS: N40°23.51′ W122°56.53′

▼ 0.0 Continue to the northwest.
▼ 0.4 SO Track on right is 29N02A.
▼ 0.6 BR Track on left is 29N03 rejoining. Undeveloped Knob Peak USFS Campground on left.
GPS: N40°23.81′ W122°56.75′

▼ 1.2 Track on right; then small track on left; then trail ends at gate. Main trail continues 0.2 miles to Knob Peak Fire Lookout. The lookout is generally gated all year.
GPS: N40°23.93′ W122°57.17′

Hall City Cave Trail

STARTING POINT Wildwood Road in Wildwood
FINISHING POINT California 36, 0.3 miles east of the intersection with Wildwood Road
TOTAL MILEAGE 5.6 miles
UNPAVED MILEAGE 5.6 miles
DRIVING TIME 30 minutes, not including the hike to the cave
ELEVATION RANGE 3,400–4,100 feet
USUALLY OPEN April to January
BEST TIME TO TRAVEL April to January

Special Attractions
Hall City Cave.
Harrison Gulch mining ruins close to the trail.

History
Hall City Cave Trail travels along an old twisting county road from Wildwood to Platina. Wildwood was a stage stop on the early wagon road to the Midas Mine, near the end of this trail. In the 1890s, Ed Landis built a sawmill with a water-driven circular saw near the trading post and inn on the banks of Hayfork Creek. His name is attached to Landis Gulch, which drains into Hayfork Creek from the west.

The old county road passes near the site of Hall City, which takes its name from the nearby Hall City Cave. A local tale relates how two miners from the vicinity of Hayfork were ambushed by Indians who made off with two sacks of gold, leaving the miners to die by the roadside. A posse pursued them, and the Indians dropped the gold into Hall City Cave. Though the assailants were captured, interrogated as to the location of the gold, and later hanged at Wildwood, the gold was never retrieved from the deep water-filled cavern.

Many ditches, tunnels, tailings, and rockwork remain deep within the forest—testimony to the high activity in the 30 mines around Hall City.

Description
This short loop passes the trailhead to Hall City Cave. The cave, set beneath a limestone cap, is reached by the easy graded dirt road and then a 0.3-mile hike.

The trail starts in the small community of Wildwood, a couple miles north of California 36. The cave is well marked as far as the final turnoff; then all markers disappear. Take the side trail and proceed to a parking area for cave visitors. A vehicle trail continues past the parking area, but it is blocked by a closure gate. The hiking trail leads out the back of the informal parking area, runs alongside Hall City Creek for a short distance, then crosses over the creek and switchbacks up the hill to the cave. If, after crossing the creek, you find yourself continuing along the creek instead of climbing up the hill, you have overshot the switchbacks.

A bit of scrambling over boulders is required to reach the cave. From the tall entrance, you will descend a rough wooden ladder into this exciting subterranean world. Inside, the narrow passageway opens up to a small cavern. The cave goes back for about 100 feet, crossing a trickling underground

Signpost to Hall City Cave

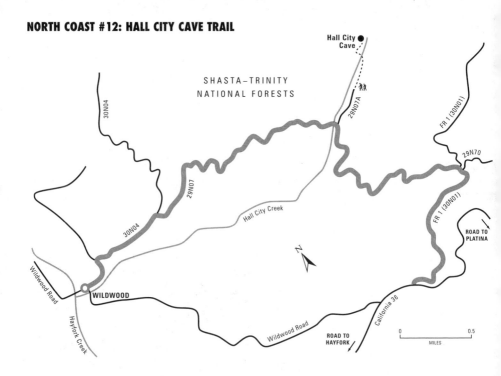

stream, and ending at a pool of deep, clear blue water. To the left of the pool, you can see a deep shaft extending beneath the water; this is supposedly the site of lost gold. The walls and ceilings of the cave have several small limestone formations. If you are planning to enter the cave, boots with good tread will help you cope with the very slippery, rough floor. A good flashlight is also essential. Allow 30 minutes round trip for the hike, plus time to explore the cave. The parking area for the cave is at GPS: N40°24.24' W123°00.59' and the coordinates of the cave are GPS: N40°24.41' W123°00.43'.

The trail can often be traveled year round, but snow is likely to block the road for short periods in January and February. Even if there is no snow, the road can be icy during winter. The trail finishes on California 36.

Current Road Information

Shasta-Trinity National Forest
Yolla Bolla Ranger District
2555 State Highway 36
Platina, CA 96076
(530) 352-4211

Map References

BLM   Garberville
USFS   Shasta-Trinity National Forests
USGS   1:24,000 Dubakella Mt.
           1:100,000 Garberville
Maptech CD-ROM: North Coast/Eureka
Northern California Atlas & Gazetteer, p. 55
California Road & Recreation Atlas, p. 51

Route Directions

▼ 0.0   From Wildwood Road in Wildwood, 2.4 miles north of California 36, zero trip meter and turn northeast on graded dirt road 30N04.

3.0 ▲   Trail ends on Wildwood Road in Wildwood. Turn left for California 36.
GPS: N40°24.03' W123°03.30'

▼ 0.3   BR Track on left.
2.7 ▲   BL Track on right.
▼ 0.8   TR Trail 30N04 continues straight ahead. Turn right on 29N07, following the sign for Hall City Caves.
2.2 ▲   TL T-intersection with 30N04.
GPS: N40°24.19' W123°02.54'

The trail follows an old logging route above Hall City Creek

▼ 0.9	SO	Track on left.
2.1 ▲	SO	Track on right.
▼ 2.9	SO	Track on left is 29N07D.
0.1 ▲	SO	Track on right is 29N07D.
▼ 3.0	SO	Cross over Hall City Creek; then track on left is 29N07A, which goes 0.3 miles to the parking area for Hall City Cave. Zero trip meter.
0.0 ▲		Continue to the northwest and cross over Hall City Creek.

GPS: N40°24.06' W123°00.91'

▼ 0.0		Continue to the southeast.
2.6 ▲	SO	Track on right is 29N07A, which goes 0.3 miles to the parking area for Hall City Cave. Zero trip meter.
▼ 0.6	BR	Track on left is 29N07C.
2.0 ▲	BL	Track on right is 29N07C.
▼ 1.1	BR	Two tracks on left.
1.5 ▲	BL	Two tracks on right.
▼ 1.6	TR	4-way intersection. FR 1 (30N01) crosses. Track straight ahead is 29N70. Turn right onto FR 1 (30N01), following the sign for California 36.
1.0 ▲	TL	4-way intersection. FR 1 (30N01) continues straight ahead. Track on right is 29N70. Turn left onto 29N07, following the sign for Hall City Cave.

GPS: N40°23.41' W123°00.25'

▼ 2.1	BR	Track on left; then track on right is 29N10.
0.5 ▲	BL	Track on left is 29N10; then track on right.
▼ 2.5	SO	Track on right under power lines.
0.1 ▲	SO	Track on left under power lines.
▼ 2.6		Trail ends at T-intersection with California 36. Turn left for Platina and Red Bluff; turn right for Hayfork.
0.0 ▲		Trail begins on California 36, 0.3 miles east of the Wildwood Store and intersection with Wildwood Road. Zero trip meter and turn northeast on graded road FR 1 (30N01), following the sign to Hall City Cave.

GPS: N40°23.02' W123°01.01'

Low Divide Road

STARTING POINT California 197, 2.2 miles north of intersection with US 199
FINISHING POINT US 101 in Smith River
TOTAL MILEAGE 14.5 miles
UNPAVED MILEAGE 12.5 miles
DRIVING TIME 1.5 hours
ELEVATION RANGE 200–2,400 feet
USUALLY OPEN Year-round
BEST TIME TO TRAVEL Year-round
DIFFICULTY RATING 1
SCENIC RATING 8
REMOTENESS RATING +0

Special Attractions

■ Views over the Pacific coast and mouth of the Smith River.
■ Easy loop east of US 101.
■ A good trail to see coastal vegetation and wildflowers in spring.

History

Northwestern California attracted a numbe of Chinese immigrants, many of whom worked at the Occident & Oriental Commercial Fish Cannery, established in De Norte County in 1857. They also worked ir the logging industry in this part of the Klamath Mountains and built wagon roads, including most of this trail, over High Divide to the mining settlements of Low Divide, Altaville, and Gasquet.

In the early 1860s, the Occidental Coppe Mining Company worked the Copper Creek Mine, just below the high point of the trail The mine was busiest during the 1860s and '70s. Some of the copper ore was shipped to Swansea, Wales, and some to Germany fo processing, returning anywhere from $41 to more than $100 per ton.

Logging above Rowdy Creek, at the northern end of Low Divide Road, was in ful swing in the early 1920s. The Del Norte Company, based in Smith River, shipped fi and redwood logs to the sawmill in Brookings, just over the state line in Oregon, b

istoric Battery Point Lighthouse is a pleasant stop near Crescent City before heading out on the trail

vay of the newly built North West Railroad. The Del Norte Company's parent organization was the California & Oregon Lumber Company, headquartered in Brookings. Logging crews were based out of Crescent City, California, and Brookings, Oregon, and mith River boomed as the social half-way oint.

Description

Low Divide Road is maintained as CR 305 and loops through the lower elevations of Six Rivers National Forest. The shrubby vegetation is different from other forest drives in this region: Much of it is manzanitas and zaleas, which produce a bright array in spring. The route has a number of views overlooking the mouth of the Smith River and he Pacific coast.

Much of the road crosses private land—racks mentioned in the route directions often go to private property and are mentioned only as points of reference for navigation. Workings of the Mountain View Mines at he top of High Divide are privately owned.

The road snakes down to meet US 101 via Rowdy Creek Road (CR 308). The southern portion of this route is shown on topographical maps as Wimer Road.

Current Road Information

Smith River National Recreation Area
Six Rivers National Forest
PO Box 228
Gasquet, CA 95543
(707) 457-3131

Map References

BLM   Crescent City
USFS   Six Rivers National Forest, Smith
       River National Recreation Area
USGS   1:24,000 Hiouchi, High Divide,
       Smith River
       1:100,000 Crescent City
Maptech CD-ROM: North Coast/Eureka
Northern California Atlas & Gazetteer, p. 22
California Road & Recreation Atlas, p. 44
Trails Illustrated, Redwood National Park,
       North Coast State Parks, Smith
       River NRA (218)

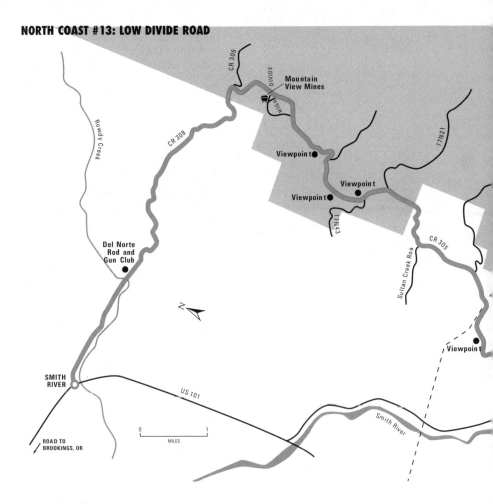

Route Directions

▼ 0.0   From the intersection of US 199 and California 197, 3.5 miles east of US 101, proceed north on California 197 for 2.2 miles. Zero trip meter and turn east on paved Low Divide Road (CR 305).

5.2 ▲   Trail ends at T-intersection with California 197. Turn left for US 199 and Crescent City; turn right for US 101 northbound.

GPS: N41°49.74′ W124°06.16′

▼ 0.3 SO Road turns to graded dirt.
4.9 ▲ SO Road becomes paved.
▼ 1.6 SO Track on left.
3.6 ▲ SO Track on right.
▼ 2.1 SO Coastal viewpoint on left.
3.1 ▲ SO Coastal viewpoint on right.

GPS: N41°51.02′ W124°05.47′

▼ 2.3 SO Track on left through seasonal closure gate.
2.9 ▲ SO Track on right through seasonal closure gate.
▼ 2.4 SO Track on left.
2.8 ▲ SO Track on right.
▼ 2.7 SO Track on left and track on right under power lines.
2.5 ▲ SO Track on left and track on right under power lines.
▼ 3.1 SO Track on right.
2.1 ▲ SO Track on left.
▼ 3.4 SO Track on right.
1.8 ▲ SO Track on left.
▼ 4.1 SO Sultan Creek Road on left. Remain on Low Divide Road.
1.1 ▲ SO Sultan Creek Road on right. Remain on Low Divide Road.

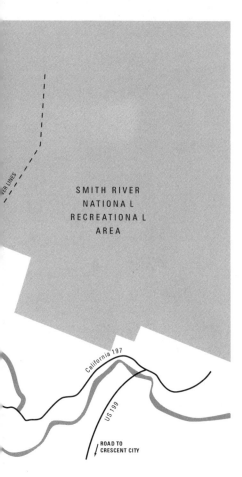

SMITH RIVER
NATIONAL
RECREATIONAL
AREA

California 197

US 199

ROAD TO
CRESCENT CITY

GPS: N41°52.16' W124°04.41'

▼ 4.3   SO   Track on left.
0.9 ▲   SO   Track on right.
▼ 5.2   SO   Graded road on right is 17N21. Zero trip meter.
0.0 ▲   Continue to the southeast on Low Divide Road (CR 305).

GPS: N41°52.80' W124°03.75'

▼ 0.0   Continue to the west on Low Divide Road (CR 305).
3.7 ▲   SO   Graded road on left is 17N21. Zero trip meter.
▼ 0.3   SO   Track on right.
3.4 ▲   SO   Track on left.
▼ 0.4   SO   Track on left is 17N43.
3.3 ▲   SO   Track on right is 17N43.
▼ 0.5   SO   Viewpoint on right over Hardscrabble

Creek Basin and Gasquet Mountain to the east.
3.2 ▲   SO   Viewpoint on left over Hardscrabble Creek Basin and Gasquet Mountain to the east.
▼ 0.7   SO   Track on left.
3.0 ▲   SO   Track on right.
▼ 0.9   SO   Viewpoint on left over mouth of the Smith River, Prince Island, and Hunter Rock to the west.
2.8 ▲   SO   Viewpoint on right over mouth of the Smith River, Prince Island, and Hunter Rock to the west.

GPS: N41°53.46' W124°04.11'

▼ 1.4   SO   Track on left; then track on right.
2.3 ▲   SO   Track on right; then track on left.
▼ 1.8   SO   Viewpoint on left over mouth of the Smith River, Prince Island, and Lake Earl State Wildlife Area to the west.
1.9 ▲   SO   Viewpoint on right over mouth of the Smith River, Prince Island, and Lake Earl State Wildlife Area to the west.

GPS: N41°53.84' W124°03.54'

▼ 2.4   SO   Track on right into active mining claims; then track on left.
1.3 ▲   SO   Track on right; then track on left into active mining claims.
▼ 2.9   SO   Track on left.
0.8 ▲   SO   Track on right.
▼ 3.0   SO   High Divide. Graded road on left to Mountain View Mines.
0.7 ▲   BL   High Divide. Graded road on right to Mountain View Mines.

GPS: N41°54.68' W124°02.92'

▼ 3.1   SO   Track on right.
0.6 ▲   SO   Track on left.
▼ 3.2   SO   Track on right.
0.5 ▲   SO   Track on left.
▼ 3.5   SO   Track on left.
0.2 ▲   SO   Track on right.
▼ 3.7   SO   Graded road on right is the continuation of CR 305. Zero trip meter.
0.0 ▲   Continue to the south on CR 305.

GPS: N41°55.16' W124°03.10'

▼ 0.0   Continue to the west on graded Rowdy Creek Road (CR 308).

5.6 ▲	BR	Graded road on left is CR 305. Zero trip meter and head uphill.
▼ 0.2	SO	Road on right.
5.4 ▲	SO	Road on left.
▼ 0.9	SO	Track on left.
4.7 ▲	SO	Track on right.
▼ 1.3	SO	Track on right.
4.3 ▲	SO	Track on left.
▼ 3.9	SO	Del Norte Rod and Gun Club on right. Road is now paved. Cross over Rowdy Creek. Remain on paved road until the end of the trail.
1.7 ▲	SO	Cross over Rowdy Creek. Del Norte Rod and Gun Club on left. Road turns to graded dirt.

GPS: N41°55.59′ W124°06.63′

▼ 5.6		Trail ends at T-intersection with US 101 in Smith River. Turn left for Crescent City; turn right for Brookings, OR.
0.0 ▲		Trail commences on US 101 at Smith River. Zero trip meter and turn northeast on Rowdy Creek Road. Remain on paved road for the first 1.7 miles.

GPS: N41°55.76′ W124°08.58′

NORTH COAST #14: HOWLAND HILL ROAD

NORTH COAST #14

Howland Hill Road

STARTING POINT Elk Valley Road, 1 mile east of US 101
FINISHING POINT US 199, 7 miles east of US 101
TOTAL MILEAGE 8.4 miles
UNPAVED MILEAGE 5.3 miles
DRIVING TIME 1 hour
ELEVATION RANGE 100–500 feet
USUALLY OPEN Year-round
BEST TIME TO TRAVEL Year-round
DIFFICULTY RATING 1
SCENIC RATING 10
REMOTENESS RATING +0

Special Attractions

■ Small winding road through giant coast redwoods in the Jedediah Smith Redwoods State Park.

■ Access to the Smith River and a number of hiking trails.
■ Excellent photo opportunities along the road.

History

Howland Hill Road weaves a path through magnificent stands of redwoods, remnants of the coastal forest traversed by Jedediah Smith in 1828. Smith, whose name graces the river at the end of this trail, was a trapper, trader, mountain man, and explorer in the 1820s. He and his men spent the better part of a month cutting a trail through the dense vegetation of these northwest California mountains.

The community of Hiouchi, near the end of the trail, was in the ancestral homeland of the Yurok and Tolowa Indians. Hiouchi is thought to mean "high clear water." Douglas Park, in the depths of the forest directly opposite Hiouchi, was formerly known as Berteleda, in memory of Bertha Brown, daughter of a Crescent City physician.

Description

On maps, Howland Hill Road appears to be a simple trail. But this easy route is a stunningly beautiful, meandering drive through large groves of moss-hung coast redwoods in Jedediah Smith Redwoods State Park. The

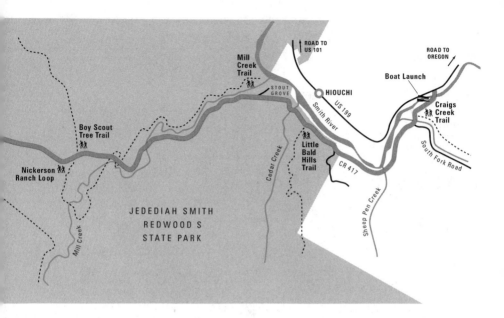

single-track road is graded dirt for most of its length, and the surface is often wet and slippery with fallen leaves. The quiet drive is surprisingly beautiful on a wet day, when mist lends it an eerie feel. Take care when it is wet—the trail can be extremely slippery.

The trail climbs steeply from the edge of Crescent City, entering Jedediah Smith Redwoods State Park and then winding among the large trees. Turnouts allow for safe parking at most of the hiking trails, which lead farther into the groves of giants.

The trail crosses Mill Creek near its halfway point, after which a short spur leads to the Stout Grove of giant redwoods. The road becomes paved after it passes the residential community of Hiouchi, most of which is on the far side of the river. River access points for boaters and anglers can be found at the east end of the trail.

Brilliant yellow banana slugs live in the forest and are valuable to the ecosystem. Try to avoid stepping on them when hiking.

Current Road Information

Jedediah Smith Redwoods State Park
1375 Elk Valley Road
Crescent City, CA 95531
(707) 464-6101 ext. 5112

Map References

BLM   Crescent City
USFS   Smith River National Recreation
       Area, Six Rivers National Forest
USGS   1:24,000   Crescent City, Hiouchi
       1:100,000   Crescent City
Maptech CD-ROM: North Coast/Eureka
Northern California Atlas & Gazetteer, p. 22
California Road & Recreation Atlas, p. 44
Trails Illustrated, Redwood National Park,
       North Coast State Parks, Smith
       River NRA (218)

Route Directions

▼ 0.0   From Elk Valley Road, 1 mile east of US 101 and Crescent City, zero trip meter and turn east on paved Howland Hill Road, following the sign for Stout Grove.

5.6 ▲   Trail ends at T-intersection with Elk Valley Road. Turn left for US 101 and Crescent City.

        GPS: N41°45.51' W124°09.98'

▼ 0.8   SO   Road on right leads to Mill Creek Horse Trail.

4.8 ▲   SO   Road on left leads to Mill Creek Horse Trail.

▼ 1.1   SO   Entering Jedediah Smith Redwoods State Park.

Coastal redwood giants

4.5 ▲   SO   Leaving Jedediah Smith Redwoods
                   State Park.
▼ 1.4   SO   Road turns to graded dirt.
4.2 ▲   SO   Road becomes paved.
▼ 1.7   SO   Closed road on right. Pass through sea-
                   sonal closure gate, following sign for
                   Stout Grove.
3.9 ▲   SO   Seasonal closure gate; then closed
                   road on left.
▼ 2.4   SO   Cross over creek. Metcalf Grove
                   plaque on left.
3.2 ▲   SO   Metcalf Grove plaque on right. Cross
                   over creek.
▼ 3.4   SO   Nickerson Ranch Loop, for hikers,
                   on right.
2.2 ▲   SO   Nickerson Ranch Loop, for hikers, on left.
                   GPS: N41º46.04' W124º06.61'

▼ 3.5   SO   Boy Scout Tree Trail, for hikers, on left.

2.1 ▲   SO   Boy Scot Tree Trail, for hikers, on right.
▼ 3.8   SO   Mill Creek Trail crosses.
1.8 ▲   SO   Mill Creek Trail crosses.
                   GPS: N41º46.23' W124º06.30'

▼ 4.3   SO   Cross over Mill Creek on bridge.
1.3 ▲   SO   Cross over Mill Creek on bridge.
                   GPS: N41º46.46' W124º05.92'

▼ 5.6   SO   Track on left goes 0.1 miles to Stout
                   Grove. Zero trip meter and follow the
                   sign to US 199.
0.0 ▲   Continue to the southwest.
                   GPS: N41º47.29' W124º05.06'

▼ 0.0   Continue to the northeast.
2.8 ▲   SO   Track on right goes 0.1 miles to Stout
                   Grove. Zero trip meter and follow the
                   sign to Crescent City.

▼ 0.5 SO Cross over Cedar Creek.

2.3 ▲ SO Cross over Cedar Creek.

▼ 0.8 SO Track on right goes to Little Bald Hills Trail.

2.0 ▲ SO Track on left goes to Little Bald Hills Trail.

▼ 1.1 SO Closure gate; then closed road on right. Leaving Jedediah Smith Redwoods State Park. Road is now paved.

1.7 ▲ SO Road turns to graded dirt. Entering Jedediah Smith Redwoods State Park. Closed road on left; then closure gate.

▼ 1.3 SO Road is now called Douglas Park Road (CR 417). Remain on paved road, which now follows alongside the Smith River.

1.5 ▲ SO Road leaves the Smith River.

▼ 1.7 SO Cross over Sheep Pen Creek on covered bridge.

1.1 ▲ SO Cross over Sheep Pen Creek on covered bridge.

▼ 2.3 TL Paved road on right is South Fork Road. Turn left and cross over South Fork Smith River on bridge; then Craigs Creek Trail (1E02) on right.

0.5 ▲ TR Craigs Creek Trail (1E02) on left; then cross over South Fork Smith River on bridge; then turn right onto Douglas Park Road. Paved road on left is South Fork Road.

JEDEDIAH SMITH

Jedediah Smith was born January 6, 1799, in New York State. Smith answered an ad in the *St. Louis Gazette and Public Advertiser* in 1822 that called for young men who wanted to explore the West. He soon became part of William Ashley's great fur-trapping and exploration venture.

Jedediah Smith

On one of Smith's first expeditions he was attacked by a grizzly bear that ripped off one ear and part of his scalp. Undeterred, he commanded a companion to sew him up, and he returned to the trail after just 10 days. For the rest of his life, he wore his hair long to conceal his scars.

In 1824, while searching for the fabled Buenaventura River, Smith and his party became the first Americans to cross overland into California. Following his arrival in the Mexican mission of San Gabriel, he was taken to the authorities in San Diego. The Mexican governor feared American intrusion into the area and ordered the party to leave California immediately. Instead of leaving, Smith entered the San Joaquin Valley via Tejon Pass and headed north. At the Stanislaus River, he left most of his party and crossed the Sierra Nevada on his way back to Utah, becoming the first American to do so. Upon returning to the group in California, Smith again ran into trouble with authorities while attempting to trade for supplies in San Jose. After a stint in a Monterey jail, he was released with strict orders to leave California immediately. This time Smith obeyed, and his party trekked north, following the Sacramento River into Oregon.

In Oregon, Smith's party was attacked by Indians, one of many such encounters that the great mountain man faced in his short career. The survivors made their way to Fort Vancouver, and eventually they were able to regain some of the goods taken during the attack. Smith was preparing to retire in 1831 when Comanche Indians attacked him and he was slain in the ensuing fight. He died before publishing an autobiography. A highly religious and strong-willed man, Jedediah Smith is remembered as one of the most important figures in the opening of the American West.

▼ 2.5	SO	Smith River access and boat launch on left.
0.3 ▲	SO	Smith River access and boat launch on right.
▼ 2.7	SO	Cross over Smith River on Neils Christensen Memorial Bridge.
0.1 ▲	SO	Cross over Smith River on Neils Christensen Memorial Bridge.
▼ 2.8		Trail ends at T-intersection with US 199. Turn left for US 101 and Crescent City; turn right for Oregon.
0.0 ▲		Trail commences on US 199, 10 miles northeast of Crescent City and 7 miles east of US 101. Zero trip meter and turn southeast on paved South Fork Road, following the sign for the Howland Hill Scenic Drive.

GPS: N41°48.13' W124°03.17'

Redwood National Park Coastal Drive

STARTING POINT Newton B. Drury Scenic Parkway, 0.8 miles south of its northern intersection with US 101

FINISHING POINT US 101 at the Klamath Beach Road, Coastal Drive exit

TOTAL MILEAGE 9.5 miles

UNPAVED MILEAGE 6 miles

DRIVING TIME 1 hour

ELEVATION RANGE 0–600 feet

USUALLY OPEN Year-round

BEST TIME TO TRAVEL Year-round

DIFFICULTY RATING 1

SCENIC RATING 9

REMOTENESS RATING +0

Special Attractions

- Whale watching in season and a chance to see seals along the coast.
- Historic World War II radar station.
- Viewpoints over the coast and mouth of the Klamath River.

History

This coastal drive overlooks the Yurok village of Requa, on the northern side of the Klamath River's mouth. The strategically positioned village once had more than 20 houses and 14 sweat houses and was the meeting point of the coastal and river members of the Yurok. The Yurok hunted sea lions, seals, bears, elk, and deer, as well as fished for salmon and gathered mollusks and crustaceans.

A World War II radar station is halfway along this scenic drive. The old station, cleverly disguised as a farmhouse, was part of a coastal surveillance operation that watched for a Japanese invasion. The farmhouse, with its false windows and shingled roof, was one of 65 such surveillance stations. A separate silo tower contained the antenna. This high security rural compound had two 50-caliber anti-aircraft machine guns, armed military guards, and a team of patrol dogs. Any movements on the

NORTH COAST #15: REDWOOD NATIONAL PARK COASTAL DRIVE

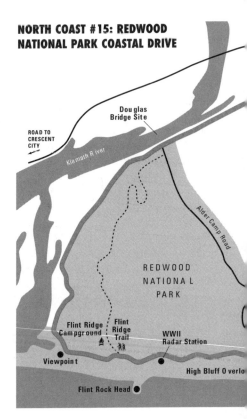

horizon were reported to San Francisco. If the approaching aircraft or vessel was thought to be hostile, fighter planes were dispatched to intercept it.

Description

The coastal drive in Redwood National Park is an easy loop on paved and gravel roads that are suitable for year-round travel. The trail's major attraction is its coastal views, which provide a chance to spot some of the larger marine mammals. Gray whales may be seen migrating between the Arctic Circle and Baja California; sea lions bask on the beaches and rocks; and you may be lucky enough to spot a school of dolphins out at sea. Binoculars are a definite help.

The first section of road is paved. Past the turnoff to Alder Camp Road, it becomes a narrow graded dirt road. The High Bluff Overlook, a short distance past the intersection, is one of the most stunning viewpoints along this part of the coast, with views of

rocky bays and headlands. There are picnic tables here for day use only. The trail then passes the old World War II radar station. The historic site can be viewed from the road, but it is worth the short scramble down the footpath to see the station up close.

The overlook above the mouth of the Klamath River is excellent, and it is also a good place to spot gray whales. All that remains of Douglas Bridge, near the end of the trail, are the surprisingly ornate stone bears that marked one end of the bridge.

Although rated a 1 for difficulty and suitable for passenger vehicles under normal conditions, this road is closed to trailers and RVs.

Current Road Information

Redwood National and State Parks
1111 Second Street
Crescent City, CA 95531
(707) 464-6101

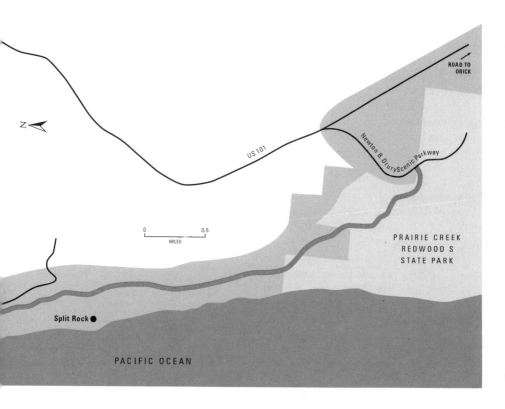

Sea lions bask on rocks below the trail

Map References

BLM   Orick, Crescent City
USFS Six Rivers National Forest
USGS 1:24,000 Fern Canyon, Requa
         1:100,000 Orick, Crescent City
Maptech CD-ROM: North Coast/Eureka
Northern California Atlas & Gazetteer,
      pp. 32, 22
California Road & Recreation Atlas, p. 44
Trails Illustrated, Redwood National Park,
      North Coast State Parks, Smith
      River NRA (218)

Route Directions

▼ 0.0   From Newton B. Drury Scenic Parkway, 0.8 miles south of its northern intersection with US 101, zero trip meter and turn southwest onto paved road, following the sign for Redwood National and State Parks Coastal Drive.

4.2 ▲   Trail ends at intersection with Newton B. Drury Scenic Parkway. Turn left to join US 101 northbound for Crescent City; turn right to join US 101 southbound for Orick.

GPS: N41°27.45′ W124°02.66′

▼ 1.2   SO Road is now a mix of pavement and graded dirt.

3.0 ▲   SO Road is now paved.

▼ 1.6   SO Coastal viewpoint on left.

2.6 ▲   SO Coastal viewpoint on right.

GPS: N41°28.43′ W124°03.76′

▼ 2.0   SO Coastal viewpoint on left.

2.2 ▲   SO Coastal viewpoint on right.

▼ 2.6   SO Coastal viewpoint on left.

1.6 ▲   SO Coastal viewpoint on right.

▼ 3.4   SO Coastal viewpoint on left.

0.8 ▲   SO Coastal viewpoint on right.

▼ 4.2   TL Road on right into state prison; then paved road continues around to the right. Zero trip meter and turn left, following the sign for the Coastal Drive North.

0.0 ▲   Continue to the southeast. Road on left goes into state prison. Road is now intermittently paved.

GPS: N41°30.64′ W124°04.47′

▼ 0.0   Continue to the west. Road is now

World War II radar station disguised as a farmhouse, part of an early warning system to watch for a Japanese invasion

graded dirt.

5.3 ▲ TR T-intersection with paved road. Zero trip meter.

▼ 0.1 BR Track on left goes 0.3 miles to High Bluff Overlook.

5.2 ▲ SO Track on right goes 0.3 miles to High Bluff Overlook.

▼ 0.9 SO Hiking trail to the WW II radar station, which can be seen below the trail on the left.

4.4 ▲ SO Hiking trail to the WW II radar station, which can be seen below the trail on the right.

GPS: N41°31.29' W124°04.65'

▼ 1.3 SO Flint Ridge Hiking Trail on right to Douglas Bridge. Parking on left of trail. Flint Ridge Campground is 0.25 miles up this trail.

4.0 ▲ SO Flint Ridge Hiking Trail on left to Douglas Bridge. Parking on right of trail. Flint Ridge Campground is 0.25 miles up this trail.

GPS: N41°31.62' W124°04.68'

▼ 1.8 SO Turnout on left is a viewpoint over the mouth of the Klamath River. Road is now paved.

3.5 ▲ SO Turnout on right is a viewpoint over the mouth of the Klamath River. Road turns to graded dirt.

GPS: N41°32.03' W124°04.66'

▼ 3.9 SO Paved road on right is Alder Camp Road. Old Douglas Memorial Bridge supports on left.

1.4 ▲ SO Paved road on left is Alder Camp Road. Old Douglas Memorial Bridge supports on right.

GPS: N41°31.45' W124°02.64'

▼ 4.1 SO Leaving Redwood National Park.

1.2 ▲ SO Entering Redwood National Park.

▼ 5.3 Trail ends at intersection with US 101. Turn north for Crescent City; turn south for Eureka.

0.0 ▲ Trail begins on US 101 at the Klamath Beach Road, Coastal Drive exit. Exit freeway and proceed to the west side. Zero trip meter and turn west on paved road.

GPS: N41°30.73' W124°01.70'

The beach below Redwood National Park Coastal Drive

SEA LIONS

Sea Lions

Sea lions are generally larger than seals and are distinguished by their external ear flaps and divided rear flippers. They breed on the Channel Islands but can be seen along the entire California coast. California sea lion males are about 7 feet in length and dark brown in color. Females are about a foot shorter and lighter in color. Although they sometimes become entangled in the nets of salmon fishers, their numbers have increased in recent years. Females give birth to a single pup in June. The dominant males form harems, leaving younger, weaker males with no mate. The species is familiar to circus goers. The northern sea lion is larger and heavier than the California sea lion. Males grow to about 10 feet in length, females to about 7 feet. They are buff-colored and shy. Northern sea lions are less commonly sighted than California sea lions because they generally stay in deep ocean water, but breeding colonies can be seen along the California coast from Santa Cruz to Oregon.

Gold Bluffs Trail

STARTING POINT US 101, 2 miles north of Orick
FINISHING POINT Fern Canyon Trailhead
TOTAL MILEAGE 6.8 miles (one-way)
UNPAVED MILEAGE 6.5 miles
DRIVING TIME 1 hour (one-way)
ELEVATION RANGE 0–400 feet
USUALLY OPEN Year-round
BEST TIME TO TRAVEL Year-round
DIFFICULTY RATING 1
SCENIC RATING 10
REMOTENESS RATING +0

Special Attractions

- Chance to see Roosevelt elk.
- Scenic hiking trail through Fern Canyon.
- Trail runs close to the beach and offers beachside picnicking and camping.

History

Arthur Davidson migrated west in the 1880s and worked at the Lower and Upper Gold Bluff Mines and helped out at a nearby dairy. Within a decade he had his own dairy on a flat beside Prairie Creek. He cleared alders and willows to create more pastures. His land and family expanded, and his descendents owned the farm until 1991.

In 1948, a sawmill was built next to the old dairy. The Arcata Redwood Company

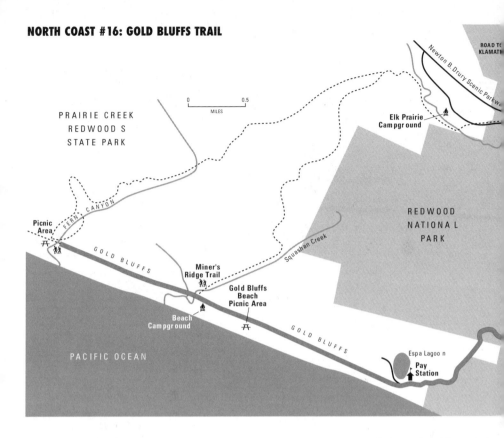

built miles of logging roads into the surrounding forests. Acres of woodlands were cleared over the next two decades, until the sawmill closed its doors in 1970. The newly established Redwood National Park stepped in to cover the logging scars and established elk habitat on what was once the mill site.

Gold Bluffs Trail ends at Fern Canyon where Home Creek has carved through layers of ancient sediments. Native Americans came to such moist areas to collect black-stemmed five-fingered ferns, valued for use in basket weaving because of their color and fine stems.

Description

Gold Bluffs Trail is an easy drive through a variety of scenery in Redwood National Park and Prairie Creek Redwoods State Park. It starts on US 101 at Elk Meadows, where you have an excellent chance of seeing Roosevelt elk. Although the elk can often be seen close to the highway, it is much safer to park and view the animals at the Elk Meadows parking

area near the start of the trail. Although the elk appear to be undisturbed by vehicles and humans, remember that they are wild animals and should not be approached. If you can't see any elk in the meadows, you may be able to see them at a spot farther down the trail, in the dunes along the beach.

The road winds through a lush coastal forest of alders, spruces, and redwoods, with a covering of moss and ferns. It enters Prairie Creek Redwoods State Park, which charges a small fee for day use, and continues close to the beach along the base of Gold Bluffs. There are coastal views and many points where you can park and walk to the beach. No vehicles are allowed on the beach. There is an exposed campground on the foreshore near the beach (additional fee required) and picnic areas for day use only.

Past the campground, low-clearance vehicles will need to take care crossing Squashan Creek. Although low-clearance vehicles often make the crossing in low water, you should walk from this point if there is any doubt.

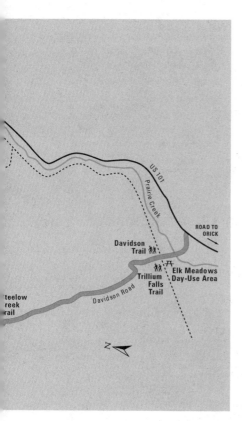

Map References
BLM Orick
USFS Six Rivers National Forest
USGS 1:24,000 Orick, Fern Canyon
1:100,000 Orick
Maptech CD-ROM: North Coast/Eureka
Northern California Atlas & Gazetteer,
pp. 32, 22
California Road & Recreation Atlas, p. 44
Trails Illustrated, Redwood National Park,
North Coast State Parks, Smith
River NRA (218)

Route Directions

▼ 0.0   From US 101, 2 miles north of Orick,
zero trip meter and turn east on paved
Davidson Road (FR 400), following the
sign for Elk Meadows and Gold Bluffs
Beach.
GPS: N41°19.28′ W124°02.29′

▼ 0.1   SO Elk Meadows parking area for elk viewing.
▼ 0.2   SO Cross over Prairie Creek on bridge.
▼ 0.3   SO Elk Meadows Day-use Area on left.
Trillium Falls Trail, for hikers, leaves
through the day-use area. Road turns
to graded dirt. Davison Trail, for hikers,
on right to Elk Prairie Campground.
GPS: N41°19.49′ W124°02.56′

▼ 2.0   SO Streelow Creek Trail, for hikers and
mountain bikers, on right to Elk Prairie
Campground.

▼ 2.8   SO Entering Gold Bluffs Beach—part of
Prairie Creek Redwoods State Park.
GPS: N41°20.96′ W124°03.84′

▼ 3.5   SO Track on right is for authorized vehicles
only. Parking area and beach access
on left. Zero trip meter at fee station.
GPS: N41°21.35′ W124°04.35′

▼ 0.0   Continue to the north.
▼ 0.1   BL Track on right goes to Espa Lagoon.
A parking area is immediately off the
trail. Bear left following the sign for
Beach Overlook.
▼ 0.2   SO Pass through gate. Trail is now running
beneath Gold Bluffs.

The trail ends at the Fern Canyon Trailhead. The 0.8-mile loop that sets out through Fern Canyon is not to be missed. The 50-foot-high canyon walls are covered with ferns, mostly five-fingered ferns, but also lady ferns and sword ferns. The canyon is habitat for eight species in all. Home Creek meanders through the canyon, and hikers have to cross it often so prepare for wet feet. The western red-legged frog and a rare species of tailed frog with a short, stumpy tail live in the canyon. These frogs can often be seen and heard along the damp banks of the creek. The Pacific giant salamander also lives in damp areas of the canyon. The hiking trail climbs out of the canyon and loops back to the parking area.

Current Road Information
Redwood National and State Parks
1111 Second Street
Crescent City, CA 95531
(707) 464-6101

Five-fingered ferns grow along the walls of Fern Canyon

Gold Bluffs Beach

▼ 1.5　SO　Gold Bluffs Beach Picnic Area on left.
　　　　　　GPS: N41°22.65′ W124°04.14′

▼ 2.0　SO　Beach Campground on left.
　　　　　　GPS: N41°23.03′ W124°04.04′

▼ 2.1　SO　Miner's Ridge Trail on right goes to
　　　　　　park headquarters; then cross through
　　　　　　Squashan Creek; then pass through
　　　　　　gate, which is open from 9 a.m. to 30
　　　　　　minutes after sunset.

▼ 2.2　SO　Cross through creek.

▼ 2.9　SO　Cross through creek.

▼ 3.1　SO　Parking area on left. In the future, the
　　　　　　trail will end here and the hiking trail
　　　　　　will extend to this point.

▼ 3.3　　　End of trail at the Fern Canyon trail-
　　　　　　head and picnic area.
　　　　　　GPS: N41°24.22′ W124°03.78

NORTH COAST #17

Bald Hills Road

STARTING POINT California 169 at Martins
　Ferry
FINISHING POINT US 101, 0.5 miles north
　of Orick
TOTAL MILEAGE 30.9 miles
UNPAVED MILEAGE 21.2 miles
DRIVING TIME 3 hours
ELEVATION RANGE 100–3,200 feet
USUALLY OPEN Year-round
BEST TIME TO TRAVEL Year-round
DIFFICULTY RATING 1
SCENIC RATING 10
REMOTENESS RATING +0

Special Attractions
- Coast redwoods and Redwood National Park.
- Historic site of Lyons Ranch.
- Schoolhouse Peak Fire Lookout.

History
Bald Hills Road begins on the Klamath River at Martins Ferry. Just upstream is Weitchpec, an important Yurok settlement at the confluence of the Trinity and Klamath Rivers. The banks of the Klamath are within two Indian reservations: the Hoopa Valley Indian Reservation and the Yurok. The forests in the drainages of these two important rivers were valuable for game and collecting seeds and firewood. Villages built by the Yurok on flats along the Klamath include Waseck, formerly called Washekw, Kenek, now spelled Kanick (at the prime fishing spot of the Kenek Rapids), Kepel, Sa'a, Murekw, and Himetl.

Once over the crest of Schoolhouse Peak, at the southeastern end of the Bald Hills, the road enters Redwood National Park, established in 1968. It passes the historic Lyons Ranch, a cattle ranch started by Jonathon and Amelia Lyons in 1860. By the 1870s, they switched to raising sheep and continued to expand their property. The Lyons entered wool at a show in Paris and won an award that brought them worldwide recognition. As a result, their sheep fetched above average prices and their ranch holdings continued to grow. The family carried on their ranching tradition for more than a century.

Some of the tallest trees in the world can be found in Redwood National Park, in groves at the western end of Bald Hills Road. At 368 feet, an ancient redwood in the Tall Trees Grove is one of the tallest recorded trees in the world.

Description
This graded dirt road starts at Martins Ferry, on the east side of the Coast Ranges, crosses the Bald Hills into Redwood National Park, and ends near the Pacific Ocean north of Orick. The Humboldt County road is sporadically maintained and is often very washboardy. Drivers should be aware that fast-moving logging trucks use this road at all hours. It snakes up a long, gradually ascending grade to French Camp Ridge and then onto the Bald Hills. From the top of the sparsely vegetated ridge, there are views to the coast and back over the Klamath River Basin toward the Klamath Mountains to the east.

A short, worthwhile side trip goes to the Schoolhouse Peak Fire Lookout (3,097 feet). You can drive the first 0.2 mile, then hike the remaining 0.2 mile to the tower, which sits on a bare peak overlooking the Bald Hills, Redwood Creek Basin, and the coast. The road enters Redwood National Park, passing the hiking trailhead to the Lyons Ranch historical site. A barn and the remains of an old bunkhouse are all that survive at this once sprawling ranch.

Additional hiking trails within the park lead to other points of interest. One popular trail is the Dolason Prairie Trail, a steep 9.5-mile round-trip for experienced hikers. The Lyons Barn is partway along this trail, which eventually connects to the Tall Trees Grove. The Tall Trees Grove can also be accessed by vehicle, but a permit is required from the national park office on the day of travel. The free permit gives the combination to a locked gate.

The trail dips into the lush, damp forest of alders and towering coast redwoods on the west side of the range. Redwoods need a mild, damp climate; coastal fog and the sheltered Redwood Creek Basin create excellent habitat.

The Redwood Creek Overlook views a patchwork of new and old growth forest along Redwood Creek. Interpretive information boards detail past and present restoration projects. The road joins the paved park road and finishes on US 101, just north of Orick.

Current Road Information
Redwood National and State Parks
1111 Second Street
Crescent City, CA 95531
(707) 464-6101

Bureau of Land Management
Arcata Field Office
1695 Heindon Road
Arcata, CA 95521
(707) 825-2300

ald Hills Road

Map References

BLM   Hoopa, Orick
USFS   Six Rivers National Forest
USGS   1:24,000   French Camp Ridge,
     Bald Hills, Holter Ridge, Orick
     1:100,000 Hoopa, Orick
Maptech CD-ROM: North Coast/Eureka
Northern California Atlas & Gazetteer,
     pp. 32, 33
California Road & Recreation Atlas, p. 44
Trails Illustrated, Redwood National Park,
     North Coast State Parks, Smith
     River NRA (218)
Other: Redwood National Park visitor map

Route Directions

▼ 0.0   From Weitchpec on California 96, at
        the intersection with California 169,

        zero trip meter and proceed west
        on California 169 for 3.4 miles to
        Martins Ferry. Zero trip meter and
        turn left (southwest) over the bridge,
        following sign for US 101 and Orick.
        Cross over the Klamath River on
        bridge.

13.7 ▲   Trail ends at T-intersection with paved
        California 169 at Martins Ferry. Turn
        right for California 96 and Weitchpec.
        GPS: N41°12.50′ W123°45.26′

▼ 0.1   TL   T-intersection. Follow the sign to Orick.
        Road turns to graded dirt.
13.6 ▲   TR   Road continues straight ahead. Turn
        right and cross over the Klamath River
        on the Martins Ferry bridge.
▼ 0.4   SO   Track on left.
13.3 ▲   SO   Track on right.

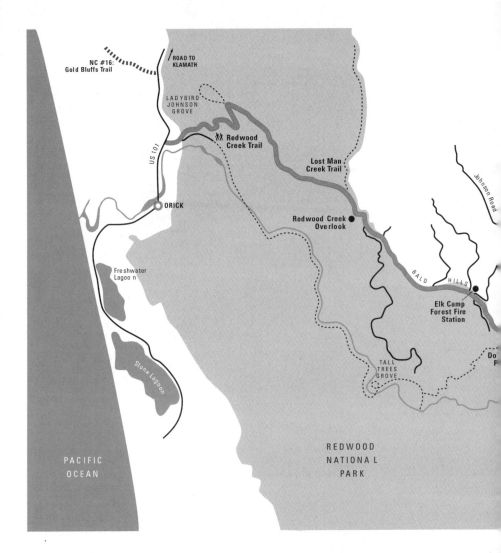

▼ 1.0   BR   Track on left.
12.7 ▲   BL   Track on right.
▼ 9.3   SO   Track on right.
4.4 ▲   SO   Track on left.
        GPS: N41°09.77' W123°49.08'

▼ 9.7   SO   Track on left.
4.0 ▲   SO   Track on right.
▼ 10.9 SO   Track on left.
2.8 ▲   SO   Track on right.
▼ 11.8 SO   Quarry on right.
1.9 ▲   SO   Quarry on left.
▼ 12.3 SO   Track on left through closure gate.
1.4 ▲   SO   Track on right through closure gate.
▼ 12.6 SO   Two tracks on left.
1.1 ▲   SO   Two tracks on right.

▼ 13.0 SO   Track on right.
0.7 ▲   SO   Track on left.
        GPS: N41°08.61' W123°51.87'

▼ 13.7 SO   Unmarked track on sharp right goes
             0.4 miles to the fire lookout on
             Schoolhouse Peak. There is a locked
             gate after 0.2 miles. Zero trip meter.
0.0 ▲   Continue to the east.
        GPS: N41°08.90' W123°52.54'

▼ 0.0   Continue to the southwest.
7.5 ▲   BR   Unmarked track on left goes 0.4 miles
             to the fire lookout on Schoolhouse
             Peak. There is a locked gate after 0.2
             miles. Zero trip meter.

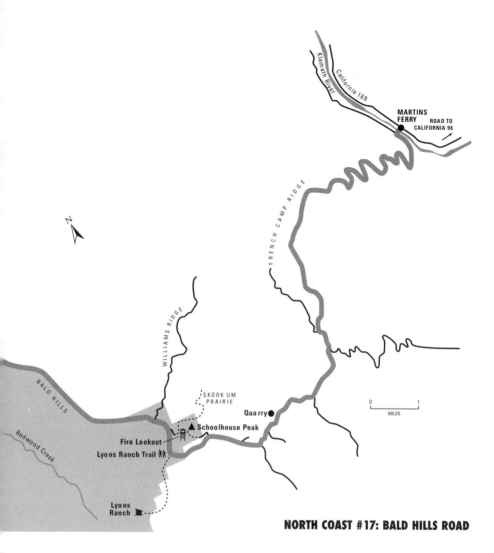

NORTH COAST #17: BALD HILLS ROAD

▼ 0.3 SO Track on left.
.2 ▲ SO Track on right.

▼ 0.6 SO Cattle guard. Entering Redwood
National Park. Lyons Barn is downhill
to the left.

9 ▲ SO Cattle guard. Leaving Redwood
National Park. Lyons Barn is downhill
to the right.
GPS: N41°08.79' W123°53.21'

0.9 BR Track on left is the parking area for the
Lyons Ranch Trailhead.

6 ▲ BL Track on right is the parking area for
the Lyons Ranch Trailhead.
GPS: N41°08.90' W123°53.52'

▼ 1.5 BL Track on right to Skookum Prairie—
no motor vehicles.

6.0 ▲ BR Track on left to Skookum Prairie—
no motor vehicles.
GPS: N41°09.36' W123°53.31'

▼ 1.8 SO Graded road on right goes to Williams
Ridge—closed to public use.

5.7 ▲ SO Graded road on left goes to Williams
Ridge—closed to public use.
GPS: N41°09.55' W123°53.55'

▼ 6.3 SO Track on left is Dolason Prairie Trail.
1.2 ▲ SO Track on right is Dolason Prairie Trail.
GPS: N41°12.35' W123°56.96'

▼ 7.5 SO Elk Camp Forest Fire Station on right. Johnson Road on right. Zero trip meter.

0.0 ▲ Continue to the southeast. Road is now sporadically paved, turning to graded dirt.

GPS: N41°13.31' W123°57.48'

▼ 0.0 Continue to the northwest. Road is now paved.

9.7 ▲ SO Elk Camp Forest Fire Station on left. Johnson Road on left. Zero trip meter and follow the sign to Weitchpec.

▼ 0.1 SO Track on right and track on left.

9.6 ▲ SO Track on right and track on left.

▼ 0.8 SO Track on right.

8.9 ▲ SO Track on left.

▼ 2.3 SO Track on right.

7.4 ▲ SO Track on left.

▼ 2.8 SO Tall Trees Grove access on left and track on right. Permit required for Tall Trees access road.

4.7 ▲ SO Tall Trees Grove access on right and track on left. Permit required for Tall Trees access road.

GPS: N41°15.24' W123°59.18'

▼ 3.3 SO Redwood Creek Overlook on left.

6.4 ▲ SO Redwood Creek Overlook on right.

GPS: N41°15.49' W123°59.27'

▼ 3.7 SO Lost Man Creek Trail for mountain bikes on right.

6.0 ▲ SO Lost Man Creek Trail for mountain bikes on left.

GPS: N41°15.83' W123°59.18'

▼ 7.1 SO Ladybird Johnson Grove parking area on left; then pass under footbridge.

2.6 ▲ SO Pass under footbridge; then Ladybird Johnson Grove parking area on right.

▼ 9.2 SO Exiting Redwood National Park. Road on left to Redwood Creek Trail.

0.5 ▲ SO Entering the Redwood National Park. Road on right to Redwood Creek Trail.

GPS: N41°18.02' W124°02.41'

▼ 9.7 Trail ends at T-intersection with US 101. Turn right for Klamath; turn left for Orick.

0.0 ▲ Trail commences on US 101, 0.5 miles

north of Orick. Zero trip meter and turn southeast on paved road at the sign for Bald Hills Road, following sign for Ladybird Johnson Grove.

GPS: N41°18.11' W124°02.79'

Shelton Butte Trail

STARTING POINT FR 10, 6.5 miles south of Orleans

FINISHING POINT Shelton Butte

TOTAL MILEAGE 9.6 miles (one-way)

UNPAVED MILEAGE 9.4 miles

DRIVING TIME 1 hour (one-way)

ELEVATION RANGE 800–3,600 feet

USUALLY OPEN June to December

BEST TIME TO TRAVEL Dry weather

DIFFICULTY RATING 2

SCENIC RATING 9

REMOTENESS RATING +0

Special Attractions

■ Views from the old fire lookout site on Shelton Butte.

■ Lightly traveled trail in Six Rivers National Forest.

History

Shelton Butte lies on the ancestral boundary of the Karok and Yurok tribal lands. Across the Klamath River from Shelton Butte, Bluff Creek, known as Iniinac in the Karok language, was the southern extent of the Karok's influence. The area downstream from Bluff Creek was considered Yuruk Veezivzaaneen (meaning "downriver country"), the ancestral domain of the Yurok.

The riverside settlement of Orleans, on California 96, is near the start of this trail. The Karok Va-araar, or "Upriver People," once had a village called Panamnik at this site. Although settlers disrupted the culture and natural environment of the Karok and Yurok, tribal members remain in this stunning deep valley country.

Description

Shelton Butte was once the site of a fire lookout tower because of its commanding views. The lookout tower is gone, and communications towers now stand on the butte. The roughly graded road to Shelton Butte's summit is lightly used, and it makes a lovely out-and-back drive for high-clearance vehicles.

Initially, the trail is easygoing, although it can be somewhat washboardy as it travels along a wide shelf road through the lush coastal forests of Six Rivers National Forest. Rockslides are common in this wet region, so be prepared to find boulders and loose rock in the road.

Past the turnoff to Hoopa (10N05), the road becomes a spur and starts the final climb up to the butte. This section is not used as much as the earlier part of the trail and is best traveled in dry weather; the shelf road can become extremely greasy and dangerous when wet. The final section spirals up to the lookout site and offers great views over Six Rivers National Forest and the coastal mountains. Below is the Klamath River and Big Bar river access point.

This trail makes for a beautiful autumn drive, with bigleaf maples providing a radiant golden color.

Current Road Information

Six Rivers National Forest
Orleans Ranger District
Highway 96
Orleans, CA 95556
(530) 627-3291

Shelton Butte

The trail climbing to Shelton Butte

NORTH COAST #18: SHELTON BUTTE TRAIL

Map References

BLM Hoopa
USFS Klamath National Forest; Six Rivers
National Forest
USGS 1:24,000 Orleans, Hopkins Butte,
Weitchpec
1:100,000 Hoopa
Maptech CD-ROM: North Coast/Eureka
Northern California Atlas & Gazetteer, p. 33
California Road & Recreation Atlas, p. 45

Route Directions

▼ 0.0   From Orleans on California 96, at the
north side of the bridge over the
Klamath River, zero trip meter and turn
southeast on paved Redcap Road and
proceed 5 miles. Pass paved road on
right and continue straight ahead.
The road becomes FR 10 (10N01).
Continue straight ahead for another 1.5
miles to the intersection with 10N02.
Zero trip meter and turn south onto
10N02, also marked CD12, following
the sign to Mill Creek Gap and Hoopa.
.5 ▲   Trail ends at intersection with paved
FR 10 (10N01). Turn left onto this road
and proceed 6.5 miles to Orleans and
California 96.
      GPS: N41°15.25′ W123°32.83′

▼ 0.8   SO   Road becomes paved.
.7 ▲   SO   Road turns back to graded dirt.
▼ 0.9   SO   Cross over Red Cap Creek on bridge.
.6 ▲   SO   Cross over Red Cap Creek on bridge.
▼ 1.0   SO   Track on left. Road turns back to

      graded dirt.
0.5 ▲   SO   Track on right. Road is now paved.
▼ 1.2   SO   Track on left.
0.3 ▲   SO   Track on right.
▼ 1.5   TR   Road 10N02 continues straight ahead
to Hoopa. Zero trip meter and turn right
onto 10N05, following the sign to
Shelton Butte.
0.0 ▲   Continue to the east.
      GPS: N41°14.08′ W123°32.85′

▼ 0.0   Continue to the northwest.
4.0 ▲   TL   T-intersection with 10N02. To the right
goes to Hoopa. Zero trip meter and fol-
low the sign to Orleans.
▼ 3.1   SO   Track on right is 10N35.
0.9 ▲   SO   Track on left is 10N35.
      GPS: N41°14.08′ W123°34.99′

▼ 4.0   BR   Track on right is 10N37; then track on
left is the continuation of 10N05 to
Hoopa. Zero trip meter and bear right
onto 10N09, following the sign to
Shelton Butte.
0.0 ▲   Continue to the east.
      GPS: N41°14.05′ W123°35.96′

▼ 0.0   Continue to the west.
▼ 2.3   SO   Seasonal closure gate.
      GPS: N41°14.10′ W123°36.97′

▼ 3.1   SO   Seasonal closure gate.
▼ 4.1   Communications towers on Shelton
Butte.
      GPS: N41°14.30′ W123°37.90′

Patterson Road

STARTING POINT Ti-Bar Road, 3.8 miles northeast of California 96
FINISHING POINT California 96, 8 miles north of Somes Bar
TOTAL MILEAGE 8.9 miles
UNPAVED MILEAGE 8.9 miles
DRIVING TIME 1 hour
ELEVATION RANGE 800–2,800 feet
USUALLY OPEN May to January
BEST TIME TO TRAVEL Dry weather
DIFFICULTY RATING 2
SCENIC RATING 8
REMOTENESS RATING +0

Special Attractions

■ Fall color viewing.
■ Can be combined with North Coast #20: Ukonom Mountain Trail for a longer trip.
■ This region of Klamath National Forest has the most Bigfoot sightings in North America.

History

Patterson Road travels along the eastern slope of the Klamath River Valley. Many Indian camps and villages once dotted the valley. Patterson Road's start near the Ti Bar Forest Service Station is near the site of a former Karok village called Tiih. Persido Bar, north of Ti Bar, was Pasiru Uuvree, another Karok village. The southern end of the trail exits the dense forest at Sandy Bar, the site of Iinpiit. The Karok relied on the Klamath River for fish and as a corridor for travel and trade. Skilled craftsmen carved canoes from redwood, taking many months to create one of the hand-hewn canoes.

Settlers disrupted life in this idyllic valley. Diseases annihilated entire villages. Mountain men who passed through the region on their way to trap beaver were surprised to find villages deserted when they returned. All of the inhabitants had died. Although the trappers moved on as quickly as possible for fear of catching an illness, it seems they themselves may have unknowingly spread the diseases.

Fall colors along the trail

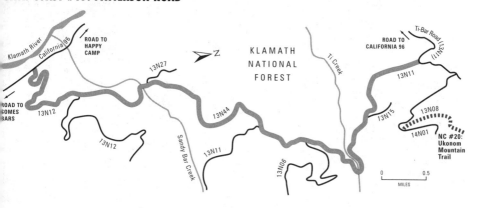

This region of California boasts the largest number of Bigfoot (Sasquatch) sightings in North America. Indeed, California 6 is called the Bigfoot Highway, and the earby town of Happy Camp hosts an annual Bigfoot Festival in summer. Whether or not you believe stories of the giant, keep an ye out as you travel these back roads. You ust never know.

escription

atterson Road travels through Klamath National Forest on the west side of the Marble Mountain Wilderness. The easy rail is a pretty drive and can be combined vith North Coast #20: Ukonom Mountain rail for a longer trip. The wet Pacific Coast forest is dense, with vine-covered rees and blackberry bushes in gullies. Trees ere include California Bays, madrones, ed alders, and bigleaf maples. Ti Creek, ear the start of the trail, flows through a ense thicket of alders.

This trail does not appear in its entirety on opographical maps of the region.

urrent Road Information
ix Rivers National Forest
)rleans Ranger District
Highway 96
)rleans, CA 95556
530) 627-3291

Map References
BLM Happy Camp, Hoopa
USFS Klamath National Forest
USGS 1:24,000 Dillon Mt., Ukonom
       Mt., Bark Shanty Gulch
       1:100,000 Happy Camp, Hoopa
Maptech CD-ROM: North Coast/Eureka
Northern California Atlas & Gazetteer,
       pp. 23, 24, 33, 34
California Road & Recreation Atlas,
       p. 45 (incomplete)
Other: "A Guide to the Marble Mountain
       Wilderness & Russian Wilderness"

Route Directions

▼ 0.0   From California 96, 25.5 miles south of
         Happy Camp at county mile marker
         12.18, zero trip meter and turn east
         onto Ti-Bar Road (13N11), following
         sign for the Wildlands Fire Station.
         Proceed 3.8 miles on Ti-Bar Road to
         the start of the trail. Zero trip meter
         and turn east on 13N11. Pass through
         seasonal closure gate.
3.3 ▲   Trail ends at intersection with 14N01.
         Turn right onto 14N01 for North Coast
         #20: Ukonom Mountain Trail; turn left
         onto 13N11 for California 96.
         GPS: N41°32.61' W123°30.11'

▼ 0.5   SO Track on right.
2.8 ▲   SO Track on left.
▼ 1.1   SO Track on left is 13N11J; then second

Ti Creek

track on left is 13N15 and track on right is 13N11D.

2.2 ▲ SO Track on left is 13N11D and track on right is 13N15; then second track on right is 13N11J.
GPS: N41°32.03′ W123°29.48′

▼ 1.8 SO Cross over Ti Creek on bridge.
1.5 ▲ SO Cross over Ti Creek on bridge.
GPS: N41°31.92′ W123°28.83′

▼ 2.7 SO Track on left is 13N06.
0.6 ▲ SO Track on right is 13N06.
GPS: N41°31.42′ W123°29.29′

▼ 3.3 TR Road 13N11 continues straight ahead. Zero trip meter and turn right onto 13N44.
0.0 ▲ Continue to the northeast.
GPS: N41°31.00′ W123°29.48′

▼ 0.0 Continue to the northwest.
5.6 ▲ TL T-intersection with 13N11. Zero trip meter.

▼ 0.1 SO Pass through seasonal closure gate.
5.5 ▲ SO Pass through seasonal closure gate.

▼ 0.7 SO Track on left.
4.9 ▲ SO Track on right.

▼ 2.4 BL Seasonal closure gate; then track on right though gate is 13N40.
3.2 ▲ BR Track on left through gate is 13N40; then pass through seasonal closure gate.
GPS: N41°30.10′ W123°30.20′

▼ 2.6 TL T-intersection. Track on right is 13N27. Turn left and cross over Sandy Bar Creek.
3.0 ▲ TR Cross over Sandy Bar Creek; then track straight ahead is 13N27. Remain on 13N44.
GPS: N41°29.96′ W123°30.21′

▼ 2.8 SO Track on left.
2.8 ▲ SO Track on right.
▼ 3.0 SO Track on left to private property.
2.6 ▲ SO Track on right to private property.
▼ 3.1 SO Track on right and track on left to private property.
2.5 ▲ SO Track on left and track on right to private property.
▼ 3.8 TR T-intersection with 13N12.
1.8 ▲ TL Turn left onto 13N44. Turn is on a sharp right-hand bend.

▼ 4.5	SO	Track on left.
.1 ▲	SO	Track on right.
▼ 5.6		Trail ends at T-intersection with California 96. Turn left for Somes Bar; turn right for Happy Camp.
.0 ▲		Trail commences on California 96, 8 miles north of Somes Bar, 0.1 miles northwest of county mile marker 8.51. Zero trip meter and turn northeast on graded dirt road, marked Patterson Road (13N12) to Sandy Bar Creek.

GPS: N41°28.91' W123°30.63'

NORTH COAST #20

Ukonom Mountain Trail

STARTING POINT 14N01, 5.4 miles northeast of California 96

FINISHING POINT Ukonom Mountain Fire Lookout

TOTAL MILEAGE 4 miles (one-way)

UNPAVED MILEAGE 4 miles

DRIVING TIME 30 minutes (one-way)

ELEVATION RANGE 3,000–4,500 feet

USUALLY OPEN Late May to mid October

BEST TIME TO TRAVEL May to October

DIFFICULTY RATING 3

SCENIC RATING 8

REMOTENESS RATING +0

Special Attractions

- Fall color viewing.
- Ukonom Mountain Fire Lookout.
- Views of the Klamath River Valley and Marble Mountain Wilderness.
- Can be combined with North Coast #19: Patterson Road to make a longer trip.

History

Ukonom Mountain (4,581 feet) was likely named for a nearby Native American village called Yuhnaam. Yuhnaam may have described the Klamath River flat on which the settlement was built. Blue Nose Bluff, another feature on the river, rises above the west bank of the Klamath at the foot of Ukonom Mountain. Nova Scotians, called Blue Noses, arrived in the vicinity in the 1890s. They established the Blue Nose Mine and built the Blue Nose Bridge across the Klamath River below the bluff in 1891.

The Ukonom Mountain Fire Lookout provides views northeast to the Kelsey Range, part of the Siskiyou Mountains. The Kelsey Pack Trail was an early mountain route that connected Crescent City with communities along the Klamath River.

Description

This short trail gradually ascends a shelf road through lush coastal forest to the fire lookout at the top of Ukonom Mountain. Vegetation includes alders, birches, madrones, and the verdant undergrowth of the moist forests found on the western, wetter slopes of these mountains.

NORTH COAST #20: UKONOM MOUNTAIN TRAIL

Ukonom Mountain Fire Lookout

As the trail climbs, the vegetation opens up to give views over the surrounding forest. The trail you see below encircles Ukonom Mountain but does not lead to the lookout.

The concrete block fire lookout on Ukonom Mountain is manned seven days a week during fire season, from late May to mid October. If you are planning to drive the trail at the start or near the end of the fire season, call ahead to see if the gate to the tower is open. The gate is locked in the off-season making the trail inaccessible to vehicles. You are normally able to climb to the tower with permission from the lookout on duty. On a clear day, you will have excellent views of the Klamath River Valley and the Marble Mountain Wilderness. Dillon Creek USFS Campground is directly below the tower on the river.

The trail's 3 rating comes from the steep climb at the end and the narrow sections of shelf road that have limited passing places. The region has abundant wildlife; look out for black bears, deer, squirrels, and smaller animals.

Current Road Information

Six Rivers National Forest
Orleans Ranger District
Highway 96
Orleans, CA 95556
(530) 627-3291

Map References

BLM   Happy Camp
USFS   Klamath National Forest
USGS   1:24,000   Ukonom Mt.
            1:100,000 Happy Camp
Maptech CD-ROM: North Coast/Eureka
Northern California Atlas & Gazetteer, p. 24
California Road & Recreation Atlas, p. 45
Other: "A Guide to the Marble Mountain
            Wilderness & Russian Wilderness"

Route Directions

▼ 0.0   From California 96, 25.5 miles south of
              Happy Camp at county mile marker
              12.18, zero trip meter and turn east
              onto Ti-Bar Road (13N11), following
              the sign for the Wildlands Fire Station.

Shelf road around the edge of Ukonom Mountain

Turn onto 14N01 after 3.8 miles, following signs for the lookout. Total distance from California 96 to the start of the trail is 5.4 miles. Zero trip meter and turn northwest on graded dirt road 13N08, following the sign to Ukonom Lookout.
GPS: N41°32.37′ W123°29.27′

▼ 0.1   SO   Seasonal closure gate.
▼ 0.5   SO   Viewpoint on left.
▼ 1.5   SO   Track on left is 13N08D—closed to vehicles.
GPS: N41°33.40′ W123°28.72′

▼ 2.2   SO   Track on right is 14N22.
▼ 2.7   SO   Track on left is 13N08B—closed to vehicles.
GPS: N41°34.08′ W123°28.55′

▼ 3.3   SO   Seasonal closure gate.
▼ 4.0   Trail ends at the Ukonom Mountain Fire Lookout.
GPS: N41°35.04′ W123°28.50′

NORTH COAST #21

Hennessy Ridge Road

STARTING POINT California 299, 2.7 miles north of Burnt Ranch
FINISHING POINT California 299 at Burnt Ranch
TOTAL MILEAGE 11.7 miles, plus 2.7-mile spur along Hennessy Ridge
UNPAVED MILEAGE 9.8 miles, plus 2.7-mile spur
DRIVING TIME 1.25 hours
ELEVATION RANGE 900–3,500 feet
USUALLY OPEN May to December
BEST TIME TO TRAVEL May to December
DIFFICULTY RATING 2
SCENIC RATING 8
REMOTENESS RATING +0

Special Attractions
■ World's largest tanoak tree.
■ Views into the South Fork of the Trinity River Valley.

History
Hennessy Ridge Road parallels a ridge-top pack trail of the late 1800s used by miners working claims along the South Fork of the Trinity River. The trail connected remote mining camps with the towns of Salyer to the north on the Trinity River and Hyampom to the south, on the South Fork of the Trinity. Hennessy Ridge is the watershed between the South Fork of the Trinity and Trinity Rivers.

Salmon from the South Fork of the Trinity River was a significant food source for the Wintun; miners also took advantage of the fish. Mining, however, reduced the number of fish spawning in the river. It wasn't until the 1910s that rivers in this vicinity recovered from the effects of mining projects.

Landslides and unstable soils are common in this region of steep slopes and deep canyons. A major landslide following heavy rains in 1890 swept away Chinese miners who were taking refuge in a cabin at Burnt Ranch.

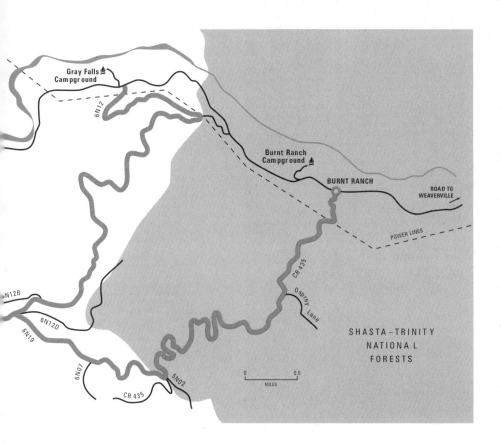

Description

This narrow graded road starts on California 299 near the Six Rivers National Forest's Gray Falls Campground on the Trinity River. The trail is easygoing, but a few rough spots make high-clearance preferable. Much of the trail is single-vehicle width shelf road with ample passing places. It ends upstream on the Trinity River, at Burnt Ranch on California 299.

The trees here are predominantly Douglas firs and bigleaf maples, which provide a nice display of golden color in the fall. California's largest tanoak is near the end of a spur. The massive tree measures more than 22 feet around its girth. The tree is marked by a small sign at the end of the spur trail. You can reach it by hiking about 100 yards or so along a steep path that can be slippery.

The forest service may close this trail during wet weather to prevent the spread of Port Orford cedar root rot.

Current Road Information

Shasta-Trinity National Forests
Big Bar Ranger District
Star Route 1, Box 10
Big Bar, CA 96010
(530) 623-6106

Map References

BLM   Hayfork
USFS   Six Rivers National Forest; Shasta-Trinity National Forests
USGS   1:24,000   Ironside Mt., Hennessy Peak, Salyer
          1:100,000 Hayfork
Maptech CD-ROM: North Coast/Eureka
Northern California Atlas & Gazetteer, pp. 43, 44
California Road & Recreation Atlas, p. 51

Route Directions

▼ 0.0   From the Trinity Scenic Byway

Hiking trail to the record California tree

▼ 0.4   SO Track on right.
5.1 ▲   SO Track on left.
▼ 1.4   SO Track on right into quarry; then track
            on left under power lines.
4.1 ▲   SO Track on right under power lines; then
            track on left into quarry.
▼ 5.1   BL Track on right is 6N12B.
0.4 ▲   SO Track on left is 6N12B.
            GPS: N40°50.73′ W123°31.80′

▼ 5.5   TL 5-way intersection. Track on right; then
            second track on right is the continuation
            of 6N12 and the spur along Hennessy
            Ridge. Track on left is 6N12D. Zero trip
            meter and turn second left onto 6N19,
            following the sign to Hennessy Peak.
0.0 ▲   Continue to the northeast.
            GPS: N40°50.92′ W123°32.13′

Spur along Hennessy Ridge

▼ 0.0   Proceed west on 6N12 from the 5-way
            intersection.
▼ 1.7   SO Track on right.
▼ 1.8   SO 6N12 continues around to the left.
            Join 6N13.
            GPS: N40°52.21′ W123°32.83′

▼ 1.9   SO Track on right.
▼ 2.7   Small sign on right points to the record
            tanoak tree. Follow the hiking trail for
            100 yards to the tree. The vehicle trail
            continues 0.6 miles past this point to a
            locked gate.
            GPS: N40°52.48′ W123°33.73′

Continuation of Main Trail

▼ 0.0   Continue to the southeast.
6.2 ▲   TR 5-way intersection. Track straight ahead
            is 6N12, the spur along Hennessy Ridge.
            Track on right is 6N12D; then second
            track on right is 6N12; then third track
            on right. Zero trip meter and turn second
            right onto 6N12, following the sign to
            California 299.
            GPS: N40°50.92′ W123°32.13′

▼ 0.9   BL Track on right is 6N07; then track on left.
5.3 ▲   BR Track on right; then track on left is 6N07.

(California 299), 2.7 miles north of
Burnt Ranch, 11.6 miles southeast of
Willow Creek, zero trip meter and turn
southwest on graded dirt road 6N12.
The turn is immediately east of the
Gray Falls USFS Campground at Trinity
County mile marker 7.73.
5.5 ▲   Trail ends at T-intersection with the
            Trinity Scenic Byway (California 299).
            Turn right for Weaverville; turn left for
            Willow Creek.
            GPS: N40°51.27′ W123°29.44′

▼ 0.2   SO Track on left.
5.3 ▲   SO Track on right.

California's largest tan oak

| ▼ 1.9 | TL | Track on left; then 4-way intersection. Straight ahead is 5N02. Track on left and track on right is Hennessy Road (CR 435). Turn left and join this road. |
| 4.3 ▲ | TR | 4-way intersection. Track on left is 5N02. CR 435 continues straight ahead. Turn right on onto 6N19; then track on right. |

GPS: N40°49.61′ W123°31.65′

▼ 3.3	BL	Turnout on right.
2.9 ▲	BR	Turnout on left.
▼ 4.0	SO	Track on left.
2.2 ▲	SO	Track on right.
▼ 4.1	SO	Track on right.
2.1 ▲	SO	Track on left.
▼ 4.3	SO	Road becomes paved; then Osprey Lane on right. Remain on main paved road.
1.9 ▲	SO	Osprey Lane on left. Road turns to graded dirt.
▼ 6.2		Trail ends at T-intersection with California 299 at Burnt Ranch. Turn right for Weaverville; turn left for Willow Creek.
0.0 ▲		Trail commences on California 299 at Burnt Ranch. Zero trip meter and turn southwest on paved Hennessy Road (CR 435). The road is opposite the Burnt Ranch post office.

GPS: N41°49.32′ W123°28.94′

Hobo Gulch Trail

STARTING POINT California 299, 8 miles east of Big Bar
FINISHING POINT Hobo Gulch USFS Campground
TOTAL MILEAGE 15.7 miles (one-way)
UNPAVED MILEAGE 11.9 miles
DRIVING TIME 1.5 hours (one-way)
ELEVATION RANGE 1,400–4,100 feet
USUALLY OPEN Year-round
BEST TIME TO TRAVEL Dry weather
DIFFICULTY RATING 2
SCENIC RATING 9
REMOTENESS RATING +1

NORTH COAST #22: HOBO GULCH TRAIL

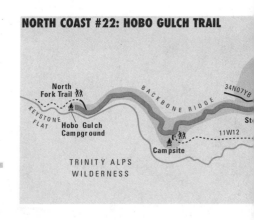

Special Attractions

- Fishing on the North Fork of the Trinity River.
- Fall color viewing.
- Access to hiking trails into the Trinity Alps Wilderness.

History

Many mines were established on the North Fork of the Trinity River in the latter half of the nineteenth century. Helena, known as North Fork until 1891, was a vital supply town for mining camps in the vicinity. This ghost town once supported a brewery, hotel, livery stable, trading post, and blacksmith shop in the 1850s. Christian Meckel's red brick hotel, built in 1858, testifies to the town's once thriving past. When North Fork was renamed, it honored Helena, Christian's wife and daughter of the postmaster.

In the 1880s, pack trains from North Fork used the narrow trails across Keystone Flat to supply miners who rushed into the vicinity of the New River deep in the Trinity Mountains. Hydraulic monitors and bucket line dredges were used in mines upstream from old North Fork. Evidence remains in the form of mine tailings along the riverbank.

Hobo Gulch may have been named for Hobo Dick, a regular at a Junction City bar. Ironically, Dick died after traversing Backbone Ridge on his way to Keystone Flat on a hot day and quenching his thirst too quickly and with too much water from the North Fork of the Trinity River.

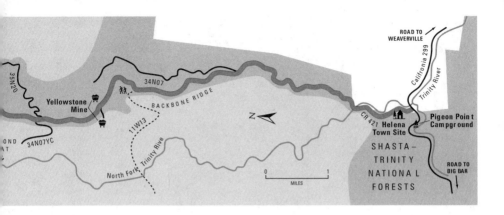

Description

Hobo Gulch Trail travels a vehicle corridor into the Trinity Alps Wilderness and ends at the Hobo Gulch USFS Campground and North Fork Trailhead.

The route starts at the site of Helena on California 299. There are a number of BLM and USFS campgrounds along the Trinity River near the start of this trail with access to rafting and fishing on the river.

North of Helena, the route turns off the paved road to follow a narrow, graded road that winds gradually up toward Backbone Ridge. The trail is spectacular in fall, when bigleaf maples turn to gold and dogwoods become salmon pink. Although trees on the ridge top may obscure some views, there are many opportunities to look down into the North Fork of the Trinity River Valley and west to Limestone Ridge.

The trail finishes at the extremely pretty wooded riverside Hobo Gulch USFS Campground. The semi-developed campground has tables and a pit toilet, but no other facilities. The North Fork Trail for hikers and equestrians leads into the Trinity Alps Wilderness sites of Bear Wallow Meadow and Grizzly Meadow. Horses are not allowed in the main campground, but there are corrals and campsites at the trailhead. A wilderness permit is required for hiking into the Trinity Alps Wilderness.

Current Road Information

Shasta-Trinity National Forests
Big Bar Ranger District
Star Route 1, Box 10

Big Bar, CA 96010
(530) 623-6106

Map References

BLM   Hayfork
USFS Shasta-Trinity National Forests
USGS 1:24,000 Helena, Deddrick,
Thurston Peaks
          1:100,000 Hayfork
Maptech CD-ROM: North Coast/Eureka
Northern California Atlas & Gazetteer, p. 44
California Road & Recreation Atlas, p. 51
Other: "A Guide to the Trinity Alps
          Wilderness" (incomplete)

Route Directions

▼ 0.0   From California 299 at the boundary of Shasta-Trinity National Forests, 8 miles east of Big Bar, zero trip meter and turn northwest on paved CR 421, following the sign to Helena.
          GPS: N40°46.19′ W123°07.62′

▼ 0.9   SO   River access point on right.
▼ 1.2   SO   Cross over North Fork Trinity River on bridge.
▼ 1.3   SO   Road on right.
▼ 3.8   BL   Paved road continues straight ahead. Zero trip meter and bear left onto dirt road 34N07, following the sign for Hobo Gulch Trailhead.
          GPS: N40°48.80′ W123°07.32′

▼ 0.0   Continue to the northwest.
▼ 2.3   SO   Waldorf Crossing Trail (11W13) on left

Hobo Gulch Campground on the North Fork of the Trinity River

Fishermen in the Trinity River

goes 3 miles to North Fork Trinity River.
GPS: N40°50.41′ W123°07.98′

▼ 3.2   SO   Track on left goes to Yellowstone Mine—private property. Diggings for the old mine are below the road to the right.

▼ 4.6   BL   Well-used track on right is 35N20.

▼ 4.9   SO   Track on left is 34N07YC.
GPS: N40°51.86′ W123°08.78′

▼ 7.4   BR   Stoveleg Gap. Track on right on right-hand bend is 34N07YB. Zero trip meter.
GPS: N40°52.89′ W123°08.69′

▼ 0.0   Continue to the north.

▼ 1.9   BR   Track on left to campsite and Raymond Flat Trail (11W12), which goes 3 miles to North Fork Trinity River.
GPS: N40°54.17′ W123°09.42′

▼ 2.2   SO   Turnout on left gives views up and down North Fork Trinity River.

▼ 4.2   SO   Track on right is 34N07YA to North Fork Trailhead. Follow the sign to Hobo Gulch Campground.
GPS: N40°55.48′ W123°09.26′

▼ 4.5   Trail ends at Hobo Gulch USFS Campground.
GPS: N40°55.64′ W123°09.23′

NORTH COAST #23

Bowerman Ridge Trail

STARTING POINT California 3, 22 miles north of Weaverville

FINISHING POINT California 3, 24.5 miles north of Weaverville

TOTAL MILEAGE 13.1 miles, plus 4-mile spur along Bowerman Ridge

UNPAVED MILEAGE 10.8 miles, plus 4-mile spur

DRIVING TIME 2 hours

ELEVATION RANGE 2,400–4,000 feet

USUALLY OPEN May 1 to October 30

Special Attractions
- The Bowerman Barn.
- Moderately challenging spur to a beautiful camp or picnic site on a narrow ridge above Trinity Lake.
- Camping, picnicking, boating, and angling at Trinity lake.

History
A barn of hand-hewn timbers on the East Fork of Stuart Creek is all that remains of the Bowerman Ranch, much of which was inundated by Trinity Lake when the Trinity Dam was completed in 1961. Jacob Bowerman, a native of Ohio, made his way west to seek his fortune in the mines. Like many others he wasn't very lucky. So he and his brother John invested in property and established a ranch to supply mining camps with food. Their timing and location at a wagon road junction were keys to their success. The road connected them to markets at Trinity Center to the north, Weaverville to the south, and Minersville, now beneath the waters of Trinity Lake, to the east. Jacob married Anna Tourtellotte, the innkeeper's daughter, at Minersville in 1872. John turned to mining and his sister-in-law established an inn on the ranch for stagecoach passengers and teamsters. Jacob expanded the ranch holdings and sold beef, corn, hay, and barrels of butter to miners.

The restored barn, first built in 1878, is all that remains of this once prosperous ranch. Jacob Bowerman died in 1917, at the age of 83; the main ranch house burned to the ground in the 1920s and Anna passed away in 1931, at the age of 80.

Description
The Central Valley Project, begun in 1935, was conceived to control floods and provide

Picnic spot at the end of Bowerman Ridge

Bowerman Barn

hydroelectric power. Trinity Lake is one of several reservoirs resulting from the long-term project. Trinity Dam, completed in 1961, now holds back the third largest man-made lake in California. When full, it has a shoreline of 145 miles and offers fishing, boating, picnicking, and camping. There are a number of full-service marinas along its shore. Although the lake is an extremely popular destination, there are some quiet, out-of-the-way spots accessible only by 4WD.

Bowerman Ridge lies between the East Fork of Stuarts Fork Arm and the southwestern side of Trinity Lake. Bowerman Ridge Trail is a loop with a one-way spur that travels down the ridge, past the site of an old fire lookout, to finish at a wonderful picnic area and campsite near the end of the spur.

The loop starts on a paved road and passes the Bowerman Barn. The trail turns to a narrow dirt road and passes the Alpine View USFS Campground as it begins to climb around the side of the ridge. There are views west over one of the arms of Trinity Lake and toward peaks in the Trinity Alps Wilderness—Granite Peak, Red Mountain, Middle Peak, and Gibson Peak among others.

The main trail joins a graded logging road on top of the ridge to return to California 3. The spur along Bowerman Ridge leads off from here, traveling to the site of an old fire lookout. Past the lookout site, the trail is rated 4 for difficulty and descends steeply along a narrow, formed spur to the turnaround point. The surface can be alternately loose and rocky in places with grades of more than 20 degrees. The turnaround at the bottom is on a narrow spit. A short hike takes you to the tip. The campsite there should be considered a single vehicle site; there is not enough room for more people to pitch a tent or share the space. From the end of the spur, the Fairview boat ramp is visible on the far side of the lake.

The entire trail can be traveled between May 1 and October 30. The section from Alpine View Campground to the ridge top is gated closed to vehicles from October 31 to April 30. However by traveling the trail in reverse, vehicles can access Bowerman Ridge year-round, weather permitting. This trail is not suitable for wet weather travel and should be avoided during rain or snow. This trail is a moderately strenuous mountain-bike route that should be attempted only by riders who are fit and experienced.

Current Road Information
Shasta-Trinity National Forests
Weaverville Ranger District
210 Main Street
Weaverville, CA 96093
(530) 623-2121

Map References
BLM   Redding
USFS   Shasta-Trinity National Forests
USGS   1:24,000   Covington Mill, Trinity
        Dam, Papoose Creek, Trinity Center
        1:100,000 Redding
Maptech CD-ROM: Shasta Lake/Redding
Northern California Atlas & Gazetteer, p. 45
California Road & Recreation Atlas, p. 52
Other: Trinity Alps Wilderness,
        Whiskeytown-Shasta-Trinity NRA:
        Trinity Unit

Route Directions

▼ 0.0   From California 3, 22 miles north of Weaverville, zero trip meter and turn east on paved Guy Covington Drive, following the sign to Alpine View Campground.

2.3 ▲   Trail ends at T-intersection with California 3. Turn left for Weaverville; turn right for Trinity Center.
        GPS: N40°54.89′ W122°46.26′

▼ 0.2 SO Covington Mill site on left. The burn cone, also known as the drying kiln, can be seen from the road.

2.1 ▲ SO Covington Mill site on right. The burn cone, also known as the drying kiln, can be seen from the road.

▼ 0.7 SO Cross over East Fork Stuart Fork Creek.

1.6 ▲ SO Cross over East Fork Stuart Fork Creek.

▼ 1.1 SO Bowerman Barn on right.

1.2 ▲ SO Bowerman Barn on left.
        GPS: N40°54.00′ W122°46.00′

NORTH COAST #23: BOWERMAN RIDGE TRAIL

▼ 1.3 SO Track on right. Road is now marked 35N14Y.

1.0 ▲ SO Track on left.

▼ 1.6 SO Graded road on left is 35N24.

0.7 ▲ SO Graded road on right is 35N24.

▼ 1.9 SO Road on right goes to Bowerman Boat Ramp.

0.4 ▲ SO Road on left goes to Bowerman Boat Ramp.
        GPS: N40°53.49′ W122°45.91′

▼ 2.3 SO Road continues to the right into Alpine View USFS Campground. Zero trip meter and pass through seasonal closure gate, remaining on 35N14Y. Road turns to dirt.

0.0 ▲   Continue to the northwest.
        GPS: N40°53.22′ W122°45.88′

▼ 0.0   Continue to the southeast.

4.6 ▲ SO Seasonal closure gate; then paved road on left goes into Alpine View USFS Campground. Zero trip meter. Road is now paved.

▼ 0.3 BR Track on left goes 1.5 miles to a dead end.

4.3 ▲ SO Track on right goes 1.5 miles to a dead end.

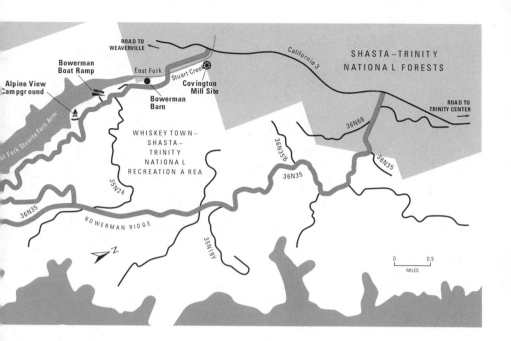

▼ 2.5 BL Track on right.
2.1 ▲ BR Track on left.
     GPS: N40°51.95′ W122°45.13′

▼ 2.9 SO Track on right.
1.7 ▲ SO Track on left.

▼ 4.6 TL Seasonal closure gate; then T-intersection with 36N35. To the right is the spur to Bowerman Ridge Lookout Spit. Zero trip meter.
0.0 ▲ Continue to the southwest.
     GPS: N40°52.81′ W122°44.59′

Spur to Bowerman Ridge Lookout Spit

▼ 0.0 Head south on 36N35.
▼ 1.4 SO Track on left is 35N15Y; then track on right is 35N38Y.
▼ 2.8 BR Track on left goes to site of the old Bowerman Ridge lookout, now a viewpoint.
     GPS: N40°50.77′ W122°45.75′

▼ 3.7 BR Track on left.
     GPS: N40°50.11′ W122°46.01′

▼ 3.8 SO Track on left.

▼ 4.0 SO Spur ends at picnic and campsite at the end of the narrow spit. A hiking trail continues a short distance to the lakeshore.
     GPS: N40°49.86′ W122°46.00′

Continuation of Main Trail

▼ 0.0 Continue to the north.
6.2 ▲ TR Track straight ahead is the continuation of 36N35, spur to Bowerman Ridge Lookout Spit. Zero trip meter and pass through seasonal closure gate onto 35N31Y.
     GPS: N40°52.81′ W122°44.59′

▼ 0.1 SO Graded road on right.
6.1 ▲ SO Graded road on left.
▼ 0.3 SO Track on left is 35N24.
5.9 ▲ SO Track on right is 35N24.
▼ 0.4 SO Track on right is 36N35D.
5.8 ▲ SO Track on left is 36N35D.
▼ 0.9 SO Track on right.
5.3 ▲ SO Track on left.
▼ 1.1 SO Track on left is 36N35C.
5.1 ▲ SO Track on right is 36N35C.
▼ 1.9 BR Track on right into private property;

Covington Mill

then two tracks on left. Bear right, remaining on major dirt road.

▲ 4.3 BR Two tracks on right; then track on left into private property. Bear right, remaining on major dirt road.

GPS: N40°54.26' W122°43.96'

▼ 2.2 SO Closed road on right is 35N19Y.
▲ 4.0 SO Closed road on left is 35N19Y.
▼ 3.7 SO Closed road on left is 36N35B.
▲ 2.5 SO Closed road on right is 36N35B.
▼ 3.9 SO Track on left.
▲ 2.3 SO Track on right.
▼ 4.4 BL Three tracks on right.
▲ 1.8 BR Three tracks on left.

GPS: N40°55.65' W122°43.55'

▼ 4.7 SO Track on right.
▲ 1.5 SO Track on left.
▼ 5.4 SO Track on right is 36N35A and track on left.
▲ 0.8 SO Track on left is 36N35A and track on right.
▼ 5.9 SO Track on left is 36N66.
▲ 0.3 SO Track on right is 36N66.
▼ 6.0 SO Track on right.
▲ 0.2 SO Track on left.
▼ 6.2 Trail ends on California 3. Turn right for Trinity Center; turn left for Weaverville.
▲ 0.0 Trail commences on California 3, 0.3 miles north of mile marker 56, 2.5 miles north of the southern end of the trail, and 24.5 miles north of Weaverville. Zero trip meter and turn east on graded dirt road 36N35, following sign for Bowerman Ridge Road.

GPS: N40°56.70' W122°44.74'

Deadwood Road

STARTING POINT CR 105, immediately south of the Trinity River Bridge
FINISHING POINT Main Street, at the southern end of French Gulch
TOTAL MILEAGE 13 miles
UNPAVED MILEAGE 12 miles

DRIVING TIME 1.25 hours
ELEVATION RANGE 1,400–4,100 feet
USUALLY OPEN Year-round
BEST TIME TO TRAVEL Dry weather
DIFFICULTY RATING 2
SCENIC RATING 8
REMOTENESS RATING +0

Special Attractions

■ Historic mining district along Deadwood Creek.

■ Trail connects the interesting settlements of Lewiston and French Gulch.

History

The Deadwood Wagon Road was built in the mid-1800s to connect the emerging mining communities of Lewiston and French Gulch. Lewis Town, named for Ford Lewis who settled there in 1853, evolved as an important supply center during the gold rush. Lewis operated an indispensable ferry on the Trinity River, complimented by his trading post near the present-day site of an old steel bridge. Many of the town's buildings such as churches, school, post office, and stores date from the 1880s. The town's first hotel, the D. B. Nielson Hotel, was built in 1899. A hardware store, printing shop, drugstore, lumberyard, restaurants, blacksmith shop, and many more commercial enterprises had been established by the 1900s. The Central Valley Project of flood control and hydroelectric power facilities was first proposed in 1919, and finally got under way in 1935. The Trinity Dam and Lewiston Dam were built concurrently, with the Trinity Dam being completed in 1961. Lewiston now flourishes as a result of the national recreation area established in 1965.

French Gulch is southeast of Lewiston and was settled by French miners in the late 1840s. Like Lewiston, the town flourished during the gold rush, and it had one of the most productive lode gold deposits in the Klamath Mountains. Charles Camden's toll road brought considerable traffic to this canyon town, which for a while rivaled Shasta. Several impressive gold rush era buildings are in French Gulch: St. Rose Catholic Church was founded in 1856, and the French Gulch Hotel, now listed on the

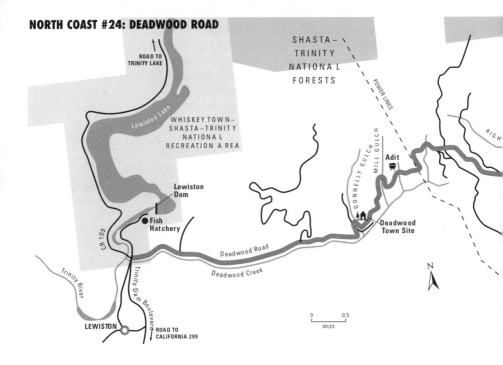

National Register of Historic Places, was built in 1886.

The Deadwood mines brought phenomenal fortune to French Gulch and Lewiston. Several high-grade ore bodies were discovered at the eastern end of Deadwood Road. The Milkmaid and Franklin Mines at the Right Fork of French Gulch Creek yielded a total of $2.5 million worth of gold. Gladstone Mine, east of town in Cline Gulch, produced more than $6 million. Total production for the entire mining district was more than $25 million.

Description

Deadwood Road is an easy run between Lewiston and French Gulch. Initially, the small single-lane road is paved because it accesses some private property, but it quickly turns to roughly graded dirt. There are many blocks of private property along this trail; side tracks given in the directions are not necessarily open for public travel.

There are only a few adits and tailings piles to indicate this was once a thriving mining district. From Deadwood, the trail climbs to a saddle. It becomes rougher and narrower on the east side and is best driven in dry weather. It can become extremely greasy in wet weather. Fall colors along this road are spectacular—predominantly the golden yellow of bigleaf maples and the yellow-brown of oaks along Deadwood Creek.

The Washington Mine, one of the earliest gold mines in the district, is still operating. The mill on the site was built in the 1930s and both the mine and mill are privately owned. There are additional mining remains farther along the trail at the Milkmaid Mine, where an old mill site sits abandoned on the far side of the Right Fork of French Gulch Creek.

The trail ends in the township of French Gulch, a pretty community with many historic buildings.

Current Road Information

Bureau of Land Management
Redding Field Office
355 Hemsted Drive
Redding, CA 96002
(530) 224-2100

Map References

BLM Redding
USFS Shasta-Trinity National Forests

5.8 ▲	SO	Track on right. Road is now paved.
1.5 ▼	BL	Track on right.
5.1 ▲	SO	Track on left.
2.4 ▼	BR	Track on left.
4.2 ▲	SO	Track on right.

GPS: N40°42.90′ W122°45.48′

3.7 ▼	SO	Track on left; then cross over Donnelly Gulch; then track on right.
2.9 ▲	SO	Track on left; then cross over Donnelly Gulch; then track on right.
4.6 ▼	SO	Track on right.
2.0 ▲	SO	Track on left.

GPS: N40°43.58′ W122°43.83′

4.7 ▼	SO	Cross over Mill Gulch at mine tailings.
1.9 ▲	SO	Cross over Mill Gulch at mine tailings.
4.9 ▼	BL	Track on right.
1.7 ▲	SO	Track on left.
5.2 ▼	SO	Adit on left; cross over creek; mine tailings on right.
1.4 ▲	SO	Mine tailings on left; cross over creek; adit on right.

GPS: N40°43.70′ W122°43.49′

5.3 ▼	SO	Track on left.
1.3 ▲	SO	Track on right.
5.4 ▼	SO	Track on right; then track on left.
1.2 ▲	SO	Track on right; then track on left.
5.6 ▼	SO	Track on left under power lines.
1.0 ▲	SO	Track on right under power lines.
6.1 ▼	SO	Track on left.
0.5 ▲	SO	Track on right.

GPS: N40°43.91′ W122°43.04′

6.2 ▼	SO	Cross over creek.
0.4 ▲	SO	Cross over creek.
6.4 ▼	BL	Two tracks on right.
0.2 ▲	BR	Two tracks on left.
6.6 ▼	SO	Unmarked 4-way intersection on saddle. Zero trip meter.
0.0 ▲		Continue to the west on Deadwood Road.

GPS: N40°43.87′ W122°42.66′

0.0 ▼		Continue to the east on French Gulch Road.
6.4 ▲	SO	Unmarked 4-way intersection on saddle. Zero trip meter.
0.2 ▼	SO	Track on left.
6.2 ▲	BL	Track on right.

USGS 1:24,000 Lewiston, French Gulch
1:100,000 Redding
Maptech CD-ROM: Shasta Lake/Redding
Northern California Atlas & Gazetteer, p. 45
California Road & Recreation Atlas, p. 52
Other: Whiskeytown-Shasta-Trinity NRA: Trinity Unit

Route Directions

| 0.0 ▼ | | From the northern end of Lewiston, immediately south of the Trinity River Bridge at the intersection of CR 105, Trinity Dam Boulevard, and Deadwood Road, zero trip meter and turn northeast on paved road, following sign to the Trinity River Fish Hatchery. Immediately turn right onto the small, paved Deadwood Road. |
| 6.6 ▲ | | Turn left at T-intersection; then trail ends at intersection with CR 105 in Lewiston. Turn Left for California 299; turn right for Trinity Lake. |

GPS: N40°43.02′ W122°48.04′

| 0.8 ▼ | BR | Track on left. Bear right onto graded dirt road. |

Deadwood Road

▼ 0.7 SO Track on left.
5.7 ▲ SO Track on right.
▼ 1.0 SO Track on left.
5.4 ▲ BL Track on right.
▼ 1.6 SO Track on right; then track on left and track on right; then track on left. Remain on main trail.
4.8 ▲ SO Track on right; then track on left and track on right; then track on left. Remain on main trail.
▼ 2.1 SO Track on left.
4.3 ▲ SO Track on right.
▼ 2.2 BL Two tracks on right.
4.2 ▲ BR Two tracks on left.
          GPS: N40°43.11′ W122°41.45′

▼ 2.3 SO Track on right.
4.1 ▲ SO Track on left.
▼ 2.6 SO Track on right.
3.8 ▲ SO Track on left.
▼ 2.7 SO Track on left.
3.7 ▲ SO Track on right.
▼ 2.8 SO Track on left; then part of the Washington Mine on right—private property.
3.6 ▲ SO Part of the Washington Mine on left—

private property; then track on right.
          GPS: N40°43.11′ W122°40.85′

▼ 2.9 SO Track on right is entrance to the Washington Mine's mill.
3.5 ▲ BR Track on left is entrance to the Washington Mine's mill.
▼ 3.1 SO Private tracks on left and right.
3.3 ▲ SO Private tracks on left and right.
▼ 3.5 SO Track on left.
2.9 ▲ SO Track on right.
▼ 3.8 TR Track straight ahead. Turn sharp right and follow along Right Fork French Gulch; then adit of the Milkmaid Mine on far side of creek.
2.6 ▲ TL Adit of the Milkmaid Mine on far side of creek on right; then track straight ahead. Turn sharp left, leaving the creek.
          GPS: N40°43.22′ W122°40.18′

▼ 4.0 SO Remains of the Milkmaid Mine's mill on the far side of the creek on left.
2.6 ▲ SO Remains of the Milkmaid Mine's mill on the far side of the creek on right.
          GPS: N40°43.08′ W122°40.14′

Historic general store in Lewiston

▼ 4.2	SO	Cross over Right Fork French Gulch.
2.2 ▲	SO	Cross over Right Fork French Gulch.
▼ 4.3	SO	Cross over the Right Fork of French Gulch then track on right.
2.1 ▲	SO	Track on left, then cross over the Right Fork of French Gulch.
▼ 4.5	SO	Cross over the Right Fork of French Gulch.
1.9 ▲	SO	Cross over the Right Fork of French Gulch.
▼ 5.4	SO	Track on left.
1.0 ▲	SO	Track on right.
▼ 6.2	SO	Road becomes paved.
0.2 ▲	SO	Road turns to graded dirt.
▼ 6.4		Trail ends at the T-intersection with Main Street in French Gulch. Turn right for California 299 and Redding.
0.0 ▲		Trail commences on Main Street at the south end of French Gulch, at the intersection with French Gulch Road. French Gulch is 3 miles north of California 299. Zero trip meter and turn west on the paved French Gulch Road.
		GPS: N40°41.87′ W122°38.25′

South Shore Drive

STARTING POINT California 299, 1 mile east of the Tower House Historic District
FINISHING POINT Intersection of J. F. Kennedy Memorial Drive and North Coast #26: Shasta Bally Trail
TOTAL MILEAGE 6.9 miles
UNPAVED MILEAGE 5.3 miles
DRIVING TIME 45 minutes
ELEVATION RANGE 1,200–1,700 feet
USUALLY OPEN Year-round
BEST TIME TO TRAVEL Year-round
DIFFICULTY RATING 1
SCENIC RATING 9
REMOTENESS RATING +0

Special Attractions

■ Boating, camping, hiking, mountain biking, and picnicking at Whiskeytown Lake.
■ Tower House Historic District.

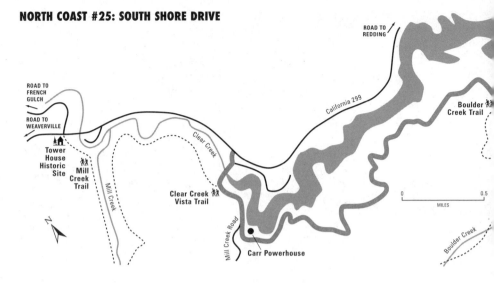

History

In the mid-1800s, wagon travel in the mountainous Whiskeytown region was far from straightforward. Charles Camden saw a need for a passable route to and from the town of Shasta. The enterprising Camden invested $20,000 to improve his franchised toll road. In 1865, he charged foot travelers 10 cents to cross his toll bridge over Clear Creek, 25 cents for those on horseback, and $1.25 for wagons. Camden complimented earnings from his toll road by extracting approximately $80,000 from a mine on Clear Creek over a 17-year period.

In 1852, Levi Tower built a 21-room hotel north of Camden's bridge. His establishment catered to travelers on the wagon road between Shasta and Weaverville until it burned down in 1919.

Description

South Shore Drive follows the southwestern shore of Whiskeytown Lake, one of the reservoirs included in the Whiskeytown-Shasta-Trinity National Recreation Area. While California 299 runs near the lake's northeastern shore, the southern shore has a quiet, remote feel to it. The graded dirt road is normally suitable for all vehicles in dry weather. It leaves California 299 a mile south of the historic site of Tower House, where you can see Charles Camden's two-story timber house and the site of his toll bridge over Clear Creek.

The main trail is paved as far as the Carr Powerhouse, after which it turns to dirt. Hiking trails access the national recreation area's backcountry, and short spurs lead down to the shore of Whiskeytown Lake. Much of the trail follows a wide shelf road high above the lake, offering great views of its shoreline.

The trail passes a marina on the western shore of the lake and a developed campground for self-contained RV units only. Campgrounds for tent campers can be found along the more difficult North Coast #26: Shasta Bally Trail at Sheep Camp and Brandy Creek; there are also campgrounds on the north shore of the lake. The trail ends at the intersection with North Coast #26: Shasta Bally Trail, a short distance west of the Whiskeytown Lake Visitor Center.

The Whiskeytown-Shasta-Trinity National Recreation Area is a fee area.

Current Road Information

Whiskeytown National Recreation Area
PO Box 188
Whiskeytown, CA 96095
(530) 246-1225

Map References

BLM   Redding
USFS   Shasta-Trinity National Forests

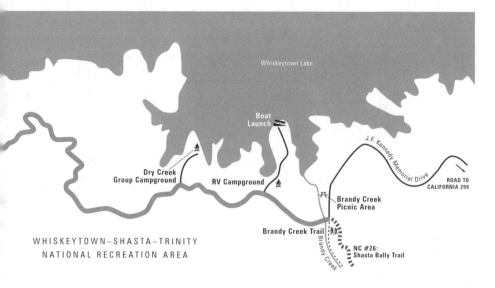

Whiskeytown Lake

Boat Launch

J.F. Kennedy Memorial Drive

ROAD TO CALIFORNIA 299

Dry Creek Group Campground

RV Campground

Brandy Creek Picnic Area

Brandy Creek Trail

Brandy Creek

NC #26: Shasta Bally Trail

WHISKEYTOWN–SHASTA–TRINITY
NATIONAL RECREATION AREA

USGS 1:24,000   Whiskeytown, French
  Gulch, Igo
  1:100,000 Redding
Maptech CD-ROM: Shasta Lake/Redding

Northern California Atlas & Gazetteer,
  pp. 45, 46
Other: Whiskeytown-Shasta-Trinity NRA:
  Whiskeytown Unit

Whiskeytown Lake

Whiskeytown

Established in 1849, the mining camp may have gotten its name when a mule loaded with two whiskey kegs lost its footing on a narrow pass and the precious cargo crashed into a ravine where it emptied into the stream below. Almost in tears, the miner leading the mule cried, "This is sure one hell of a whiskey creek now." The stream became known as Whiskey Creek and the camp, Whiskeytown. Refusing to accept Whiskeytown as a legitimate name, the town's post office was named Blair in 1881, Stella in 1885, and Schilling in 1917. Finally, in 1952, Whiskeytown residents could receive mail with Whiskeytown as an address.

Jedediah Smith passed this way in 1826, and prospectors following his trail to Oregon some 30 years later found nuggets of gold in the gravel. The rich gold deposits were more important to prospectors than the difficulty of getting to the camp. The town, as the name implies, grew into a free-spirited place that produced great wealth, which was typically spent without restraint. The vicinity's mines and streams are estimated to have yielded $25 million in gold.

In order to create Whiskeytown-Shasta-Trinity National Recreation Area, the Bureau of Reclamation diverted the Trinity River in 1963, submerging the old Whiskeytown beneath the icy 200-foot-deep Whiskeytown Lake. Old Whiskeytown was located east of Weaverville and west of Redding off California 299. New Whiskeytown sits on the banks of the lake. The post office from old Whiskeytown was relocated to the lake's eastern shore before the original settlement site was flooded.

Yachting and fishing on Whiskeytown Lake

Route Directions

▼ 0.0 From California 299 near the north-western end of Whiskeytown Lake, 1 mile east of the Tower House Historic Site (which is opposite the road to French Gulch), zero trip meter and turn south on paved Carr Powerhouse Road. Remain on paved road for next 1.1 miles.

5.9 ▲ Trail ends at intersection with California 299. Turn right for Redding; turn left for Weaverville.
GPS: N40°39.28' W122°37.36'

▼ 0.1 BR Paved road on left.
5.8 ▲ BL Paved road on right.

▼ 0.2 SO Cross over Clear Creek on bridge.
5.7 ▲ SO Cross over Clear Creek on bridge.

▼ 0.3 SO Clear Creek Vista Trail for hikers on right.
5.6 ▲ SO Clear Creek Vista Trail for hikers on left.

▼ 0.5 SO Track on right is Mill Creek Road, which goes to Boulder Creek Trail and Mill Creek Trail, and two tracks on left.
5.4 ▲ SO Track on left is Mill Creek Road, which goes to Boulder Creek Trail and Mill Creek Trail, and two tracks on right.

▼ 0.6 SO Carr Powerhouse on left.
5.3 ▲ SO Carr Powerhouse on right.
GPS: N40°38.86' W122°37.62'

▼ 1.1 BL Road turns to graded dirt.
4.8 ▲ BR Road becomes paved. Remain on paved road for next 1.1 miles.

▼ 1.2 SO Track on left.
4.7 ▲ SO Track on right.

▼ 3.4 SO Track on left. Boulder Creek Trail fopr hikers on right.
2.5 ▲ SO Track on right. Boulder Creek Trail for hikers on left.
GPS: N40°38.50' W122°35.78'

▼ 3.5 SO Cross over Boulder Creek.
2.4 ▲ SO Cross over Boulder Creek.

▼ 5.0 SO Track on right.
0.9 ▲ SO Track on left.

▼ 5.1 SO Track on right is gated closed.
0.8 ▲ SO Track on left is gated closed.

▼ 5.4 SO Track on left. Service road on right.
0.5 ▲ SO Track on right. Service road on left.

▼ 5.9   TR   T-intersection with paved road. To the left is the Dry Creek Group Campground (reservations only). Zero trip meter.

0.0 ▲   Continue to the west.

GPS: N40°37.42′ W122°35.02′

▼ 0.0   Continue to the south.

1.0 ▲   TL   Paved road continues straight ahead to the Dry Creek Group Campground (reservations only). Zero trip meter and turn left onto graded dirt road, following sign for South Shore Drive.

▼ 0.6   SO   Paved road on left goes to marina, boat launch, and self-contained RV campsites.

0.4 ▲   SO   Paved road on right goes to marina, boat launch, and self-contained RV campsites.

GPS: N40°37.10′ W122°34.65′

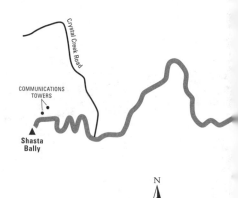

▼ 1.0   Trail ends at intersection with the start of North Coast #26: Shasta Bally Trail. Continue straight ahead to exit to California 299 and Redding. The Brandy Creek Trailhead for hikers is at the intersection.

0.0 ▲   Trail commences at intersection with J. F. Kennedy Memorial Drive and North Coast #26: Shasta Bally Trail, 4.5 miles west of the Whiskeytown Lake Visitor Center beside California 299. The Brandy Creek Trailhead for hikers is at the intersection. Zero trip meter and continue southwest on paved road.

GPS: N40°36.78′ W122°34.42′

DRIVING TIME   45 minutes (one-way)
ELEVATION RANGE   1,400–6,200 feet
USUALLY OPEN   May to early December
BEST TIME TO TRAVEL   Dry weather only
DIFFICULTY RATING   4
SCENIC RATING   10
REMOTENESS RATING   +0

Special Attractions

- Moderately difficult, steep trail that climbs to a summit.
- Panoramic views from Shasta Bally.
- Boating, camping, hiking, mountain biking, and picnicking at Whiskeytown Lake.

History

Shasta Bally (6,209 feet) provides an excellent view over the lands once held by the Wintun Indians, whose territory stretched from lands west of Weaverville, east of Redding, north of La Moine (located along I-5), and south to Cottonwood Creek. The region around Shasta Bally—bally is derived from the Wintun word *buli*, meaning "mountain"—had much game and fish, including deer, rabbits, salmon, ducks, and geese. The Indians used acorns to make bread and soups. The Wintun had a strong regard for the landscape in which they lived,

NORTH COAST #26

Shasta Bally Trail

STARTING POINT   J. F. Kennedy Memorial Drive, 4.5 miles west of the visitor center on California 299
FINISHING POINT   Shasta Bally summit
TOTAL MILEAGE   7.9 miles (one-way)
UNPAVED MILEAGE   7.8 miles

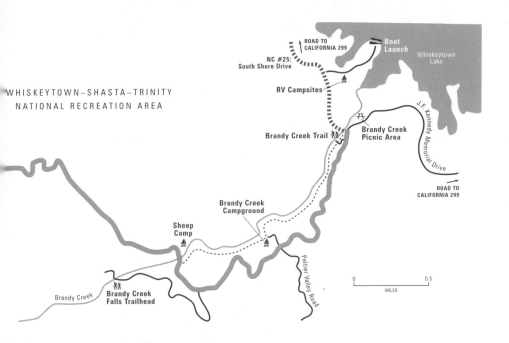

WHISKEYTOWN–SHASTA–TRINITY
NATIONAL RECREATION AREA

ROAD TO
CALIFORNIA 299

Boat
Launch

Whiskeytown
Lake

NC #25:
South Shore Drive

RV Campsites

J.F. Kennedy Memorial Drive

Brandy Creek Trail

Brandy Creek
Picnic Area

ROAD TO
CALIFORNIA 299

Brandy Creek
Campground

Sheep
Camp

Peltier Valley Road

0   0.5
MILES

Brandy Creek

Brandy Creek
Falls Trailhead

Northerly view of Mount Shasta from the summit of Shasta Bally

believing it was essential to maintain harmony with Mother Earth. Much of their mythology was based on features such as pools, rocks, caves, and mountains like Shasta Bally.

The Wintun's lifestyle came to an abrupt end with the arrival of settlers in the mid-1800s. Diseases swept through villages as miners rushed into the region following the 1848 discovery of gold at Readings Bar, off to the west on the Trinity River. The mining camp of Whiskeytown was established near the base of Shasta Bally in 1849. The town got its unusual name after a keg of whiskey fell into a nearby creek.

Work on the Whiskeytown Dam, part of the Central Valley Project, began in 1959 and ended in 1963. Some of Whiskeytown was torn down, and the rest disappeared as the reservoir filled.

Description

Shasta Bally Trail is a wonderful addition to the easier North Coast #25: South Shore Drive for those with high-clearance 4WDs. The trail winds past Sheep Camp, an undeveloped camping area alongside Brandy Creek (permit required), and then starts to climb a steep and unrelenting 15- to 25-degree grade all the way to the summit of Shasta Bally. The surface is rough in spots and not suitable for wet weather travel. The trail is also narrow and has few passing places. As you approach the summit, the forest gives way to shrubby manzanitas. At the summit, the panorama includes Lassen Peak and the town of Redding to the east. To the north, Mount Shasta dominates the view with the Castle Crags in front. To the northwest is the Trinity Alps Wilderness, and to the south is the Yolla Bolly Middle Eel Wilderness.

Be careful as you descend the steep grade back to Whiskeytown Lake. Judicious use of the transmission will help avoid overheating brakes. Keep in mind that vehicles traveling uphill have the right of way. This may necessitate a quick stop and even an uphill reverse on sections of the single-lane road.

Current Road Information

Whiskeytown National Recreation Area
PO Box 188
Whiskeytown, CA 96095
(530) 246-1225

Map References

BLM   Redding
USFS   Shasta-Trinity National Forests
USGS   1:24,000   Igo, Shasta Bally
1:100,000 Redding
Maptech CD-ROM: Shasta Lake/Redding
Northern California Atlas & Gazetteer,
pp. 46, 45
California Road & Recreation Atlas, p. 52
Other: Whiskeytown-Shasta-Trinity NRA:
Whiskeytown Unit

Route Directions

▼ 0.0   From paved J. F. Kennedy Memorial Drive on the south side of Whiskeytown Lake, 4.5 miles west of the visitor center on California 299 and 0.1 miles west of the Brandy Creek Picnic Area, zero trip meter and turn south on paved road, following the sign for Sheep Camp and Shasta Bally. Pass through closure gate. The Brandy Creek Trailhead for hikers is at the intersection. Paved road straight ahead to the southwest is North Coast #25: South Shore Drive.
GPS: N40°36.78' W122°34.42'

▼ 0.1   BL   Road turns to graded dirt. Track on right goes 0.1 miles to Brandy Creek and additional trailhead parking.

▼ 0.2   SO   Track on right.

▼ 1.3   SO   Track on left is Peltier Valley Road. Track on right goes into Brandy Creek Campground. Follow the sign for Shasta Bally.
GPS: N40°36.08' W122°34.85'

▼ 1.8   SO   Brandy Creek Trail for hikers and mountain bikes on right.

▼ 2.2   BR   Track on left goes 1 mile to Brandy Creek Falls Trailhead. Bear right, following the sign for Shasta Bally.

The steep trail climbs grades of up to 22 degrees

▼ 2.4 SO Brandy Creek Trail on left; then season-
           al closure gate; then cross over Brandy
           Creek on bridge.
▼ 2.5 BL Sheep Camp on right (permit required).
           Zero trip meter. Trail starts to climb.
           GPS: N40°36.01' W122°35.62'

▼ 0.0   Continue to the northwest.
▼ 0.2 SO Seasonal closure gate.
▼ 1.0 SO Track on right.
▼ 1.8 SO Turnout on right.
▼ 3.0 SO Track on left.
▼ 3.7 SO Turnout on left.
▼ 4.5 SO Crystal Creek Road on right—closed to
           motor vehicles.
           GPS: N40°36.01' W122°38.59'

▼ 5.3 SO Communications towers on right.
▼ 5.4   Trail ends at summit of Shasta Bally.
           GPS: N40°36.05' W122°39.04'

NORTH COAST #27

Backbone Road

STARTING POINT Dry Creek Road, 0.2 miles
north of the intersection with Bear
Mountain Road
FINISHING POINT California 299, 5 miles
southwest of Round Mountain
TOTAL MILEAGE 17.6 miles
UNPAVED MILEAGE 17.1 miles
DRIVING TIME 2 hours
ELEVATION RANGE 1,000–2,200 feet
USUALLY OPEN Year-round
BEST TIME TO TRAVEL Dry weather
DIFFICULTY RATING 3
SCENIC RATING 8
REMOTENESS RATING +0

Special Attractions

- Views of Mount Shasta and Lassen Peak.
- Ridge-top trail with spectacular views to
  the north and south.

History

Clikapudi Creek, near the start of the trail
was the site of a Wintun village and the scene
of a battle with the Yana, who moved through
this region while hunting and gathering. The
Yana attacked the village, claiming it was on
their tribal lands. With assistance from other
Wintun nearby, the villagers managed to fend
off the Yana. The Wintun word for fight
clikapudi, survives as the creek's name.

Backbone Road travels the crest of Backbone Ridge, immediately south of Shasta
Lake's Pit River Arm. Work on Shasta Dam
another of the great Central Valley Project's
dams, began in 1938 and was completed in
1945, with the lake finally filling in 1948
Some 6,000 workers combined to build the
dam, which is more than 600 feet high and
nearly 900 feet thick at its base. The dam
flooded the Pit, Shasta, and McCloud Rivers
and Squaw Creek. The dam at Fenders Flat
at the northeastern end of the Pit River Arm
is one of three dams supplementing Shasta
Dam. The great reservoir flooded many mining claims. It also covers much of the right of
way of the Sacramento & Eastern Railroad
which was built along the Pit River to the
copper mine at Bully Hill Mine. Bully Hill
operated from 1901 to 1910. Its smelter was
closed by court order in 1919. The sulphur
fumes from the smelter were very destructive
to forests and fish.

Description

Backbone Road travels through a mix of private land and Shasta-Trinity National Forests
south of Shasta Lake and north of California
299. Although marked as forest road 34N02
on maps, much of it travels through private
land. Please respect landowners' rights and do
not trespass. The best camping is in the developed campgrounds beside Shasta Lake,
near the start of the trail.

Backbone Road begins in Jones Valley and
immediately starts climbing away from it. The
pavement ends after a short distance, and the
road immediately becomes rough enough to
make 4WD preferable. Once on the ridge top,
the trail switches from one side of the spine to
the other, crossing at saddles. Mount Shasta

ackbone Road

ominates the view to the north, and Lassen 'eak to the east. The trail crosses paved Sugar 'ine Camp Road, which serves as access to a tate prison. You can usually travel south down his road to California 299. However, the road , private and access should not be relied upon.

The trail gets rougher on the east side of Sug- r Pine Camp Road, before once again becom- ng a graded dirt road. It travels down McCan- less Gulch Road to finish on California 299.

urrent Road Information

hasta-Trinity National Forests
hasta Lake Ranger District
4225 Holiday Road
tedding, CA 96003
530) 275-1589

1ap References

sLM   Redding
JSFS   Shasta-Trinity National Forests
JSGS   1:24,000   Bella Vista, Oak Run,
       Devils Rock
       1:100,000 Redding
Maptech CD-ROM: Shasta Lake/Redding

Northern California Atlas & Gazetteer,
   pp. 46, 47
California Road & Recreation Atlas, pp. 52, 53
Other: Whiskeytown-Shasta-Trinity NRA:
   Shasta Unit

Route Directions

▼ 0.0   From Dry Creek Road on the southern
           shore of Shasta Lake in Jones Valley,
           0.2 miles north of the intersection with
           Bear Mountain Road, zero trip meter
           and turn northeast on paved Backbone
           Road (34N02). Backbone Road leads
           off from the general store and is also
           at the intersection with Hidden Valley
           Drive. Remain on Backbone Road for
           0.5 miles.

5.4 ▲   Trail ends on Dry Creek Road in Jones
           Valley. Turn right for Shasta Lake; turn
           left for California 299, I-5, and Redding.
           GPS: N40°43.10' W122°14.39'

▼ 0.5   SO Road turns to roughly graded dirt; then
            track on left to water tank.

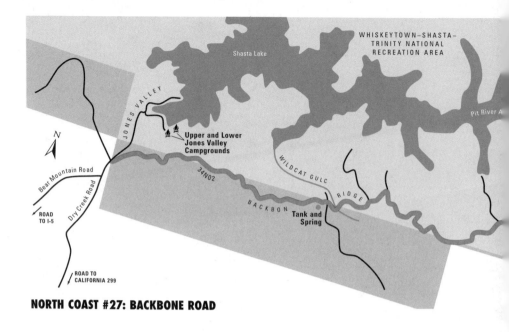

NORTH COAST #27: BACKBONE ROAD

4.9 ▲   SO Track on right to water tank; then road
            becomes paved. Remain on paved
            Backbone Road for the next 0.5 miles.
▼ 3.4   SO Track on right.
2.0 ▲   SO Track on left.
▼ 4.0   SO Tank and spring on right. Tank was
            built by the CCC in 1939.
1.4 ▲   SO Tank and spring on left. Tank was built
            by the CCC in 1939.
            GPS: N40°43.39′ W122°10.90′

▼ 4.1   SO Private tracks on left and right on saddle.
1.3 ▲   SO Private tracks on left and right on saddle.
▼ 4.4   SO Track on right; then cross over Wildcat
            Gulch.
1.0 ▲   SO Cross over Wildcat Gulch; then track
            on left.
▼ 4.8   SO Two tracks on right.
0.6 ▲   SO Two tracks on left.
▼ 5.1   BR Well-used track on left.
0.3 ▲   BL Well-used track on right.
            GPS: N40°43.59′ W122°10.10′

▼ 5.4   TR Unmarked, well-used T-intersection.
            Track on left goes to private property.
            Zero trip meter.
0.0 ▲   Continue to the south.
            GPS: N40°43.74′ W122°09.91′

▼ 0.0   Continue to the east.
5.3 ▲   TL Unmarked intersection. Well-used
            track continues straight ahead to
            private property. Zero trip meter.
▼ 0.5   SO Track on right.
4.8 ▲   SO Track on left.
▼ 1.1   SO Track on right is private.
4.2 ▲   SO Track on left is private.
▼ 2.1   SO Track on left.
3.2 ▲   SO Track on right.
▼ 2.2   SO Track on left.
3.1 ▲   SO Track on right.
▼ 2.4   SO Track on right.
2.9 ▲   BR Track on left.
▼ 2.7   SO Track on left to private property.
2.6 ▲   BL Track on right to private property.
            GPS: N40°43.81′ W122°07.96′

▼ 2.8   SO Track on right is private.
2.5 ▲   SO Track on left is private.
▼ 3.1   SO Two tracks on right are private.
2.2 ▲   SO Two tracks on left are private.
▼ 5.3   SO Cross over paved Sugar Pine Camp
            Road. To the left is the state prison; to
            the right leads to California 299—the
            gates on this private road may be
            locked at any time. Zero trip meter.
0.0 ▲   Continue to the southwest on
            Backbone Road.

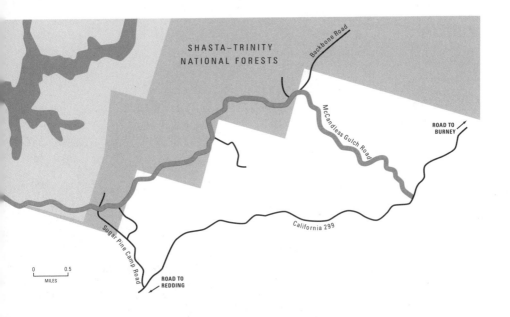

SHASTA–TRINITY
NATIONAL FORESTS

Backbone Road

McCandless Gulch Road

ROAD TO
BURNEY

California 299

Sugar Pine Camp Road

0   0.5
MILES

ROAD TO
REDDING

Manzanitas, oaks, and pines on Backbone Ridge

The distinctive shape of snow-capped Mount Shasta rises above the fall colors on backbone ridge

GPS: N40°44.53' W122°05.65'

▼ 0.0   Continue to the east on Backbone Road.
4.1 ▲   SO   Cross over paved Sugar Pine Camp Road. To the right is the state prison; to the left leads to California 299—the gates on this private road may be locked at any time. Zero trip meter.
▼ 0.3   SO   Track on right.
3.8 ▲   SO   Track on left.
▼ 0.7   SO   Track on left is private.
3.4 ▲   SO   Track on right is private.
▼ 2.3   SO   Track on right is private.
1.8 ▲   SO   Track on left is private.

GPS: N40°45.76' W122°04.16'

▼ 3.9   SO   Two tracks on left are private.
0.2 ▲   SO   Two tracks on right are private.
▼ 4.1   BR   Graded road on left is the continuation of Backbone Road. Zero trip meter and bear right onto McCandless Gulch Road.
0.0 ▲   Continue to the southwest.

GPS: N40°46.61' W122°02.98'

▼ 0.0   Continue to the east.
2.8 ▲   SO   Graded road on right is second entrance to Backbone Road. Zero trip meter and join Backbone Road.
▼ 0.1   SO   Second entrance to Backbone Road on left. Remain on McCandless Gulch Road.
2.7 ▲   BL   Track on right is first entrance to Backbone Road.
▼ 0.5   SO   Track on left.
2.3 ▲   SO   Track on right.
▼ 0.7   SO   Two tracks on right, the second is 300-A3.
2.1 ▲   SO   Two tracks on left, the first is 300-A3.
▼ 1.2   SO   Track on right.
1.6 ▲   SO   Track on left.
▼ 2.0   SO   Track on left.
0.8 ▲   BL   Track on right.
▼ 2.8   Track on left is private; then trail ends at T-intersection with California 299. Turn right for Redding; turn left for Burney.
0.0 ▲   Trail commences on California 299, 5 miles southwest of Round Mountain, 0.2 miles south of Shasta County mile marker 48.00. Zero trip meter and turn west on graded dirt road, marked McCandless Gulch Road (small sign after the turn). Track on right is private.

GPS: N40°45.71' W122°00.69'

Backbone Ridge Trail

STARTING POINT 35N08, where the trail turns to graded dirt, 6 miles west of Lakeshore

FINISHING POINT Saddle on Backbone Ridge

TOTAL MILEAGE 8.4 miles (one-way)

UNPAVED MILEAGE 8.4 miles

DRIVING TIME 1 hour (one-way)

ELEVATION RANGE 1,200–2,900 feet

USUALLY OPEN May to November

BEST TIME TO TRAVEL Dry weather

DIFFICULTY RATING 3

SCENIC RATING 8

REMOTENESS RATING +1

Special Attractions

■ Boating, fishing, camping, and other water-related activities at Shasta Lake.

■ Panoramic views from Backbone Ridge.

History

The 370-mile shoreline of Shasta Lake spreads out far below the twisting Backbone Ridge Trail. The lake impounds water from three major river systems: the Sacramento, McCloud, and Pit. Construction of the Shasta Dam commenced in 1938 and was completed in 1945. It took three more years to fill the mammoth reservoir. Many mines, sections of the Central Pacific Railroad and Oregon Trail, and a multitude of historic buildings in the mining town of Kennett, which once supported a population of more than 10,000, lie below the lake's waters.

Shasta Lake lies 2,000 feet below the trail

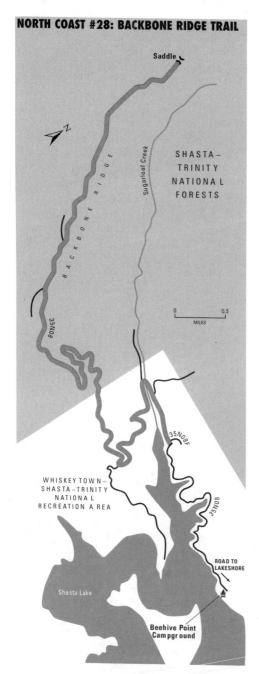

Elmore Mountain, on the east side of the Sacramento Arm and beyond this trail's route, was on the impressive Elmore Ranch, much of which is now under water. The settlement of Lakehead, passed en route to the start of Backbone Ridge Trail, was named in 1950, five years after Shasta Dam was com-

pleted. The hilltop town became a lakeshore town as the waters of Shasta Lake rose to meet it. Initially, the town site was called Pollock Bridge, for a span across the Sacramento River. As the Shasta Dam project continued the site was moved upriver in 1939 and again in 1940. In 1944, Pollock Bridge was renamed Loftus, to avoid confusion with a town in El Dorado County. Finally, once the waters rose, the site became Lakehead.

Realignment of the Central Pacific Railroad, which later became the Southern Pacific Railroad, required blasting a series of tunnels to circumvent the rising waters of Shasta Lake. The original railroad, a feat in its own right, was built in 1872. The line followed part of the Oregon Trail.

Description

Backbone Ridge Trail (not to be confused with North Coast #27: Backbone Road on the south side of Shasta Lake, or North Coast #22: Hobo Gulch Trail, which travels along another Backbone Ridge) begins on the western shore of Shasta Lake's Sacramento Arm, south of Lakeshore. There are campgrounds and boat launches along the road from Lakeshore. Anglers will enjoy fishing for rainbow trout, brown trout, and salmon; the best time is in spring and early summer. Bass fishing is good year-round, and crappie and catfish can also be caught.

The trail starts at the end of the paved road and immediately starts to climb a narrow shelf road onto the ridge. The trail runs along the top of Backbone Ridge for a few miles, offering great views over the surrounding area. Passing places are limited, and vehicles must be prepared to back up for oncoming traffic.

The trail enters privately owned forest managed for timber harvesting and has been blocked before it intersects with any other roads.

Current Road Information

Bureau of Land Management
Redding Field Office
355 Hemsted Drive
Redding, CA 96002
(530) 224-2100

Shasta-Trinity National Forests
Shasta Lake Ranger District
4225 Holiday Road
Redding, CA 96003
(530) 275-1589

Iron Canyon Reservoir Trail

Map References

BLM Redding
USFS Shasta-Trinity National Forests
USGS 1:24,000 Bohemotash Mt.,
Lamoine
1:100,000 Redding
Maptech CD-ROM: Shasta Lake/Redding
Northern California Atlas & Gazetteer, p. 46
California Road & Recreation Atlas, p. 52
Other: Whiskeytown-Shasta-Trinity NRA:
Shasta Unit

STARTING POINT FR 11, at the intersection
with 38N04Y
FINISHING POINT FR 11, at the intersection
with 37N78
TOTAL MILEAGE 13.2 miles
UNPAVED MILEAGE 8.8 miles
DRIVING TIME 1 hour
ELEVATION RANGE 2,400–4,100 feet
USUALLY OPEN May to December
BEST TIME TO TRAVEL May to December
DIFFICULTY RATING 2
SCENIC RATING 9
REMOTENESS RATING +0

Special Attractions

■ Camping, boating, angling, and picnicking at Lake McCloud and Iron Canyon Reservoir.

Route Directions

▼ 0.0   Trail commences on 35N08, where the road turns to graded dirt, 6 miles west of Lakeshore. Zero trip meter and proceed northwest on 35N08. Immediately track on right is 35N08F.
     GPS: N40°51.12′ W122°25.91′

▼ 0.5   SO   Track on right.
▼ 0.6   SO   Cross over Sugarloaf Creek; then track on right.
▼ 1.1   SO   Cross over creek.
▼ 2.0   BR   Track on left on right-hand bend. Zero trip meter.
     GPS: N40°50.68′ W122°26.04′

▼ 0.0   Continue to the northwest and start to climb ridge.
▼ 3.7   TR   End of climb. Trail is now on top of Backbone Ridge. Track on left. Zero trip meter.
     GPS: N40°50.94′ W122°28.16′

▼ 0.0   Continue to the northwest.
▼ 0.5   BR   Track on left.
▼ 2.7   Road is blocked at saddle where it enters privately owned forest.
     GPS: N40°52.89′ W122°29.47′

Tall firs line the trail

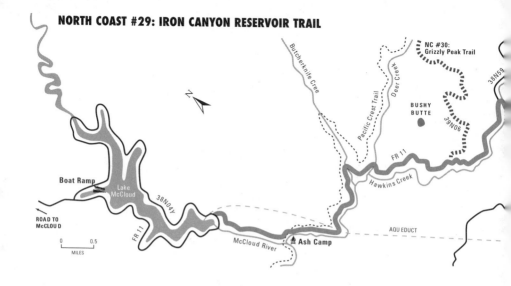

- Access to the Pacific Crest National Scenic Trail and a network of dirt roads and 4WD trails.

History

The Pacific Crest National Scenic Trail crosses Iron Canyon Reservoir Trail at the shady Ash Camp and continues to cross a high arched footbridge over the McCloud River on its way to Ah-Di-Na, the site of a Native American village. The Wintun, Pit River, and Okwanuchu people have associations with the riverside site, which was bought by the Whittier family in the late 1890s. They turned it into a hunting camp, planted an orchard, and built guest cabins. The property changed hands in 1919. The new owner William M. Fitzhugh built a cabin; all that remains of a second cabin he built in 1923 is its stone cellar. Little occurred at the riverside property and the buildings eventually fell into disrepair.

Description

This winding trail in Shasta-Trinity National Forests links two very pretty reservoirs. Both offer boating, developed sites for camping and picnicking, and a variety of fishing opportunities. The trail is initially a rough shelf road that follows the McCloud River. Ash Camp, an undeveloped USFS camping area,

has a couple of riverside sites. It is a popular place with anglers who fish for rainbow and brown trout in the McCloud River. The Pacific Crest National Scenic Trail crosses this trail at Ash Camp—there is a footbridge to the far side of the river. The trail becomes a narrow paved road for the last couple of miles to Iron Canyon Reservoir. Set in a basin, the multiarmed lake has excellent fishing for rainbow and German brown trout.

Many 4WD trails lead off into the forest from this road. One of note is North Coast #30: Grizzly Peak Trail, which can be combined with this route to loop back to California 89.

Current Road Information

Shasta-Trinity National Forests
McCloud Ranger District
2019 Forest Road
McCloud, CA 96057
(530) 964-2184

Map References

BLM   Mt. Shasta, McArthur
USFS   Shasta-Trinity National Forests
USGS   1:24,000   Lake McCloud,
        Shoeinhorse Mt., Big Bend
        1:100,000 Mt. Shasta, McArthur
Maptech CD-ROM: Shasta-Trinity/Modoc
Northern California Atlas & Gazetteer, p. 37
California Road & Recreation Atlas, p. 53

Route Directions

▼ 0.0　　From FR 11, at the intersection with
　　　　　38N04Y at the northeast side of Lake
　　　　　McCloud's dam, 13.5 miles south of
　　　　　McCloud, zero trip meter and turn east
　　　　　on paved FR 11.

5.8 ▲　　Trail ends at the intersection with
　　　　　38N04Y at the northeast side of Lake
　　　　　McCloud's dam. Continue on paved FR
　　　　　11 to McCloud.
　　　　　GPS: N41°07.94' W122°04.16'

▼ 0.3　SO　Track on right.
5.5 ▲　SO　Track on left.
▼ 1.1　BL　Road on right is 38N11H to Ash Camp.
　　　　　Follow sign to Iron Canyon Reservoir.
　　　　　Road turns to graded dirt.
4.7 ▲　SO　Road on left is 38N11H to Ash Camp.
　　　　　Road becomes paved.
　　　　　GPS: N41°07.12' W122°03.68'

▼ 1.4　SO　Pacific Crest Trail crosses.
4.4 ▲　SO　Pacific Crest Trail crosses.
▼ 1.9　SO　Track on right.
3.9 ▲　SO　Track on left.
▼ 2.0　SO　Two tracks on right.
3.8 ▲　SO　Two tracks on left.
▼ 2.1　SO　Cross over aqueduct pipeline linking
　　　　　Lake McCloud and Iron Canyon
　　　　　Reservoir.

3.7 ▲　SO　Cross over aqueduct pipeline linking
　　　　　Lake McCloud and Iron Canyon
　　　　　Reservoir.
　　　　　GPS: N41°06.55' W122°02.81'

▼ 2.2　SO　Wide track on right.
3.6 ▲　SO　Wide track on left.
▼ 3.4　SO　Cross over Butcherknife Creek.
2.4 ▲　SO　Cross over Butcherknife Creek.
　　　　　GPS: N41°07.07' W122°01.88'

▼ 4.0　SO　Cross over Deer Creek.
1.8 ▲　SO　Cross over Deer Creek.
　　　　　GPS: N41°06.81' W122°01.53'

▼ 5.8　SO　Track on left is North Coast #30:
　　　　　Grizzly Peak Trail (39N06). Zero trip
　　　　　meter and follow the sign to Iron
　　　　　Canyon Reservoir and California 299.
0.0 ▲　　Continue to the west, remaining on FR 11.
　　　　　GPS: N41°06.04' W122°00.58'

▼ 0.0　　Continue to the north, remaining on FR 11.
7.4 ▲　SO　Track on right is North Coast #30:
　　　　　Grizzly Peak Trail (39N06). Zero trip
　　　　　meter.
▼ 1.1　SO　Cross over creek.
6.3 ▲　SO　Cross over creek.
▼ 1.3　SO　Track on right is 38N11C.
6.1 ▲　SO　Track on left is 38N11C.
▼ 1.5　BR　Graded road on left is 38N59 to Mica
　　　　　Gulch. Follow sign to Iron Canyon
　　　　　Reservoir and cross over Hawkins
　　　　　Creek.
5.9 ▲　BL　Cross over Hawkins Creek; then grad-
　　　　　ed road on right is 38N59 to Mica
　　　　　Gulch.
　　　　　GPS: N41°06.11' W121°59.25'

▼ 2.2　SO　Track on right is 37N48 to Van Sicklin
　　　　　Butte.
5.2 ▲　SO　Track on left is 37N48 to Van Sicklin
　　　　　Butte.
　　　　　GPS: N41°05.90' W121°58.81'

▼ 2.9　SO　Track on left is 38N59.
4.5 ▲　SO　Track on right is 38N59.
▼ 3.1　SO　Road is now paved.
4.3 ▲　SO　Road turns to graded dirt.
▼ 4.1　SO　Track on right is 38N60.

Iron Canyon Reservoir

3.3 ▲ SO Track on left is 38N60.
        GPS: N41°05.13' W121°58.02'

▼ 5.2 SO Track on left is 37N29.
2.2 ▲ SO Track on right is 37N29.
▼ 6.1 SO Paved road on right goes 1 mile to
           Deadlun USFS Campground. Follow the
           sign to Big Bend.
1.3 ▲ BR Paved road on left goes 1 mile to
           Deadlun USFS Campground. Follow the
           sign to Lake McCloud.
▼ 6.3 SO Track on right is 37N66Y to Hawkins
           Landing USFS Campground and boat
           ramp.
1.1 ▲ SO Track on left is 37N66Y into Hawkins
           Landing USFS Campground and boat
           ramp.
        GPS: N41°03.47' W121°58.13'

▼ 7.4 SO Trail ends at intersection with 37N78
           to Pit 5 Powerhouse on right. Continue
           on straight ahead on FR 11 to exit to
           Big Bend.
0.0 ▲   Trail commences on FR 11 at the inter-
           section with 37N78 to Pit 5

Powerhouse, 5 miles northwest of Big
Bend and 21 miles north of California
299. Zero trip meter and proceed north
on paved FR 11, following sign to
Hawkins Landing and McCloud.
        GPS: N41°02.98' W121°57.95'

NORTH COAST #30

Grizzly Peak Trail

STARTING POINT North Coast #29: Iron
    Canyon Reservoir Trail, 5.8 miles from
    the northern end
FINISHING POINT California 89, 13 miles east
    of McCloud
TOTAL MILEAGE 19.3 miles
UNPAVED MILEAGE 18.4 miles
DRIVING TIME 2.25 hours
ELEVATION RANGE 3,600–6,200 feet
USUALLY OPEN May to November
BEST TIME TO TRAVEL May to November
DIFFICULTY RATING 3

Special Attractions
- Panoramic views from Grizzly Peak.
- Angling in the McCloud River at Algoma USFS Campground.

History
Built in the early 1950s, Grizzly Peak Fire Lookout provides excellent 360-degree views from its lofty perch at 6,275 feet. The twisting course of the McCloud River, some 3,300 feet below, is off to the northwest. The Wyntoon villa estate of William Randolph Hearst, built alongside the river in the 1930s, is just north of Lake McCloud. The elaborate retreat was designed as a Bavarian village by renowned San Francisco architect Julia Morgan. Morgan completed several hundred impressive buildings throughout her working life; many of her commissions followed the San Francisco earthquake of 1906.

The Wyntoon property had three groups of buildings centered around a green with tennis and croquet courts, a swimming pool, and a variety of entertaining buildings scattered along the McCloud River. The ornate complex was built to showcase Hearst's German art collection. Called Hearst Castle, the estate was frequented by the Hearst family during World War II because they feared that their coastal San Simeon property would be a target for enemy bombers.

The name Wyntoon comes from Wintun, the Native Americans who inhabited this region.

Description
Grizzly Peak's summit, covered with manzanitas, stands high above the surrounding forests and valleys. However, Mount Shasta dwarfs it because it is nearly twice as high. The trail leaves North Coast #29: Iron Canyon Reservoir Trail and starts to climb through Shasta-Trinity National Forests along a roughly graded road. There are sections of shelf road and enough uneven ground to require a high-clearance vehicle. As you climb, the conifer forest is gradually left behind, and the trail travels across a man-

Grizzly Peak Fire Lookout

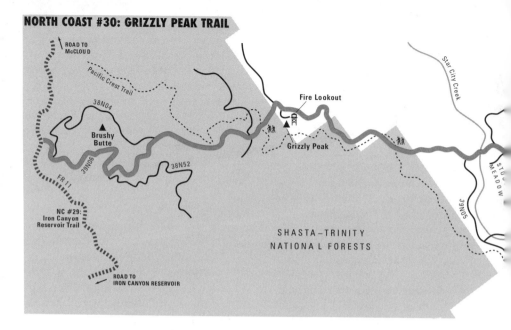

NORTH COAST #30: GRIZZLY PEAK TRAIL

zanita-covered ridge. Mount Shasta dominates views to the north. A short 0.1-mile side trail leads to the fire lookout, which is occasionally manned during thunderstorms.

Past Grizzly Peak, the loose, scrabbly trail descends back into the forest. This part of the trail is a good place to see fall colors. Part of the trail travels through privately owned forests managed for timber harvesting. The road is currently open for public travel, but you are not permitted to trespass on the private land off the thoroughfare. Be sure that you are on public land before camping or venturing off the main trail.

Two old wooden cabins can be seen a short distance off the main trail at Stouts Meadow, along 39N05. These cabins are privately owned. The larger of the two has an ornate veranda and roof. Please admire them from the public road.

Re-entering Shasta-Trinity National Forests, the trail passes Algoma USFS Campground, on the banks of the McCloud River. The river is popular among fishermen, and it contains some brook trout below Lakin Dam (found along North Coast #31: McCloud River Road) and is regularly stocked with rainbow trout.

The trail ends on paved California 89. Watch out for deer, numerous chipmunks, and even black bears along this trail.

Current Road Information

Shasta-Trinity National Forests
McCloud Ranger District
2019 Forest Road
McCloud, CA 96057
(530) 964-2184

Map References

BLM Mt. Shasta, McArthur
USFS Shasta-Trinity National Forests
USGS 1:24,000 Shoeinhorse Mtn., Big
      Bend, Grizzly Peak, Kinyon
      1:100,000 Mt. Shasta, McArthur
Maptech CD-ROM: Shasta-Trinity/Modoc
Northern California Atlas & Gazetteer, p. 37
California Road & Recreation Atlas, pp. 53, 47

Route Directions

▼ 0.0   From FR 11, 19.3 miles south of McCloud and 5.8 miles from the start of North Coast #29: Iron Canyon Reservoir Trail, zero trip meter and turn northwest on graded dirt road 39N06, following sign for Grizzly Peak.

4.8 ▲   Trail ends at T-intersection with North Coast #29: Iron Canyon Reservoir Trail (FR 11). Turn right for McCloud; turn left for Iron Canyon Reservoir

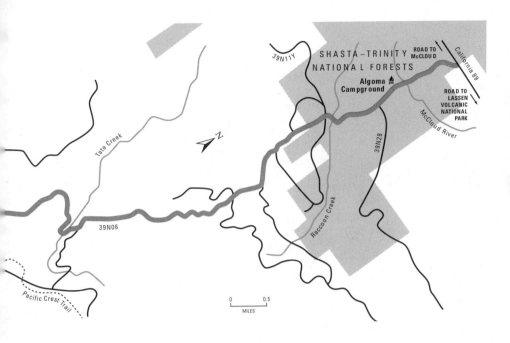

and California 299.

GPS: N41°06.04' W122°00.58'

▼ 0.4   SO   Track on left is 38N04.
4.4 ▲   SO   Track on right is 38N04.
▼ 2.0   BL   Track on right is 38N52.
2.8 ▲   BR   Track on left is 38N52.

GPS: N41°06.50' W121°59.52'

▼ 2.7   BL   Track on right is 39N06E.
2.1 ▲   SO   Track on left is 39N06E.
▼ 3.1   SO   Track on left is 38N04.
1.7 ▲   SO   Track on right is 38N04.

GPS: N41°07.19' W121°59.57'

▼ 3.3   SO   Track on left.
1.5 ▲   SO   Track on right.
▼ 3.8   SO   Start of shelf road.
1.0 ▲   SO   End of shelf road.
▼ 4.8   SO   Graded road on right and left under power lines. Zero trip meter.
0.0 ▲   Continue to the southwest.

GPS: N41°08.14' W121°58.69'

▼ 0.0   Continue to the north.
1.0 ▲   SO   Graded road on right and left under power lines. Zero trip meter.
▼ 0.3   SO   Pacific Crest Trail crosses.
0.7 ▲   SO   Pacific Crest Trail crosses.

▼ 0.6   SO   Track on left.
0.4 ▲   SO   Track on right.
▼ 0.7   BR   Track on left.
0.3 ▲   BL   Track on right.
▼ 0.9   SO   Track on left.
0.1 ▲   SO   Track on right.
▼ 1.0   TL   Track on right is 39N06A, which goes 0.1 mile to Grizzly Peak Fire Lookout. Zero trip meter.
0.0 ▲   Continue to the southwest, remaining on 39N06.

GPS: N41°08.66' W121°58.73'

▼ 0.0   Continue to the north, remaining on 39N06.
3.3 ▲   TR   Track straight ahead is 39N06A, which goes 0.1 mile to Grizzly Peak Fire Lookout. Zero trip meter.
▼ 0.6   BR   Track on left.
2.7 ▲   BL   Track on right.
▼ 2.3   SO   Pacific Crest Trail crosses.
1.0 ▲   SO   Pacific Crest Trail crosses.

GPS: N41°09.54' W121°57.11'

▼ 2.8   SO   Cross over creek; then track on right. Trail enters private forest.
0.5 ▲   SO   Track on left; then cross over creek. Trail re-enters Shasta-Trinity National Forests.

Mount Shasta and Konwakiton Glacier from Grizzly Peak

▼ 3.3   BL Stouts Meadow. Track on right is 39N05. Two privately owned cabins are a short distance down this trail on the edge of the meadow. Zero trip meter.

0.0 ▲   Continue to the west, remaining on 39N06.
        GPS: N41°10.14′ W121°56.40′

▼ 0.0   Continue to the north, remaining on 39N06. Trail is now marked G Line as well as 39N06.

6.3 ▲ BR Stouts Meadow. Track on left is 39N05. Two privately owned cabins are a short distance down this trail on the edge of the meadow. Zero trip meter.

▼ 0.2 SO Cross over Star City Creek; then track on right.

6.1 ▲ SO Track on left; then cross over Star City Creek.

▼ 0.5 BR Graded road on left.

5.8 ▲ BL Graded road on right.

▼ 0.7 SO 4-way intersection. Graded road on left through closure gate. Track on right. Remain on G Line (39N06).

5.6 ▲ SO 4-way intersection. Graded road on right through closure gate. Track on left. Remain on G Line (39N06).
        GPS: N41°10.56′ W121°56.11′

▼ 0.9 SO Track on left.

5.4 ▲ SO Track on right.

▼ 1.3 SU Track on left and track on right.

5.0 ▲ SO Track on left and track on right.

▼ 1.9 SO Two tracks on right. Remain on 39N06.

4.4 ▲ SO Two tracks on left. Remain on 39N06.
        GPS: N41°10.38′ W121°55.12′

▼ 2.6 SO Track on right.

3.7 ▲ SO Track on left.

▼ 3.7 SO Cross through Tate Creek.

2.6 ▲	SO	Cross through Tate Creek.
		GPS: N41°11.04' W121°54.27'

▼ 4.0	BL	Track on right; then cross over creek.
2.3 ▲	BR	Cross over creek; then track on left.
▼ 4.1	SO	Track on left.
2.2 ▲	SO	Track on right.
▼ 5.6	SO	Cross over creek.
0.7 ▲	SO	Cross over creek.
▼ 6.1	SO	Track on left.
0.2 ▲	SO	Track on right.
▼ 6.3	SO	Well-used track on left passes under power lines. Track on right. Zero trip meter and pass under power lines.
0.0 ▲		Continue to the south.
		GPS: N41°12.89' W121°53.10'

▼ 0.0		Continue to the north.
3.9 ▲	SO	Pass under power lines; then well-used track on right passes under power lines. Track on left. Zero trip meter.
▼ 0.2	SO	Track on left.
3.7 ▲	SO	Track on right.
▼ 0.4	SO	Track on left.
3.5 ▲	SO	Track on right.
▼ 0.5	BL	Graded road on right.
3.4 ▲	BR	Graded road on left.
▼ 1.0	SO	Track on right.
2.9 ▲	SO	Track on left.
▼ 1.1	SO	Track on right.
2.8 ▲	SO	Track on left.
▼ 1.3	SO	Track on left and track on right.
2.6 ▲	SO	Track on left and track on right.
▼ 1.4	SO	Track on left.
2.5 ▲	SO	Track on right.
▼ 1.8	SO	Track on left is 39N11Y and track on right. Re-entering Shasta-Trinity National Forests. Track on right to campsite; then cross over Raccoon Creek.
2.1 ▲	SO	Cross over Raccoon Creek; then track on left to campsite. Entering private forest. Track on left. Track on right is 39N11Y.
		GPS:N41°14.37' W121°53.28'
▼ 2.0	SO	Two tracks on right.
1.9 ▲	SO	Two tracks on left.
▼ 2.1	SO	Track on left.
1.8 ▲	SO	Track on right.

▼ 2.2	SO	Track on right is 39N06B.
1.7 ▲	SO	Track on left is 39N06B.
▼ 2.3	SO	Track on left.
1.6 ▲	SO	Track on right.
▼ 2.6	SO	Track on right is 39N28.
1.3 ▲	SO	Track on left is 39N28.
▼ 3.0	SO	Algoma USFS Campground on left on the McCloud River. Road is now paved. Remain on paved road until the end of the trail.
0.9 ▲	SO	Algoma USFS Campground on right on the McCloud River. Road turns to graded dirt.
▼ 3.1	SO	Cross over McCloud River on bridge.
0.8 ▲	SO	Cross over McCloud River on bridge.
		GPS: N41°15.39' W121°52.92'

▼ 3.9		Trail ends at T-intersection with paved California 89. Turn right for Lassen Volcanic National Park; turn left for McCloud.
0.0 ▲		Trail commences on California 89, 0.1 mile west of county mile marker 11 and 0.2 mile east of Sheephaven Road, 13 miles east of McCloud. Zero trip meter and turn south on paved road, marked Stouts Meadow Road (39N06). Remain on paved road for the next 0.9 mile.
		GPS: N41°15.99' W121°52.69'

NORTH COAST #31

McCloud River Road

STARTING POINT California 89, 9.8 miles east of McCloud

FINISHING POINT California 89, 2.6 miles east of McCloud

TOTAL MILEAGE 8.3 miles, plus 0.5-mile spur to Lakin Dam and 1.2-mile spur to Lower Falls

UNPAVED MILEAGE 5.9 miles, plus spurs

DRIVING TIME 1 hour

ELEVATION RANGE 3,300–3,700 feet

USUALLY OPEN May to December

BEST TIME TO TRAVEL Spring and fall

DIFFICULTY RATING 1

McCloud River Railroad with Mount Shasta behind

SCENIC RATING 8

REMOTENESS RATING +0

Special Attractions

- Many access points for angling, picnicking, swimming, and wildlife watching along the McCloud River.
- Excellent trail for family bicycling.
- Upper, Middle, and Lower Falls and the start of a canoe run to Lake McCloud.

History

In 1854, Ross McCloud purchased land in this area from Harry and Samuel Lockhart, brothers who operated a ferry north of today's Fall River Mills. McCloud built a camp to cater to the passing traffic on the pack trail that led north to Yreka. He went on to become a prominent figure in the community that developed on his land.

In the 1890s, William W. VanArsdale and George W. Scott built a railroad to connect McCloud with Sisson, the original name of the city of Mount Shasta. They also purchased a sawmill in Squaw Valley from A. F. George and began what would evolve into a massive business called the McCloud River Lumber Company. Their railroad network became the McCloud River Railroad Company.

With seemingly endless timber to harvest and a transportation system to reach outside markets, the businesses thrived. Because people could count on finding and keeping a job at McCloud, the town flourished. The railroad network expanded and added passenger service for the public. Steam-powered excursion trains brought many tourists who just wanted to take in the spectacular scenery; guesthouses and hotels in McCloud catered to their needs. McCloud River Road travels a riverside section of the railroad that was built east to Hambone. This river corridor was acquired by the forest service in 1989 in a land exchange deal with Champion International Corporation, then owners of the railroad.

Description

This short, easy trail, suitable for all vehicles in dry weather, gives accesses to the McCloud River at a number of points. Although the trail only takes an hour to drive, it is a perfect trail for a full day's outing, allowing time to hike,

Handicapped fishing access at Lakin Dam

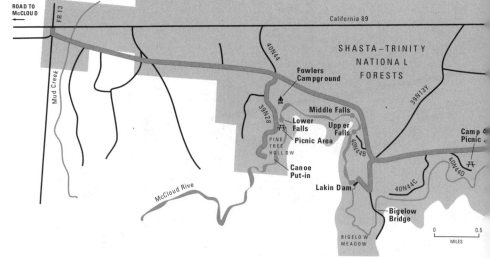

swim, fish, and view the waterfalls. Campers will find two developed USFS campgrounds: one at the start and one at the end of the trail. There is no camping permitted at any of the picnic areas along the route; this includes Camp 4, which is a group site for day use only.

The route is an easy graded road with short spurs leading to points of interest along the way. Cattle Camp Picnic Area has a wonderful clear blue swimming hole on a bend in the river. This is a great spot to relax, have a picnic, and enjoy a cool dip.

Of the three waterfalls along the trail, Upper Falls, which cuts through black volcanic rock to plunge sharply into the pool below, is the most dramatic and has fewer visitors than the other waterfalls. Middle Falls has a large paved parking area and a short walk to a viewpoint over the falls. Lower Falls has a very popular USFS campground as well as a day-use picnic area beside the cascades. A short distance downstream is the put-in for canoes and kayaks. From here, a gentle trip takes paddlers downstream to Lake McCloud. There are short stretches of whitewater, but generally the trip is considered to be easy. The best time of year to make the run is May and June. Around July the water level starts to drop and quickly becomes too low. Anglers will enjoy fishing for rainbow and brook trout below Lakin Dam. This lower section of the

river is stocked with rainbow trout. Above the dam, redband trout can be caught.

The final section of the trail follows an old railroad grade, one of the lumber company's many, to finish a short distance east of McCloud back on California 89.

Current Road Information

Shasta-Trinity National Forests
McCloud Ranger District
2019 Forest Road
McCloud, CA 96057
(530) 964-2184

Map References

BLM   Mcarthur, Mt. Shasta
USFS   Shasta-Trinity National Forests
USGS   1:24,000   Kinyon, Grizzly Peak,
       Lake McCloud, Elk Spring
       1:100,000 McArthur, Mt. Shasta
Maptech CD-ROM: Shasta-Trinity/Modoc
Northern California Atlas & Gazetteer, p. 37
California Road & Recreation Atlas, p. 47

Route Directions

▼ 0.0   From California 89, 9.8 miles east of McCloud, zero trip meter and turn south onto paved road 40N44, following the sign to McCloud River Loop Road and Cattle Camp USFS Campground.

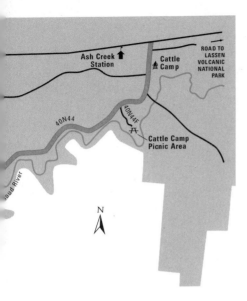

Ash Creek Station

Cattle Camp

ROAD TO LASSEN VOLCANIC NATIONAL PARK

40N44

40N44F

Cattle Camp Picnic Area

N

▼ 3.4	SO	Track on left is 40N44D, which goes 0.3 miles to Camp 4 Picnic Area, angling point, and swimming hole. Zero trip meter.
0.0 ▲		Continue to the northeast.
		GPS: N41°14.31' W121°59.26'

▼ 0.0		Continue to the southwest.
0.8 ▲	SO	Track on right is 40N44D, which goes 0.3 miles to Camp 4 Picnic Area, angling point, and swimming hole. Zero trip meter.
▼ 0.2	SO	Track on left is 40N44C.
0.6 ▲	SO	Track on right is 40N44C.
▼ 0.3	SO	Track on right.
0.5 ▲	SO	Track on left.
▼ 0.8	SO	4-way intersection. Graded road on right and left is Bigelow Meadow Road (39N13Y). To the left is the spur to Bigelow Bridge and Lakin Dam. To the right goes to California 89. Zero trip meter.
0.0 ▲		Continue to the east. Road turns to graded dirt.
		GPS: N41°14.16' W122°00.16'

Spur to Bigelow Bridge and Lakin Dam

▼ 0.0		Continue to the south.
▼ 0.3	TR	Road continues ahead for 0.3 miles to Bigelow Bridge, which is blocked to public access. Turn right, following sign to Lakin Dam.
		GPS: N41°13.87' W122°00.22'

▼ 0.5		Lakin Dam.
		GPS: N41°13.99' W122°00.37'

Continuation of Main Trail

▼ 0.0		Continue to the west. Road becomes paved.
1.6 ▲	SO	4-way intersection. Graded road on right and left is Bigelow Meadow Road (39N13Y). To the right is the spur to Bigelow Bridge and Lakin Dam. To the left goes to California 89. Zero trip meter.
		GPS: N41°14.16' W122°00.16'

▼ 0.2	SO	Track on left is 40N44B, which goes

3.4 ▲		Trail ends back on California 89. Turn left for McCloud; turn right for Lassen Volcanic National Park.
		GPS: N41°15.83' W121°56.49'

▼ 0.1	SO	Track on left is 39N10.
3.3 ▲	SO	Track on right is 39N10.
▼ 0.3	SO	Cattle Camp USFS Campground on left.
3.1 ▲	SO	Cattle Camp USFS Campground on right.
▼ 0.4	SO	Track on right.
3.0 ▲	SO	Track on left.
▼ 0.6	BR	Track on left crosses McCloud River. Remain on paved road.
2.8 ▲	BL	Track on right crosses McCloud River. Remain on paved road.
		GPS: N41°15.32' W121°56.50'

▼ 0.7	SO	Road turns to graded dirt.
2.7 ▲	SO	Road becomes paved.
▼ 0.9	SO	Track on left is 40N44F, which goes 0.2 miles to Cattle Camp Picnic Area, angling point, and swimming hole.
2.5 ▲	SO	Track on right is 40N44F, which goes 0.2 miles to Cattle Camp Picnic Area, angling point, and swimming hole.
		GPS: N41°15.21' W121°56.78'

▼ 1.4	SO	Track on left is 40N44E.
2.0 ▲	SO	Track on right is 40N44E.
▼ 2.1	SO	Track on right.
1.3 ▲	SO	Track on left.

0.3 miles to Upper Falls. Hike 0.1 miles farther downstream to view the falls.

1.4 ▲   SO Track on right is 40N44B, which goes 0.3 miles to Upper Falls. Hike 0.1 miles farther downstream to view the falls.

GPS: N41°14.32' W122°00.28'

▼ 0.4   SO Upper Falls can be seen between the trees on the left.

1.2 ▲   SO Upper Falls can be seen between the trees on the right.

▼ 0.7   SO Parking area for Middle Falls on left. The falls are a short distance past the parking lot.

0.9 ▲   SO Parking area for Middle Falls on right. The falls are a short distance past the parking lot.

▼ 0.9   SO Track on right.
0.7 ▲   SO Track on left.
▼ 1.5   SO Track on left.
0.1 ▲   SO Track on right.
▼ 1.6   SO Paved road on left is 39N28, spur to Lower Falls. To the right is 40N44, which goes to California 89. Zero trip meter.

0.0 ▲   Continue to the east on paved road.

GPS: N41°14.94' W122°01.52'

Spur to Lower Falls

▼ 0.0   Proceed south on 39N28.
▼ 0.1   TR Turn right, following sign to Lower Falls.
▼ 0.3   SO Track on right.
▼ 0.6   BR Lower Falls on left; then picnic area on left. Road turns to graded dirt.

GPS: N41°14.44' W122°01.45'

▼ 1.0   TL Turn left to access Pine Tree Hollow Hiking Trail and canoe put-in.

GPS: N41°14.18' W122°01.68'

▼ 1.2   Canoe put-in access and hiking trail.

GPS: N41°14.14'W122°01.53'

Continuation of Main Trail

▼ 0.0   Continue to the west on graded dirt road.
2.5 ▲   SO Paved road on right is 39N28, spur to Lower Falls. To the left is 40N44, which goes to California 89. Zero trip meter.

GPS: N41°14.94' W122°01.52'

▼ 0.6   SO Track on right.
1.9 ▲   SO Track on left.
▼ 1.3   SO Track on left and track on right.
1.2 ▲   SO Track on left and track on right.
▼ 1.5   SO Track on right.
1.0 ▲   SO Track on left.
▼ 1.6   SO Track on left.
0.9 ▲   SO Track on right.
▼ 1.9   SO Track on left and track on right.
0.6 ▲   SO Track on left and track on right.
▼ 2.1   SO Track on left and track on right.
0.4 ▲   SO Track on left and track on right.
▼ 2.2   SO Cross over Mud Creek.
0.3 ▲   SO Cross over Mud Creek.

GPS: N41°15.12' W122°04.19'

▼ 2.4   TR Paved road on right and left. Track straight ahead.
0.1 ▲   TL Paved road continues ahead. Track on right. Turn left onto dirt road.
▼ 2.5   Trail finishes at intersection with California 89. Pilgrim Creek Road (FR 13) is opposite. Turn left for McCloud; turn right for Lassen Volcanic National Park.

0.0 ▲   Trail starts on California 89, 2.6 miles east of McCloud. Zero trip meter and turn southeast on paved road. The turn is opposite Pilgrim Creek Road (FR 13), which is signed to the snowmobile park and Mount Shasta Wilderness trailheads.

GPS: N41°15.25' W122°04.43'

Toad Lake Trail

STARTING POINT FR 26, 8.1 miles southwest of Mount Shasta
FINISHING POINT Hiking trailhead, 0.4 mile east of Toad Lake
TOTAL MILEAGE 10.4 miles (one-way)
UNPAVED MILEAGE 10.4 miles
DRIVING TIME 1 hour (one-way)
ELEVATION RANGE 3,700–6,800 feet
USUALLY OPEN May to November

Toad Lake

Special Attractions
- Fishing, picnicking, and camping at Toad Lake.
- Views of Mount Shasta from the shelf road.
- Hiking access to the Pacific Crest National Scenic Trail.

History
Toad Lake, in the Trinity Mountains, is due west of Mount Shasta and the Sacramento Valley. Though Indians used the important north-south corridor of the Sacramento River, it eluded settlers for some time. In 1850, gold was discovered in Scott Valley, to the west of the Trinity Mountains, drawing attention to the region. The site that became the town of Mount Shasta was established in the 1850s. The Central Pacific Railroad reached Mount Shasta in 1887. On June 11, 1903, a Dr. Thompson and Manuel Perry drove the first automobile up the Sacramento Valley to Yreka.

Description
The long climb to Toad Lake follows a snaking path above the South Fork of the Sacramento River, starting at an approximate elevation of 3,700 feet. The trail also crosses the Middle Fork of the Sacramento. As the trail climbs an additional 3,000 feet to Toad Lake, the river corridors come clearly into view.

The trail follows roughly graded forest roads to the trailhead to Toad Lake. The beautiful natural lake is set in a bowl below the ridge top, south of Mount Eddy. Much of the trail is shelf road that travels toward The Eddys, a range of volcanic peaks that is part of the Trinity Mountains. The vegetation is predominantly mixed conifers, but the serpentine soils have a high magnesium content, which is not conducive to plant growth. Because of this, the ridge tops are less vegetated than might be expected.

There are few markers along the trail, but navigation is generally easy because there are few turns. The climbs are gradual, and much of the trail wraps around the mountainside, descending to cross over the Middle Fork of the Sacramento River before as-

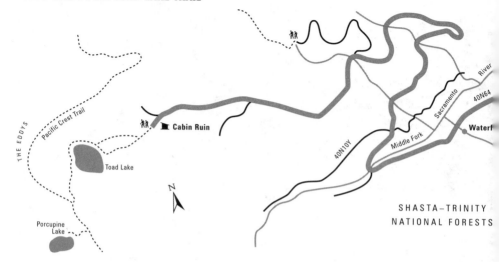

cending again. Landslides have made some sections of the trail uneven, but generally it is easygoing. The final mile earns most of the 3 difficulty rating, with loose, rubbly rocks on the final climb to the trailhead. There is plenty of parking at the trailhead, as well as some undeveloped backcountry campsites.

The 0.4-mile hiking trail to Toad Lake follows an old jeep trail now closed to vehicles. The surface is loose and rubbly, with a moderate grade. The hiking trail continues around the lake to join the Pacific Crest National Scenic Trail. There is a lovely walk-in campsite by the lake beneath some pine trees. The lake offers angling for rainbow and brown trout. It is stocked by air with fingerling trout once or twice a year.

Current Road Information

Shasta-Trinity National Forests
Mount Shasta Ranger District
204 West Alma
Mount Shasta, CA 96067
(530) 926-4511

Map References

BLM   Mt. Shasta
USFS   Shasta-Trinity National Forests
USGS   1:24,000 Mt. Eddy
          1:100,000 Mt. Shasta

Maptech CD-ROM: Shasta-Trinity/Modoc
Northern California Atlas & Gazetteer, p. 36
California Road & Recreation Atlas, p. 46

Route Directions

▼ 0.0   From FR 26, 8.1 miles southwest of Mount Shasta, past Siskiyou Lake and 0.1 mile southwest of where the paved road crosses over South Fork Sacramento River on a bridge, zero trip meter and turn north on graded dirt road 41N53.
            GPS: N41°16.25' W122°24.17'

▼ 0.2   BL Road continues straight ahead. Bear left onto unmarked road.
▼ 1.8   SO Track on right.
▼ 2.2   BR Track on left is 39N84.
            GPS: N41°15.76' W122°25.04'

▼ 3.2   SO Turnout on right with a view of Mount Shasta.
▼ 4.2   SO Well-used track on left. Track is now marked as 40N64.
            GPS: N41°16.45' W122°26.21'

▼ 4.8   SO Small waterfall on left.
            GPS: N41°16.39' W122°26.85'

▼ 5.6   SO Track on left; then cross over Middle

```
0        0.5
|_____|
   MILES
```

Fork Sacramento River on bridge.
Zero trip meter.
GPS: N41°16.29′ W122°27.69′

▼ 0.0   Continue to the northwest.

▼ 0.4   SO   Track on left is 40N10Y and track on right.
                  GPS: N41°16.49′ W122°27.41′

▼ 0.6   SO   Cross over creek.
▼ 1.2   SO   Cross over creek.
▼ 2.6   SO   Track on left.
▼ 2.8   SO   Track on right goes to trailhead accessing the Sisson Calahan National Recreation Trail; then cross over creek.
                  GPS: N41°17.04′ W122°27.47′

▼ 3.9   SO   Track on left.
▼ 4.6   BL   Track on right.
                  GPS: N41°17.07′ W122°29.30′

▼ 4.7   SO   Track on left to campsite; then collapsed log cabin on left.
▼ 4.8   Hiking trail on left goes 0.4 mile to Toad Lake. The vehicle trail continues another 0.1 mile to a couple of campsites and a turnaround.
                  GPS: N41°17.00′ W122°29.41′

Bridge over the Middle Fork of the Sacramento River

Mount Shasta Loop

STARTING POINT FR 19, 10.5 miles southeast of US 97

FINISHING POINT South Mount Shasta Boulevard in the town of Mount Shasta

TOTAL MILEAGE 31.2 miles

UNPAVED MILEAGE 28.1 miles

DRIVING TIME 3 hours

ELEVATION RANGE 3,600–6,400 feet

USUALLY OPEN May to October

BEST TIME TO TRAVEL May to October

DIFFICULTY RATING 2

SCENIC RATING 9

REMOTENESS RATING +0

Special Attractions

- Easy trail around the east and south sides of Mount Shasta.
- Excellent views of the mountain and access to hiking trails that climb to the summit.
- The trail is part of a network of winter snowmobile routes and is close to the Deer Mountain Snowmobile Staging Area.
- Mount Shasta Ski Park and cross-country ski area.

History

Mount Shasta, a volcanic summit in the Cascade Range, rises to 14,162 feet and is the centerpiece of the Mount Shasta Wilderness and Mount Shasta Natural Landmark (see Mount Shasta, page 159). The Konwakiton Glacier, on the south face of Mount Shasta, is subject to mud flows. A particularly devastating flow occurred in 1924.

Mud flows occur when especially warm weather rapidly melts a glacier's ice. Melted water accumulates mud and debris as it flows down its usual channels, but, given the massive amount, Konwakiton's melt overflowed and carried huge rocks and blocks of ice with it. The 1924 flow fanned out of Mud Creek Canyon before it reached the concrete Mud Creek Dam, east of McKenzie Butte, beside the described trail. The flow carried debris nearly 13 miles from the glacier, some 8,000 feet below the mountain's summit. The McCloud River Railroad was engulfed, stalling a train east of McCloud.

Description

This trail travels easy, graded forest roads on the east side of Mount Shasta before swinging around the south side of the mountain to finish in the town of Mount Shasta. Although most of the trail is suitable for passenger vehicles in dry weather, there are a couple of places where high-clearance is preferable: A section of wide shelf road around the south side of the mountain is a little rough for passenger vehicles and the Ash Creek crossing is in a dip on a slight rise. It is impossible to see until you are right on top of it, and vehicles traveling at more than a few miles an hour will risk damage on the sharp dip. Although a small, carefully driven passenger vehicle may be able to negotiate this crossing when the water level is low, high-clearance is definitely preferable. If the water level is high, usually in spring and early summer, the crossing may be impassable to all vehicles.

The trail begins on FR 19, a short distance past the end of the pavement. Initially, the trail travels within the Deer Mountain–Whaleback Road Management Area. From August 15 to March 31 each year, motorized travel is restricted to roads and tracks marked with a green arrow on a white background. Side tracks mentioned in the route directions are for navigation purposes only. If you intend to explore the side trails, you should purchase a current forest service map that shows year-round vehicle travel routes.

The trail passes the eastern end of North Coast #34: Military Pass Trail, a 2-rated trail that leads west to US 97 along the north side of Mount Shasta. The main trail remains on FR 19 before turning onto FR 31 at the turnoff to the Brewer Creek Trailhead, which provides access to Mount Shasta's summit. A fee is required to use this trail. Access to the Clear Creek Trailhead is farther south.

The trail passes a wide variety of scenery and a number of exceptional viewpoints along its length. The mountain dominates the landscape, and photographers should be

Mount Shasta rises above the trail

Mount Shasta

MOUNT SHASTA

The splendid snowcapped summit of Mount Shasta, at an elevation of 14,162 feet, is visible for more than 100 miles on a clear day. This volcanic mountain, one of the largest volcanoes in the Cascades, began to form around 590,000 years ago. The mountain is a stratovolcano, or stratocone, made up of four overlapping volcanic cones, which formed on remnants of an older stratocone, toppled more than 300,000 years ago by an immense landslide estimated to have been 20 times greater than the slide created by the eruption of Mount Saint Helens in 1980. Each of the cones that form Mount Shasta had independent volcanic activity, although they are not all individually recognizable.

Sargents Ridge, Misery Hill, Shastina, and Hotlum Cone comprise Mount Shasta. The oldest cone, Sargents Ridge, formed when a now-extinct vent erupted about 50,000 years ago. The cone's size increased with frequent eruptions over hundreds to thousands of years. The cone's activity continued through two major glaciations, and glaciers and streams eroded its slopes. During this period, vents formed on the north, west, and south sides of Sargents Ridge.

Misery Hill, north of Sargents Ridge, erupted about 130,000 years ago and almost buried the cone of Sargents Ridge. This cone makes up most of what we recognize as Mount Shasta today. The volcanic episode that established today's Misery Hill occurred when thick hot lava filled the interior of the cone and pushed upwards to create a lava dome supported by a ridge of the eroded cone's rim.

The most individually recognizable cone is Shastina, which grew from a vent on the western slope of Misery Hill between 9,700 and 9,400 years ago. Shastina Cone developed in the relatively short span of 300 years, after the close of the Ice Age.

Hotlum Cone, the fourth cone, is slightly younger than Shastina and forms the north and northwest flank of Mount Shasta. Layers of lava on the north side of the mountain indicate that Hotlum's formation began during Shastina's period of volcanic activity, but most of what we recognize as the cone today developed from eruptions within the last 6,000 years. The remaining heat from such recent activity has created steam vents, sulfur deposits, and a hot spring just below the summit. French navigator Jean La Pérouse may have witnessed Hotlum Cone's most recent volcanic explosion in 1786.

Black Butte is another distinct feature associated with Mount Shasta. It is at the foot of the mountain's western slope and formed about 9,500 years ago as a group of overlapping domes. As lava cooled on the exterior of Black Butte, the interior lava continued to rise, shattering the surface into angular boulders. Part of Black Butte collapsed sending large volumes of volcanic ash and debris down its south and west slopes. The towns of Weed and Mount Shasta are built on that debris.

able to get many good shots on a clear day. On the southern part of the trail, the section of shelf road around McKenzie Butte offers views south over McCloud Valley. The trail briefly intersects with paved Ski Park Highway, which leads to the Mount Shasta Ski Park, and passes through the cross-country ski area before joining the paved road to the town of Mount Shasta.

Those intending to climb Mount Shasta should be well prepared and not underestimate the mountain. It is essential that you check with the forest service for permits and other related information. The mountain attracts approximately 30,000 climbers a year, many of whom are novices, making it one of the most popular climbs in the United States. A Mount Shasta Summit Pass is required for ascents above 10,000 feet. These are limited and a fee is required. Most climbers make the ascent between May and October and take one to two days for the round trip. The most popular route is Avalanche Gulch, reached from Bunny Flat on the southwest slope. This route is usually covered in two days with a camp at Helen Lake.

Another attraction of this region is the abundance of rare matsutake mushrooms. This valuable cash crop is harvested by Japanese and Koreans who use the very pungent mushroom for ceremonial purposes as well as for seasoning. Traditionally, it is given as a gift of great worth—either a wedding gift or to seal a business deal. The mushroom is harvested between late August and the first frost, typically around October. Matsutake mushrooms grow at high elevations in light, rocky soils typically associated with volcanic regions. A permit is required to collect the mushrooms.

Much of this trail is a marked snowmobile route in winter, and the Deer Mountain Snowmobile Staging Area is a short distance north of the trail.

Current Road Information

Shasta-Trinity National Forests
Mount Shasta Ranger District
204 West Alma
Mount Shasta, CA 96067
(530) 926-4511

Map References

BLM   Yreka, Mt. Shasta
USFS   Shasta-Trinity National Forests;
       Klamath National Forest
USGS   1:24,000   West Haight Mtn., Ash
       Creek Butte, Elk Spring, McCloud,
       City of Mt. Shasta
       1:100,000 Yreka, Mt. Shasta
Maptech CD-ROM: Shasta-Trinity/Modoc
Northern California Atlas & Gazetteer,
       pp. 27, 37, 36
California Road & Recreation Atlas, pp. 46, 47
Other: Mount Shasta Wilderness, Tom
       Harrison Maps—Mt. Shasta
       Wilderness Trail Map (incomplete)

Route Directions

▼ 0.0   Trail begins on FR 19 at the intersection with 42N16, which leads to the north and is marked to Butte Creek and Alder Creek. The starting point is a short distance past the end of the paved road, 10.5 miles southeast of US 97 and 6.5 miles south of the Deer Mountain Snowmobile Staging Area. Zero trip meter and proceed northeast, following sign to California 89.
5.2 ▲   Trail finishes at intersection with 42N16. Continue straight ahead on FR 19, which becomes paved, to exit to US 97.
         GPS: N41°30.82′ W122°05.50′

▼ 0.9   SO Track on left.
4.3 ▲   SO Track on right.
▼ 1.3   SO Track on right is 42N23 and track on left.
3.9 ▲   SO Track on left is 42N23 and track on right.
▼ 1.8   SO Track on left; then cattle guard.
3.4 ▲   SO Cattle guard; then track on right.
         GPS:N41°30.48′ W122°03.89′

▼ 3.0   SO Track on right.
2.2 ▲   SO Track on left.
▼ 3.1   SO Leaving Deer Mountain–Whaleback Road Management Area.
2.1 ▲   SO Entering Deer Mountain–Whaleback Road Management Area.
▼ 4.6   SO Track on left is 42N12B.

.6 ▲ SO Track on right is 42N12B.
▼ 4.9 SO Track on right.
.3 ▲ SO Track on left.
▼ 5.2 SO Track on right is North Coast #34: Military Pass Trail (43N19). Track on left is 42N20. Zero trip meter and follow the sign for California 89.
.0 ▲ Continue to the west, remaining on FR 19.
GPS: N41°28.61' W122°05.14'

▼ 0.0 Continue to the east, remaining on FR 19.
.7 ▲ SO Track on left is North Coast #34: Military Pass Trail (43N19). Track on right is 42N20. Zero trip meter and follow the sign for US 97.
▼ 0.3 SO Track on right.
.4 ▲ SO Track on left.
▼ 0.4 SO Track on right.
.3 ▲ SO Track on left.
▼ 0.6 SO Track on right and track on left.
.1 ▲ SO Track on right and track on left.
▼ 1.0 SO Track on left is 42N09.
.7 ▲ SO Track on right is 42N09.
GPS: N41°28.03' W122°04.56'

▼ 1.9 BL Track on right is 43N19X. Follow the sign for California 89.
.8 ▲ BR Track on left is 43N19X. Remain on main graded road, following sign for Deer Mountain Snowmobile Park.
▼ 2.2 SO Track on left is 42N70.
.5 ▲ SO Track on right is 42N70.
▼ 2.8 SO Track on right is 42N05.
.9 ▲ SO Track on left is 42N05.
GPS: N41°26.45' W122°04.92'

▼ 3.0 SO Track on right; then track on left.
.7 ▲ SO Track on right; then track on left.
▼ 3.5 SO Track on left is 41N19XD.
.2 ▲ SO Track on right is 41N19XD.
▼ 3.7 TR Graded road on right is 42N02 to Brewer Creek Trailhead. Track on left. Then turn right onto FR 31 (41N31) and zero trip meter.
.0 ▲ Continue to the north.
GPS: N41°25.85' W122°04.40'

▼ 0.0 Continue to the west.
.9 ▲ TL T-intersection with FR 19. Zero trip meter and turn left. Then graded road

on left is 42N02 to Brewer Creek Trailhead. Also track on right.
▼ 0.5 SO Track on right.
5.4 ▲ SO Track on left.
▼ 1.1 SO Track on right.
4.8 ▲ SO Track on left.
▼ 1.4 SO Track on left.
4.5 ▲ SO Track on right.
▼ 2.0 SO Graded road on right is 42N61.
3.9 ▲ SO Graded road on left is 42N61.
GPS: N41°24.59' W122°04.83'

▼ 2.2 SO Cross through Ash Creek. Caution— creek crossing is in a dip and is hard to see, so keep your approach speed slow.
3.7 ▲ SO Cross through Ash Creek. Caution— creek crossing is in a dip and is hard to see, so keep your approach speed slow.
▼ 2.3 BR Road on left is 41N16. Remain on FR 31, now marked Sugar Pine Butte Road.
3.6 ▲ SO Road on right is second entrance to 41N16. Remain on FR 31.
GPS: N41°24.34' W122°04.87'

▼ 2.5 SO Track on right and second entrance to 41N16 on left.
3.4 ▲ SO Track on right is 41N16 and track on left.
▼ 3.5 SO Cross over Cold Creek; then track on right.
2.4 ▲ SO Track on left; then cross over Cold Creek.
▼ 3.7 SO Track on left.
2.2 ▲ SO Track on right.
▼ 3.8 SO Track on right is 41N61.
2.1 ▲ SO Track on left is 41N61.
GPS: N41°23.34' W122°04.84'

▼ 3.9 SO Track on right.
2.0 ▲ SO Track on left.
▼ 4.2 SO Track on right; then cross over Pilgrim Creek.
1.7 ▲ SO Cross over Pilgrim Creek; then track on left.
▼ 4.8 SO Track on left is 41N85.
1.1 ▲ SO Track on right is 41N85.
▼ 4.9 SO Track on right.
1.0 ▲ SO Track on left.
▼ 5.1 SO Track on right.
0.8 ▲ SO Track on left.

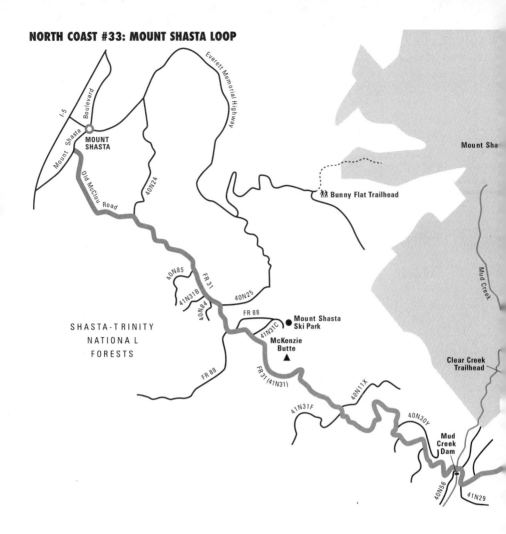

▼ 5.3   SO   Cross through wash.

1.6 ▲   SO   Cross through wash.

▼ 5.4   SO   Track on left.

0.5 ▲   SO   Track on right.

▼ 5.9   SO   4-way intersection. Graded road on
             right is 41N61 to Clear Creek Trailhead
             (fee required). Graded road on left is
             41N15. Zero trip meter.

0.0 ▲   Continue to the north, remaining on FR 31.

             GPS: N41°21.79' W122°05.15'

▼ 0.0   Continue to the south, remaining on FR 31.

5.1 ▲   SO   4-way intersection. Graded road on
             right is 41N15. Graded road on left is
             41N61 to Clear Creek Trailhead (fee
             required). Zero trip meter.

▼ 0.4   SO   Track on right and track on left.

4.7 ▲   SO   Track on right and track on left.

▼ 1.2   SO   Track on right.

3.9 ▲   SO   Track on left.

▼ 1.9   SO   Track on right.

3.2 ▲   SO   Track on left.

▼ 2.1   SO   Track on left.

3.0 ▲   SO   Track on right.

▼ 2.2   SO   Track on left.

2.9 ▲   SO   Track on right.

▼ 2.3   TR   T-intersection. Track on left is 41N29.
             Remain on FR 31.

2.8 ▲   TL   Track straight ahead is 41N29. Remain
             on FR 31.

             GPS: N41°20.00' W122°06.24'

▼ 2.7   SO   Track on right.

2.4 ▲   SO   Track on left.

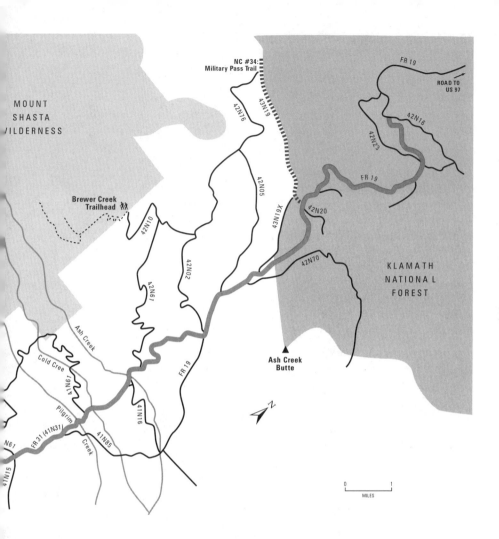

▼ 2.8   SO   Cross over Mud Creek Dam; then track
              on left is 40N56.

.3 ▲   SO   Track on right is 40N56; then cross
              over Mud Creek Dam.

            GPS: N41°20.10′ W122°06.61′

▼ 3.4   SO   Track on left.

.7 ▲   SO   Track on right.

▼ 3.7   SO   Track on right.

.4 ▲   SO   Track on left.

▼ 4.1   SO   Track on left.

.0 ▲   SO   Track on right.

▼ 4.6   SO   Track on right.

.5 ▲   SO   Track on left.

▼ 4.8   SO   Track on left.

.3 ▲   SO   Track on right.

▼ 4.9   SO   Track on left is 41N31H.

0.2 ▲   SO   Track on right is 41N31H.

            GPS: N41°19.69′ W122°08.06′

▼ 5.1   TL   T-intersection. Graded road on right is
              40N30Y. Zero trip meter.

0.0 ▲   Continue to the east, remaining on FR 31.

            GPS: N41°19.70′ W122°08.25′

▼ 0.0   Continue to the south, remaining on FR 31.

6.3 ▲   TR   Graded road ahead is 40N30Y. Zero
              trip meter.

▼ 0.5   SO   Track on right is 41N31E and track
              on left.

5.8 ▲   SO   Track on left is 41N31E and track
              on right.

▼ 1.2   SO   Track on right.

5.1 ▲   SO   Track on left.

South end of Mount Shasta Loop

▼ 2.0	SO	Track on right; then track on left.
.3 ▲	SO	Track on right; then track on left.
▼ 2.5	SO	Track on right.
.8 ▲	SO	Track on left.
▼ 2.8	BL	Track on left is 41N31F; then track on right is 40N11X.
.5 ▲	BR	Track on left is 40N11X; then track on right is 41N31F.
▼ 3.4	SO	Track on left.
.9 ▲	SO	Track on right.
▼ 5.6	SO	Track on left.
.7 ▲	SO	Track on right.
▼ 5.8	SO	Track on right is 41N31C.
.5 ▲	SO	Track on left is 41N31C.

GPS: N41°18.75' W122°12.28'

▼ 6.1	TL	Intersection with paved Ski Park Highway (FR 88). To the right goes to Mount Shasta Ski Park. Turn left joining FR 88/31.
.2 ▲	TR	Paved FR 88 continues to Mount Shasta Ski Park. Turn right onto graded dirt FR 31. Turn is on a left-hand bend.

GPS: N41°18.63' W122°12.54'

▼ 6.3	TR	Paved FR 88 continues straight ahead. Turn right onto graded dirt FR 31 at the sign for Mount Shasta Cross Country Ski Center. Zero trip meter.
.0 ▲		Continue to the northeast on FR 88/31.

GPS: N41°18.47' W122°12.67'

▼ 0.0		Continue to the west. Track on right.
.0 ▲	TL	Track on left; then T-intersection with paved Ski Park Highway (FR 88). Zero trip meter.
▼ 0.2	SO	Track on right.
.8 ▲	SO	Track on left.
▼ 0.4	SO	Track on left.
.6 ▲	SO	Track on right.
▼ 0.6	SO	Track on right is 40N25.
.4 ▲	SO	Track on left is 40N25.

GPS: N41°18.65' W122°13.27'

▼ 0.8	SO	Track on left is 40N84.
.2 ▲	SO	Track on right is 40N84.
▼ 1.0	SO	Track on left is 41N31B.
.0 ▲	SO	Track on right is 41N31B.
▼ 1.4	SO	Track on right.
.6 ▲	SO	Track on left.

▼ 1.5	SO	Track on left is 40N85.
3.5 ▲	SO	Track on right is 40N85.
▼ 1.8	SO	Track on right is 40N01X.
3.2 ▲	SO	Track on left is 40N01X.
▼ 1.9	SO	Tank on left.
3.1 ▲	SO	Tank on right.
▼ 2.0	SO	Two tracks on left.
3.0 ▲	SO	Two tracks on right.
▼ 2.1	SO	Track on right. Road becomes paved. Remain on paved FR 31.
2.9 ▲	SO	Track on left. Road turns to graded dirt.
▼ 3.5	SO	Track on right is 40N24; then cross over railroad.
1.5 ▲	SO	Cross over railroad; then track on left is 40N24.

GPS: N41°18.42' W122°16.31'

▼ 5.0		Trail ends at intersection with South Mount Shasta Boulevard in Mount Shasta.
0.0 ▲		Trail commences in Mount Shasta at the intersection of South Mount Shasta Boulevard and Old McCloud Road. Zero trip meter and turn east on paved Old McCloud Road. Remain on paved road for 2.9 miles.

GPS: N41°18.32' W122°18.51'

NORTH COAST #34

Military Pass Trail

STARTING POINT US 97, 14.3 miles northeast of Weed

FINISHING POINT North Coast #33: Mount Shasta Loop, 5.2 miles south of the northern end

TOTAL MILEAGE 9.9 miles

UNPAVED MILEAGE 9.9 miles

DRIVING TIME 1 hour

ELEVATION RANGE 4,400–6,100 feet

USUALLY OPEN June to October

BEST TIME TO TRAVEL Dry weather

DIFFICULTY RATING 2

SCENIC RATING 10

REMOTENESS RATING +0

Special Attractions
- Historic military trail.
- Trail traverses the north slope of Mount Shasta, offering fantastic views of the mountain.
- Access to hiking trails on the north side of the mountain.

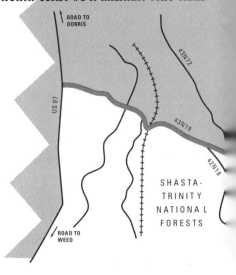

History

Military Pass Road follows a route first used by Indians and trappers. Over the years, the pass has been part of many longer trails such as the 1850s Lockhart Wagon Road and Red Bluffs to Yreka Wagon Road, the 1880s Yreka to Fort Crook Road, the 1900s Fall City and Yreka Road, the Shasta Valley Road in the 1910s, and Sheep Rock–Pilgrim Camp Road for a period in the 1940s. In the mid-1940s it was renamed Military Pass Road on Siskiyou County maps because local information indicated that the army was first to use the route.

Hudson's Bay Company trappers such as John Work may have traveled through this mountain pass in the 1830s. The Lockhart brothers, Harry and Samuel, operated a ferry at today's Fall River Mills in the 1850s and attempted to establish a through road, via their ferry, between Red Bluff and Yreka using this particular pass. Emigrant wagons were noted as passing through the gap in 1855. Teamsters and stagecoache lines chose this route on a regular basis, though the California Stage Company eased up on service because of harassment and attacks by Indians in the late 1850s.

Additional skirmishes broke out in the vicinity of the Pit River to the south. One of these resulted in the death of Harry Lockhart, among others, at his ferry in early 1857, apparently at the hands of Pit River Indians. The infantry stationed farther north at Fort Jones patrolled the road through the pass, and troops from Fort Crook were mobilized to forestall raids. These measures brought a level of security to this hazardous route, enabling stages and freighters to once again travel safely through the pass.

Description

The dominant feature of Shasta-Trinity National Forests, and indeed of the region for miles around, is the volcanic cone of Mount Shasta. Towering above the forests at 14,16: feet, Mount Shasta has permanent glaciers and year-round snow on its peak.

Military Pass Trail travels across the mountain's northern slope, passing through mixed conifer forests to join graded North Coast #33: Mount Shasta Loop. The trail leaves US 97 along a roughly graded dir road. For the first few miles it travels along the border of Klamath National Forest and Shasta-Trinity National Forests. The part of Klamath National Forest (to the north of the trail) is a restricted travel area. From August 15 to March 31, motorized travel is restricted to roads and tracks marked with a green arrow on a white background. Side tracks mentioned in the route directions are for navigation purposes only. If you intend to explore the side trails, you should purchase a current forest service map that shows year-round vehicle travel routes.

The graded road sees a lot of use, and it can be very washboardy. The climb to the pass is gradual. Military Pass is a long gap between Mount Shasta to the south and The Whaleback to the north. East of the pass, the

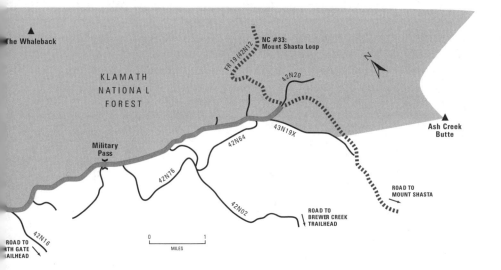

mall, formed trail can be very sandy in dry
weather. It travels through sections of privately owned forest managed for timber harvesting.

The trail accesses two hiking trails, North
Gate and Brewer Creek, that lead to the summit of Mount Shasta. A fee and permit is required for both. Campers will find many
backcountry campsites along this trail.

The trail ends at the intersection with
North Coast #33: Mount Shasta Loop.

Current Road Information

Shasta-Trinity National Forests
Mount Shasta Ranger District
204 West Alma
Mount Shasta, CA 96067
(530) 926-4511

Map References

BLM   Yreka, Mt. Shasta
USFS Shasta-Trinity National Forest;
      Klamath National Forest
USGS 1:24,000 The Whaleback, Mt.
      Shasta, Ash Creek Butte
      1:100,000 Yreka, Mt. Shasta
Maptech CD-ROM: Shasta-Trinity/Modoc
Northern California Atlas & Gazetteer,
      pp. 26, 27, 37
California Road & Recreation Atlas, p. 46

Other: Mount Shasta Wilderness
(incomplete), Tom Harrison
Maps—Mt. Shasta Wilderness
Trail Map (incomplete)

Route Directions

▼ 0.0   From US 97 on the boundary of
         Shasta-Trinity and Klamath National
         Forests, 14.3 miles northeast of Weed
         and 2.5 miles north of the intersection
         with CR A12, zero trip meter and turn
         east on graded dirt Military Pass Road
         (43N19). Cross cattle guard. Track on
         left along fence line. There is a sign for
         Military Pass Road on US 97.
4.5 ▲   Trail ends at intersection with US 97.
         Turn left for Weed; turn right for Dorris
         and Klamath Falls.
         GPS: N41°33.55′ W122°12.49′

▼ 0.1   SO Track on left at information board.
4.4 ▲   SO Track on right at information board.
▼ 0.3   SO Track on left.
4.2 ▲   SO Track on right.
▼ 0.4   SO Track on right.
4.1 ▲   SO Track on left.
▼ 1.2   SO Track on left and track on right.
3.3 ▲   SO Track on left and track on right.
▼ 1.5   SO Track on left and track on right.

View of Mount Shasta from Military Pass Trail

3.0 ▲	SO	Track on left and track on right.
▼ 1.8	SO	Track on left and track on right; then pass under railroad; then track on left and track on right.
2.7 ▲	SO	Track on left and track on right; then pass under railroad; then track on left and track on right.

GPS: N41°32.16′ W122°11.76′

▼ 2.3	SO	Track on left.
2.2 ▲	SO	Track on right.
▼ 2.9	SO	Track on right is 42N18; then track on left.
1.6 ▲	SO	Track on right; then track on left is 42N18.

GPS: N41°31.41′ W122°11.09′

▼ 3.4	SO	Track on left is 43N72.
1.1 ▲	SO	Track on right is 43N72.

▼ 4.5	BL	Track on right is Andesite Logging Road (42N16) to North Gate Trailhead. Zero trip meter and follow the sign to McCloud.
0.0 ▲		Continue to the northwest, remaining on 43N19.

GPS: N41°30.21′ W122°10.73′

▼ 0.0		Continue to the east, remaining on 43N19.
2.3 ▲	BR	Track on left is Andesite Logging Road (42N16) to North Gate Trailhead. Zero trip meter.
▼ 0.5	SO	Track on right.
1.8 ▲	SO	Track on left.
▼ 0.7	SO	Leaving motor travel restricted area.
1.6 ▲	SO	Entering motor travel restricted area.
▼ 2.0	SO	Military Pass. Track on right.
0.3 ▲	SO	Military Pass. Track on left.

GPS: N41°29.75′ W122°08.69′

Herd Peak Trail

▼ 2.3	SO	Track on right is 42N76 to Brewer Creek Trailhead. Zero trip meter and follow sign to McCloud.
▲		Continue to the west, remaining on 43N19.

GPS: N41°29.56′ W122°08.41′

▼ 0.0		Continue to the east, remaining on 43N19.
▲	SO	Track on left is 42N76 to Brewer Creek Trailhead. Zero trip meter and follow the sign to US 97.
▼ 0.4	SO	Track on right.
▲	SO	Track on left.
▼ 0.8	SO	Track on right.
▲	SO	Track on left.
▼ 0.9	SO	Track on right.
▲	SO	Track on left.
▼ 1.6	SO	Track on right.
▲	SO	Track on left.
▼ 1.8	SO	Track on left.
▲	SO	Track on right.
▼ 2.3	SO	Track on left.
▲	SO	Track on right.
▼ 2.4	SO	Track on right is 42N64.
▲	SO	Track on left is 42N64.

GPS: N41°28.77′ W122°05.77′

▼ 2.7	BL	Track on right is 43N19X.
▲	BR	Track on left is 43N19X. Follow sign to Military Pass.

GPS: N41°28.61′ W122°05.59′

▼ 3.1		Trail ends at 4-way intersection. Graded road on left and right is North Coast #33: Mount Shasta Loop (FR 19). Straight ahead is 42N20. Turn right for the town of Mount Shasta; turn left to exit to US 97.
▲ 0.0		Trail commences on North Coast #33: Mount Shasta Loop (FR 19), 5.2 miles from the north end. Zero trip meter at 4-way intersection and turn southwest onto 43N19. Track opposite is 42N20. The formed trail is unmarked, but is well-used. There are directional signs on FR 19 to California 89 to the east and US 97 to the west at the intersection.

GPS: N41°28.61′ W122°05.14′

STARTING POINT US 97, 0.5 miles south of Grass Valley Maintenance Station
FINISHING POINT Herd Peak Fire Lookout
TOTAL MILEAGE 5.5 miles (one-way)
UNPAVED MILEAGE 5.5 miles
DRIVING TIME 30 minutes (one-way)
ELEVATION RANGE 5,100–7,000 feet
USUALLY OPEN June to October
BEST TIME TO TRAVEL Fire season (when the lookout is manned)
DIFFICULTY RATING 1
SCENIC RATING 8
REMOTENESS RATING +0

Special Attractions

■ Views of Mount Shasta and the surrounding forests.
■ Herd Peak Fire Lookout.

History

This short trail to the summit of Herd Peak (7,071 feet) offers spectacular views of nearby Mount Shasta to the east. The trail and peak overlook the route of the Yreka Trail, an emigrant trail developed in 1852 as part of a network that brought gold seekers to California. The Yreka Trail branched off from the Applegate Trail near Oklahoma Flat, just south of Klamath Lake. From there it headed southwest through the Cascade Range to Butte Creek, which is visible from Herd Peak Trail. The wagon road continued west, skirting the southern edge of Grass Lake along a route similar to today's US 97. It passed over the rise at the start of the described vehicle trail. The emigrant trail then swung south, gradually dropping to traverse the southern side of Sheep Rock (5,705 feet) heading due south of Herd Peak. At this point it joined a fur trappers' trail and headed northwest, descending near Yellow Butte to roughly follow the course of the old Cutoff Road, known today as CR A12. Shortly after this, the trail forked: One branch went north to Little Shasta and the other made its way to Yreka.

Easygoing shelf road goes to the lookout on Herd Peak

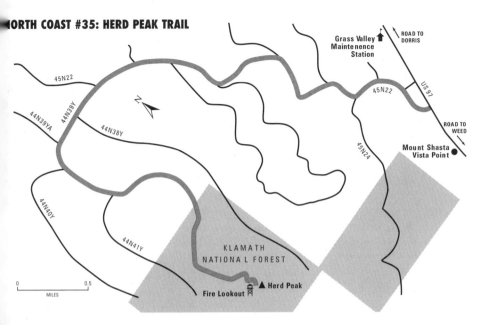

Description

This trail follows a graded dirt road through privately owned forest before entering Klamath National Forest for the climb to Herd Peak's summit. Fire spotters occupy the lookout tower during the fire season—normally late May to mid September. During this time, the gate is open and you can visit the lookout in your vehicle. Visiting hours are from 9:30 A.M. to 5:30 P.M. You are normally welcome to climb the tower with permission from the lookout on duty. The gate is closed outside fire season or these hours, in which case it is a 1-mile hike from the locked gate to the lookout tower.

The trail forms part of a loop used by mountain bikers that starts and ends at the start of the vehicle route. It is rated for moderate to advanced riders.

Current Road Information

Bureau of Land Management
Redding Field Office
355 Hemsted Drive
Redding, CA 96002
(530) 224-2100

Klamath National Forest
Goosenest Ranger District

37805 Highway 97
Macdoel, CA 96058
(530) 398-4391

Map References

BLM Yreka
USFS Klamath National Forest
USGS 1:24,000 Grass Lake, The
Whaleback
1:100,000 Yreka
Maptech CD-ROM: Shasta-Trinity/Modoc
Northern California Atlas & Gazetteer, p. 26
California Road & Recreation Atlas, p. 46

Route Directions

▼ 0.0   From US 97, 0.5 miles south of Grass Valley Maintenance Station and 0.3 miles north of the Mount Shasta Vista Point, zero trip meter and turn east on 45N22. Cross cattle guard.
         GPS: N41°37.47' W122°11.84'

▼ 0.3   SO Track on right.
▼ 0.4   SO Track on right.
▼ 0.6   BR Track on left is 45N24.
         GPS: N41°37.83' W122°12.13'

▼ 0.8   SO Track on right.
▼ 1.1   SO Track on left.

▼ 1.4	SO	Track on right.
▼ 1.7	SO	Track on left.
▼ 2.3	SO	Track on left.
▼ 2.5	SO	Track on right.
▼ 2.8	BL	Road straight ahead is continuation of 45N22. Bear left onto 44N39Y, following the sign to Herd Peak. Small track on left. Zero trip meter.

GPS: N41°39.15′ W122°13.30′

▼ 0.0		Continue to the west.
▼ 0.3	SO	Track on left is 44N38Y.
▼ 0.5	SO	Track on right is 44N39YA.
▼ 0.7	SO	Track on right is 44N40Y.
▼ 1.0	SO	Track on right is 44N41Y.

GPS: N41°38.70′ W122°13.94′

▼ 1.7	SO	Gate. Entering Klamath National Forest.

GPS: N41°38.33′ W122°13.53′

▼ 2.7		Trail ends at the Herd Peak Fire Lookout.

GPS: N41°37.69′ W122°13.80′

NORTH COAST #36

Klamath River Road

STARTING POINT California 96 at Ash Creek Bridge, 1.8 miles west of the intersection with California 263

FINISHING POINT California 96 at Walker Bridge, 0.9 miles west of the Klamath River Post Office

TOTAL MILEAGE 18.1 miles

UNPAVED MILEAGE 16.1 miles

DRIVING TIME 2 hours

ELEVATION RANGE 1,700–2,000 feet

USUALLY OPEN Year-round

BEST TIME TO TRAVEL Year-round

DIFFICULTY RATING 2

SCENIC RATING 9

REMOTENESS RATING +0

Special Attractions

- Road parallels the Klamath River and is great for mountain bikes as well as vehicles.
- Excellent fishing in the Klamath River.
- Many raft put-ins.

History

The gold rush to Yreka in 1851 saw miners scouring the entire vicinity in search of a lucky strike. The Klamath River did not escape their scrutiny, and in time camps sprang up along the river. Klamath River Road, also known as Walker Road, passes the site of Walker, long gone from today's maps. The old settlement was at the mouth of Barkhouse Creek, not far from the western end of this road.

In 1851, a rough pack trail was built from the coast up through the river's deep valley. Rocks, boulders, and trees were pushed aside to establish this trail. The earliest wagon road to enter the Klamath River Valley did so from Yreka, north to Hawkinsville, up and over to Humbug, and down along Humbug Creek. Freshour Ferry took wagons across the Klamath near the mouth of Dutch Creek, just east of Gottville. Wagon roads then traveled north up Dutch, Empire, and Lumgrey Creeks before reverting to pack trails that climbed into the Siskiyou Mountains.

The Honolulu School was established just west of Kanaka Bar and Cemetery in 1890. These names reflect the presence of Hawaiian miners in the region. Rather than mine, Chinese settlers started market gardens near Humbug Point. The Trees of Heaven Campground on the north side of the river was the site of one of the gardens that supplied fresh produce to mining camps. The Chinese introduced trees of heaven, also called ailanthus, to California.

The Ash Creek Bridge, at the east end of the road, was built in September 1901, a project supported in part by Abner Weed, a county supervisor and Civil War veteran for whom the town of Weed is named.

Description

For travelers wanting a leisurely drive along the Klamath River, California 96 can be a disappointment. The mostly graded dirt Klamath River Road, on the south side of the river, is a much better alternative. The rougher surface ensures a slow speed, with time to appreciate vibrant colors in fall or to find a perfect fishing spot. Great blue herons and eagles are commonly sighted here.

The trail starts at Ash Creek Bridge. The

The Ash Creek Bridge, built in 1901

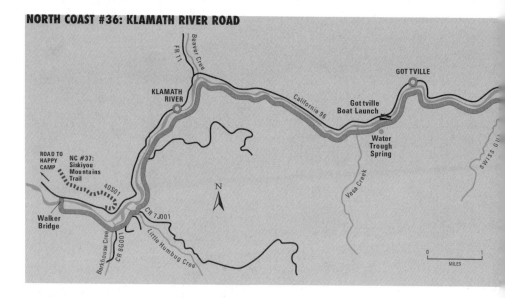

road is mainly single-vehicle width, and some sections, especially where the road passes around rocky outcroppings high above the river, are rough enough to make high-clearance preferable. Passing places are limited on some of these sections, and there is often quite a drop below the shelf road.

The trail accesses many fishing spots and marked boat put-ins along the river. Campers will enjoy the developed USFS Trees of Heaven Campground on the far side of the river, just west of the start of the trail. Mountain bikers can also take advantage of this easy, scenic riverside route.

The trail ends by crossing the Walker Bridge to rejoin California 96.

Current Road Information
Klamath National Forest
Scott River Ranger District
11263 North Highway 3
Fort Jones, CA 96032
(530) 468-5351

Map References
BLM   Yreka
USFS Klamath National Forest
USGS 1:24,000   Hawkinsville, Badger
      Mt., McKinley Mtn.
      1:100,000   Yreka
Maptech CD-ROM: Shasta-Trinity/Modoc

Northern California Atlas & Gazetteer,
   pp. 26, 25
California Road & Recreation Atlas, p. 46

Route Directions

▼ 0.0   From California 96 at the Klamath
           National Forest boundary, 1.8 miles
           west of the intersection with California
           263 and 9 miles north of Yreka, zero
           trip meter and turn south. Cross over
           the Klamath River on Ash Creek Bridge
           and proceed on CR 8J001.
3.4 ▲   Cross over Ash Creek Bridge; then trail
           ends at intersection with California 96.
           Turn left for Happy Camp; turn right for
           Yreka and I-5.
           GPS: N41°50.05′ W122°37.15′

▼ 0.4   SO   Ash Creek River Access on right.
3.0 ▲   SO   Ash Creek River Access on left.
▼ 1.8   BL   Track on right to Garvey Bar.
1.6 ▲   BR   Track on left to Garvey Bar.
             GPS: N41°49.65′ W122°38.79′

▼ 2.1   SO   Track on right.
1.3 ▲   SO   Track on left.
▼ 2.4   SO   Track on right to river; then track on
             left; then second track on right.
1.0 ▲   SO   Track on left; then track on right; then
             second track on left to river.

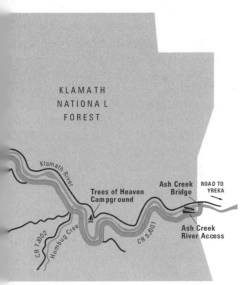

KLAMATH
NATIONAL
FOREST

Klamath River

Trees of Heaven
Campground

Ash Creek
Bridge

ROAD TO
YREKA

Ash Creek
River Access

CR 7J002

Humbug Creek

CR 8J001

▼ 3.4   BR Cross over Humbug Creek on bridge;
            then graded road on left is CR 7J002.
            Zero trip meter.
0.0 ▲   Continue to the east and cross over
            Humbug Creek on bridge.
            GPS: N41°49.97′ W122°39.97′

▼ 0.0   Continue to the north on 46N13Y.
6.3 ▲   BL Graded road on right is CR 7J002.
            Zero trip meter.
▼ 0.2   SO Track on left.
6.1 ▲   SO Track on right.
▼ 1.0   SO Track on left.
5.3 ▲   SO Track on right.
▼ 1.3   SO Track on right.
5.0 ▲   SO Track on left.
            GPS: N41°50.58′ W122°41.00′

Water Trough Spring

Trout fishing in the Klamath River

▼ 2.5 SO Track on right.
3.8 ▲ SO Track on left.
▼ 2.6 SO Track on right.
3.7 ▲ SO Track on left.
▼ 3.4 SO Swiss Gulch on left.
2.9 ▲ SO Swiss Gulch on right.
▼ 5.5 SO Track on right. Gottville is on the far side of the river.
0.8 ▲ SO Track on left. Gottville is on the far side of the river.
       GPS: N41°51.91' W122°44.54'

▼ 6.2 SO Gottville Boat Launch on far side of the river.
0.1 ▲ SO Gottville Boat Launch on far side of the river.
       GPS: N41°51.48' W122°44.93'

▼ 6.3 SO Track on right; then Water Trough Spring on left. Zero trip meter.
0.0 ▲   Continue to the north. Track on left.
       GPS: N41°51.42' W122°45.11'

▼ 0.0   Continue to the south. Track on left.
6.5 ▲ SO Track on right; then Water Trough Spring on right. Zero trip meter.
▼ 0.4 SO Cross over Vesa Creek; then track on left.
6.1 ▲ SO Track on right; then cross over Vesa Creek.
▼ 1.2 SO Track on right.
5.3 ▲ SO Track on left.
▼ 3.6 SO Track on right. Beaver Creek is on the far side of the river.
2.9 ▲ SO Track on left. Beaver Creek is on the far side of the river.
       GPS: N41°52.10' W122°48.91'

▼ 5.6 SO Track on left.
0.9 ▲ SO Track on right.
       GPS: N41°50.85' W122°50.11'

▼ 6.4 SO Road becomes paved.
0.1 ▲ SO Road turns to graded dirt.
▼ 6.5 TR T-intersection with paved CR 7J001 (45N30). Zero trip meter.
0.0 ▲   Continue to the northwest.
       GPS: N41°50.09' W122°50.23'

▼ 0.0   Continue to the southwest. Eagles

Grass Lake in the valley below

       Nest Golf Course on right; then cross over Little Humbug Creek on bridge.
1.9 ▲ TL Cross over Little Humbug Creek on bridge; then Eagles Nest Golf Course on left. CR 7J001 (45N30) continues straight ahead. Zero trip meter and turn left onto Walker Road (CR 8J001).
▼ 0.2 SO Lockhaven Drive on left.
1.7 ▲ SO Lockhaven Drive on right.
▼ 0.3 SO Barkhouse Court on left.
1.6 ▲ SO Barkhouse Court on right.
▼ 0.6 BR Graded road on left is CR 8G001 (46N38); then cross over Barkhouse Creek on bridge.
1.3 ▲ BL Cross over Barkhouse Creek on bridge; then graded road on right is CR 8G001 (46N38).
▼ 1.6 TR Paved road continues ahead.
0.3 ▲ TL T-intersection.
       GPS: N41°50.11' W122°51.83'

▼ 1.9   Cross over Klamath River on Walker Bridge; then trail ends at T-intersection with California 96. Turn right for Yreka; turn left for Happy Camp.
0.0 ▲   Trail commences on California 96, 0.9 miles west of Klamath River Post Office. Zero trip meter and turn south on paved road, following the sign for Walker Bridge Road. Immediately cross over the Klamath River on Walker Bridge.
       GPS: N41°50.30' W122°51.81'

Siskiyou Mountains Trail

STARTING POINT California 96, 4.4 miles west of the community of Klamath River
FINISHING POINT Beaver Creek Road (FR 11), 5.4 miles north of California 96
TOTAL MILEAGE 31.6 miles
UNPAVED MILEAGE 30.9 miles
DRIVING TIME 3.5 hours
ELEVATION RANGE 1,800–6,900 feet
USUALLY OPEN June to December
BEST TIME TO TRAVEL June to December
DIFFICULTY RATING 2
SCENIC RATING 10
REMOTENESS RATING +1

Special Attractions

- Condrey Mountain Blueschist Geological Area.
- Site of the Dry Lake Fire Lookout.
- Panoramic ridge-top views over California and Oregon.
- Access to a network of trails within the Klamath and Rogue River National Forests.

History

Siskiyou Mountains Trail begins in the homeland of the Karok. The tribal name Karok means "upriver" and refers to their territory on the upper section of the Klamath River. The river defined the Karok's way of life, providing transportation and abundant salmon and trout. The Karok were exceptional basket makers who wove baskets so tight they were capable of carrying water. Their traditional way of life was disrupted by the arrival of miners in the early 1850s, and their fishing grounds were spoiled with dams, dredging, diversion canals, and hydraulic monitors.

The settlement of Klamath River, near the end of this trail, was a commercial center for the region in the 1920s. In the mid-1920s, Willis Quigley built a riverside store and the Klamath River Lodge. The lodge became a popular fishing destination, and Quigley, al-so known as Moon, took guests to prime fishing spots along the river.

Description

The Siskiyou Mountains are part of the Klamath Mountains, which straddle the California-Oregon state line. The region is rugged and quiet; the nearest town, Yreka, is a twisting highway away, and most drivers stick to paved California 96. The trail begins on California 96 west of the community of Klamath River. The pavement ends after the Oak Knoll Work Station, and the trail becomes a narrow, roughly graded shelf road that winds into the mountains. The road passes through privately owned forest, maintained for timber harvesting, interspersed with patches of Klamath National Forest. Trail markings are sporadic. Many well-used tracks are unmarked or have signs that have fallen into disrepair. GPS coordinates have been given for these intersections.

As the trail climbs into the range, the views get better and better. Mount Shasta dominates the skyline to the south, and there are fantastic views over the convoluted ridges and mountains of Klamath National Forest to the west.

Deer Camp, a designated undeveloped USFS camping area, is in the shade at the edge of Deer Camp Meadows. Once on the ridge tops, the trees give way to sparser vegetation. The site of an old fire lookout, which operated until 1970, is passed at Dry Lake. As you might expect, views from this spot are tremendous. The lookout site marks the southern end of the Condrey Mountain Blueschist Geological Area, which contains metamorphic blue schist. The rock is flaky and has a high percentage of mica. Twisted ridges of blue schist can be seen along the northwestern end of the trail.

The trail turns northeast near Alex Hole and runs along the crest of a ridge, paralleling the course of the Pacific Crest National Scenic Trail. This part of the trail provides wonderful views into Oregon. The Siskiyou Mountains Trail leaves the ridge at Wards Fork Gap and descends a shelf road to the south, traveling above the West Fork of Beaver Creek. Two lonely graves can be

Mount Shasta rises above the Condrey Mountain Blueschist Geological Area

found beside the trail near the confluence of Trapper and West Fork Beaver Creeks.

Fall colors along Beaver Creek and the Klamath River are particularly brilliant, making the crisp days of early autumn an excellent time to travel this route. Campers must be sure they are on public land before pitching their tents; Deer Camp is the best site along the trail. Other sites are scarce because of the shelf road and sections of privately owned forest.

Snowmobiles use parts of this route in winter.

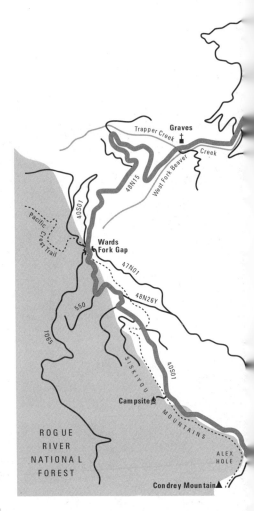

Current Road Information

Klamath National Forest
Scott River Ranger District
11263 North Highway 3
Fort Jones, CA 96032
(530) 468-5351

Map References

BLM Yreka
USFS Klamath National Forest, Rogue River National Forest
USGS 1:24,000 McKinley Mtn., Horse Creek, Buckhorn Bally, Condrey Mtn.
1:100,000 Yreka
Maptech CD-ROM: Shasta-Trinity/Modoc
Northern California Atlas & Gazetteer, p. 25
California Road & Recreation Atlas, p. 46

Route Directions

▼ 0.0   From California 96, 4.4 miles west of Klamath River (measured from the bridge over Beaver Creek), zero trip meter and turn northeast on paved road 40S01. The turn is 0.1 miles east of the Klamath River Post Office. Note that this road is shown as FR 20 on the forest map.

2.3 ▲   Trail ends at T-intersection with paved California 96. Turn left for Yreka; turn right for Happy Camp.

        GPS: N41°50.14′ W122°50.90′

▼ 0.6   SO Pass Oak Knoll USFS Work Station.
1.7 ▲   SO Pass Oak Knoll USFS Work Station.

▼ 0.7   SO Cattle guard. Road turns to graded dirt.
1.6 ▲   SO Cattle guard. Road is now paved.

        GPS: N41°50.41′ W122°51.04′

▼ 0.8   BL Track on right is 46N82.
1.5 ▲   BR Track on left is 46N82.
▼ 2.3   BR Graded road on left is 46N42. Zero trip meter.
0.0 ▲   Continue to the south, remaining on 40S01.

        GPS: N41°51.04′ W122°51.97′

▼ 0.0   Continue to the northeast, remaining on 40S01.
4.9 ▲   SO Graded road on right is 46N42. Zero

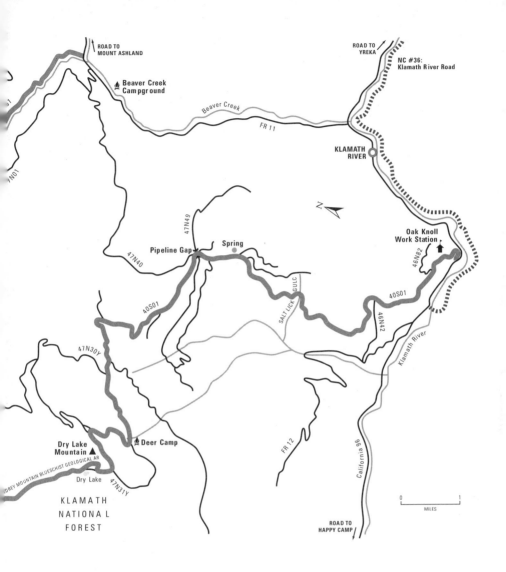

trip meter.

▼ 0.1   SO   Track on right.
4.8 ▲   SO   Track on left.
▼ 2.3   SO   Cross through Salt Lick Gulch.
2.6 ▲   SO   Cross through Salt Lick Gulch.

       GPS: N41°52.20′ W122°52.26′

▼ 2.9   SO   Track on left is 47N55.
2.0 ▲   SO   Track on right is 47N55.
▼ 3.9   SO   Track on right.
1.0 ▲   BR   Track on left.
▼ 4.1   TL   Turn left at T-intersection. Spring at intersection.
0.8 ▲   TR   Graded road continues straight ahead. Spring at intersection.

       GPS: N41°53.28′ W122°51.97′

▼ 4.3   SO   Track on right is 47N55Y.
0.6 ▲   SO   Track on left is 47N55Y.
▼ 4.5   BR   Track on left through gate. Remain on 40S01, following the sign to Deer Camp.
0.4 ▲   SO   Track on right through gate. Remain on 40S01, following the sign to California 96.

       GPS: N41°53.55′ W122°52.13′

▼ 4.9   BL   6-way intersection at Pipeline Gap. Track on right, second track on right is 47N49, and graded road on right is 47N40 to Beaver Creek USFS

		Campground. Also track on left. Bear left, following the sign to Deer Camp, and zero trip meter.
0.0 ▲		Continue to the southeast, remaining on 40S01.
		GPS: N41°53.84' W122°52.12'

▼ 0.0		Continue to the west, remaining on 40S01.
3.8 ▲	BR	6-way intersection at Pipeline Gap. Graded road on left is 47N40 to Beaver Creek USFS Campground, second track on left is 47N49, and third track on left. Also track on right. Bear right, following the sign to Oak Knoll Work Station, and zero trip meter.
▼ 0.5	SO	Track on right.
3.3 ▲	SO	Track on left.
▼ 1.1	SO	Track on left.
2.7 ▲	SO	Track on right.
▼ 1.7	SO	Track on left is 47N59.
2.1 ▲	SO	Track on right is 47N59.
		GPS: N41°54.39' W122°53.84'

▼ 1.9	SO	Track on left.
1.9 ▲	SO	Track on right.
▼ 2.2	SO	Track on left.
1.6 ▲	SO	Track on right.
▼ 2.4	SO	Track on right.
1.4 ▲	SO	Track on left.
▼ 2.8	SO	Track on right.
1.0 ▲	SO	Track on left.
▼ 2.8	BR	Track on left; then track on right.
1.0 ▲	SO	Track on left; then track on right.
▼ 3.1	SO	Two tracks on right.
0.7 ▲	SO	Two tracks on left.
▼ 3.2	SO	Track on right.
0.6 ▲	SO	Track on left.
▼ 3.4	SO	Track on left.
0.4 ▲	SO	Track on right.
▼ 3.8	SO	Track on right is 47N30Y. Entering travel restricted area. Zero trip meter.
0.0 ▲		Continue to the northeast.
		GPS: N41°54.59' W122°54.77'

▼ 0.0		Continue to the southwest.
3.6 ▲	SO	Track on left is 47N30Y. Leaving travel restricted area. Zero trip meter.
▼ 0.4	SO	Track on left.
3.2 ▲	SO	Track on right.

▼ 1.0	SO	Track on right.
2.6 ▲	SO	Track on left.
▼ 1.1	BR	Track on left; then smaller track on left into Deer Camp (unmarked).
2.5 ▲	SO	Track on right into Deer Camp (unmarked); then second track on right.
		GPS: N41°54.06' W122°55.68'

▼ 1.2	SO	Cross over creek; then track on left is 47N31Y. Passing through Deer Camp Meadows.
2.4 ▲	SO	Passing through Deer Camp Meadows. Track on right is 47N31Y; then cross over creek.
▼ 2.2	SO	Track on right.
1.4 ▲	SO	Track on left.
▼ 2.3	SO	Track on right.
1.3 ▲	SO	Track on left.
▼ 2.8	SO	Track on left.
0.8 ▲	SO	Track on right.
▼ 3.0	SO	Track on left is 47N31Y.
0.6 ▲	SO	Track on right is 47N31Y.
		GPS: N41°54.17' W122°56.42'

▼ 3.3	TR	Track continues straight ahead around Dry Lake. Turn right onto smaller track to pass the site of Dry Lake Fire Lookout.
0.3 ▲	TL	T-intersection with 40S01.
		GPS: N41°54.40' W122°56.49'

▼ 3.5	SO	Site of Dry Lake Fire Lookout.
0.1 ▲	SO	Site of Dry Lake Fire Lookout.
		GPS: N41°54.48' W122°56.37'

▼ 3.6	TR	T-intersection. Zero trip meter.
0.0 ▲		Continue to the southeast. Trail leaves Condrey Mountain Blueschist Geological Area.
		GPS: N41°54.56' W122°56.49'

▼ 0.0		Continue to the northwest, rejoining 40S01. Trail now passes through Condrey Mountain Blueschist Geological Area.
1.9 ▲	TL	Track continues straight ahead. Zero trip meter and turn left onto smaller track to pass the site of Dry Lake Fire Lookout.
▼ 0.6	SO	Track on left.

1.3 ▲	SO	Track on right.
▼ 1.9	BR	Track on left to Alex Hole. Zero trip meter and follow the sign to Mount Ashland.
0.0 ▲		Continue to the east, remaining on 40S01.
		GPS: N41°55.85′ W122°57.85′

▼ 0.0		Continue to the northwest, remaining on 40S01.
5.6 ▲	SO	Track on right to Alex Hole. Zero trip meter and follow the sign to Klamath River.
▼ 0.3	SO	Leaving Condrey Mountain Blueschist Geological Area on right.
5.3 ▲	SO	Passing through Condrey Mountain Blueschist Geological Area on left.
▼ 1.3	SO	Track on left.
4.3 ▲	SO	Track on right.
▼ 2.0	SO	Track on left at campsite. Pacific Crest Trail crosses and now runs parallel to the vehicle route on the north side.
3.6 v	SO	Track on right at campsite. Pacific Crest Trail crosses.
		GPS: N41°57.34′ W122°57.19′

▼ 3.2	SO	Track on right.
2.4 ▲	SO	Track on left.
▼ 3.4	SO	Track on left.
2.2 ▲	SO	Track on right.
▼ 3.7	BR	Track on left. Leaving travel restricted area.
1.9 ▲	BL	Track on right. Entering travel restricted area.
		GPS: N41°58.35′ W122°55.90′

▼ 3.9	SO	Track on right is 48N26Y.
1.7 ▲	SO	Track on left is 48N26Y.
▼ 4.5	TR	T-intersection. Track 550 on left goes into Rogue River National Forest.
1.1 ▲	TL	Track 550 continues straight ahead into Rogue River National Forest.
		GPS: N41°58.71′ W122°55.78′

▼ 4.8	SO	Track on left.
0.8 ▲	SO	Track on right.
▼ 5.1	SO	Track on right.
0.5 ▲	BR	Track on left
		GPS: N41°58.89′ W122°55.28′

▼ 5.2	SO	Track on left.
0.4 ▲	BL	Track on right.
▼ 5.4	SO	Pacific Crest Trail crosses on a sharp left-hand bend.
0.2 ▲	SO	Pacific Crest Trail crosses on a sharp right-hand bend.
▼ 5.6	BR	6-way intersection at Wards Fork Gap. First track on left is 1065 to Upper Applegate in Rogue River National Forest. Second track on left is 48N16. Straight ahead is 40S01 to Mount Ashland. Track on immediate right is 47N01. Zero trip meter and bear right onto lower shelf road 48N15 to Klamath River. Pacific Crest Trail crosses through this intersection.
0.0 ▲		Continue to the south.
		GPS: N41°59.03′ W122°54.99′

▼ 0.0		Continue to the northeast.
6.5 ▲	BL	6-way intersection at Wards Fork Gap. Track on immediate right is 40S01 to Mount Ashland. Second track on right is 48N16. Straight ahead is 1065 to Upper Applegate in Rogue River National Forest. First track on left is 47N01. Zero trip meter and bear second left onto 40S01. Pacific Crest Trail crosses through this intersection.
▼ 1.5	SO	Track on left.
5.0 ▲	SO	Track on right.
▼ 1.8	SO	Track on left through closure gate.
4.7 ▲	SO	Track on right through closure gate.
▼ 2.6	SO	Track on left.
3.9 ▲	SO	Track on right.
▼ 2.7	BR	Track on left through closure gate.
3.8 ▲	BL	Track on right through closure gate.
		GPS: N41°59.11′ W122°52.82′

▼ 5.2	SO	Cross over Trapper Creek on bridge; then grave on right of trail.
1.3 ▲	SO	Grave on left of trail; then cross over Trapper Creek on bridge.
		GPS: N41°58.13′ W122°52.72′

▼ 5.4	SO	Graded road on right; then grave surrounded by wooden fence on hillside on left.
1.1 ▲	BR	Grave surrounded by wooden fence on hillside on right; then graded road

on left.

GPS: N41°57.95′ W122°52.66′

▼ 6.1   SO   Track on right.
0.4 ▲   BR   Track on left.
▼ 6.3   SO   Graded road on left.
0.2 ▲   SO   Graded road on right.

GPS: N41°57.32′ W122°52.23′

▼ 6.5   SO   Graded road on right is 47N01. Zero
             trip meter.
0.0 ▲   Continue to the northwest.

GPS: N41°57.28′ W122°52.00′

▼ 0.0   Continue to the east, joining 47N01.
3.0 ▲   BR   Graded road on left is the continuation
             of 47N01. Zero trip meter and bear
             right onto 48N15, following sign to
             Wards Fork Gap.
▼ 2.3   SO   Track on left.
0.7 ▲   SO   Track on right.
▼ 3.0   Trail ends at T-intersection with Beaver
             Creek Road (FR 11, 48N01). Turn left
             for Mount Ashland; turn right for
             California 96.
0.0 ▲   Trail commences on Beaver Creek Road
             (FR 11, 48N01) immediately west of the
             bridge over Beaver Creek, 0.7 miles north
             of Beaver Creek USFS Campground and
             5.4 miles north of California 96. Zero trip
             meter and turn northwest onto graded
             dirt road 47N01.

GPS: N41°56.24′ W122°49.23′

NORTH COAST #38

Medicine Lake Trail

STARTING POINT Modoc Volcanic Scenic Byway
(FR 49), 1 mile east of Medicine Lake
FINISHING POINT Davis Road (FR 15) at
Junction 37
TOTAL MILEAGE 7.6 miles
UNPAVED MILEAGE 6.8 miles
DRIVING TIME 1 hour
ELEVATION RANGE 6,400–7,000 feet
USUALLY OPEN June to November
BEST TIME TO TRAVEL June to November

DIFFICULTY RATING 2
SCENIC RATING 9
REMOTENESS RATING +0

Special Attractions

■ Fishing, boating, swimming, camping,
  and picnicking at Medicine Lake.
■ Rockhounding for obsidian at the volcanic lava flow of Little Glass Mountain.
■ Little Mount Hoffman Fire Lookout
  (available for overnight rental).

History

Medicine Lake lies in the center of the collapsed caldera of a massive ancient volcano
called Mount Hoffman, whose lava flows are
known as the Medicine Lake Highlands. The
collapse of Mount Hoffman's summit formed
the 25-square-mile caldera. Subsequent eruptions from smaller cones on the caldera's rim
have obscured the giant volcano's original
shape.

The summit of Little Mount Hoffman
has been the site of a lookout tower since
1924, and it was in use until 1978. The original building was a simple 8 x 8 foot cabin.
One fire spotter, George Dunlap, repeatedly
walked a portion of the Medicine Lake Trail,
from his home at Medicine Lake to the lookout. A larger improved cabin was built in
1930, and a decade later the structure under-
went a general overhaul and concrete footings were installed. Little Mount Hoffman
was renovated in 1994 as part of the National Forest Lookout rental program. The structure offers basic accommodations in a stunning location, at an elevation of 7,310 feet.
The cabin building is not perched on a tower, but it does have a wooden catwalk.

To the west of Little Mount Hoffman, the
trail passes the northern rim of Little Glass
Mountain, named for the type of lava comprising it: obsidian. Indians used obsidian for
arrowheads and other tools. Having such a
supply in their hunting grounds was quite an
asset.

Description

Medicine Lake, in Modoc National Forest, is
a wonderful spot for camping, fishing, and

Little Mount Hoffman Fire Lookout

picnicking. In addition, the trail passes short hiking trails, views over the Medicine Lake Lava Flow, and Little Medicine Lake. A hiking trail of less than half a mile takes you to the edge of the Medicine Lake Lava Flow.

The trail immediately enters the Medicine Lake Recreation Area. Camping is permitted in designated sites only, and there are four developed campgrounds to choose from. These are extremely popular in summer and can be very busy on weekends. They are shady, and some sites have lake views. The day-use area has a boat launch and picnic tables on the lakeshore. There is also a beach for swimming. Medicine Lake and Little Medicine Lake are both stocked with trout, and although it is popular, the fishing is generally good.

The trail passes through a restricted area, where travel is permitted year-round on roads and tracks marked with a green arrow on a white background. Other trails are closed to vehicles, and it is your responsibility to know which roads are open. The forest map shows the open network of trails; they are also posted as you enter the restricted area. However, maps become outdated and policies change. Tracks mentioned in the route description are for navigational purposes only. If you plan to explore the region further, you should purchase a current forest map and be sure that the roads you wish to travel are legally open.

The trail enters Klamath National Forest at the turn for Little Mount Hoffman Fire Lookout. The lookout can be rented for overnight use from the forest service. Contact the McCloud Ranger District of Shasta-Trinity National Forests for details. The lookout is situated on the boundaries of three national forests: Shasta-Trinity, Klamath, and Modoc. You can visit the lookout in the daytime, but the forest service requests that you give

renters privacy between 8 P.M. and 8 A.M.

The shelf road to the lookout provides fantastic views to the south over Little Glass Mountain, a barren area of jagged lava rock with little vegetation. Rockhounds will find it easy to pick up specimens of obsidian.

As the main trail wraps around the northern edge of Little Glass Mountain, you can see the abrupt halt of the lava, which looks like a cliff beside the trail. Those looking for an undeveloped backcountry campsite will find some pleasant ones tucked into the trees on the edge of the lava flow.

The trail ends on paved Davis Road (FR 15). The route is marked for snowmobile use in winter.

Current Road Information

Klamath National Forest
Goosenest Ranger District
37805 Highway 97
Macdoel, CA 96058
(530) 398-4391

Map References

BLM Tule Lake
USFS Modoc National Forest; Klamath National Forest; Shasta-Trinity National Forests
USGS 1:24,000 Medicine Lake, Little Glass Mtn.
1:100,000 Tule Lake
Maptech CD-ROM: Shasta-Trinity/Modoc
Northern California Atlas & Gazetteer, p. 28
California Road & Recreation Atlas, p. 47
Other: Modoc Country USFS/BLM Map

Route Directions

▼ 0.0   From Modoc Volcanic Scenic Byway (FR 49), 1 mile east of Medicine Lake, zero trip meter and turn west on paved 43N48, following the sign to Medicine Lake. Trail immediately enters the Medicine Lake Recreation Area.

4.2 ▲   Trail ends at T-intersection with paved Modoc Volcanic Scenic Byway (FR 49). Turn left for Lava Beds National Monument; turn right for California 89.

  GPS: N41°35.11′ W121°34.83′

▼ 0.3   TR   Turn right, following sign for the campgrounds. To the left goes 0.2 miles to the day-use areas, which include a swimming area and boat ramp.

3.9 ▲   TL   Road straight ahead goes 0.2 miles to the day-use areas, which include a swimming area and boat ramp.

▼ 0.5   SO   Hemlock USFS Campground on left.

4.7 ▲   SO   Hemlock USFS Campground on right.

▼ 0.7   SO   A. H. Hogue USFS Campground on left. Hiking trail on right goes 0.4 miles to the Medicine Lake Lava Flow.

3.5 ▲   SO   A. H. Hogue USFS Campground on right. Hiking trail on left goes 0.4 miles to the Medicine Lake Lava Flow.

  GPS: N41°35.30′ W121°35.56′

▼ 0.8   SO   Medicine Lake USFS Campground on left. Hiking trail on right goes 0.8 miles to Little Medicine Lake. Road turns to graded dirt. Follow the sign for Schonchin Springs.

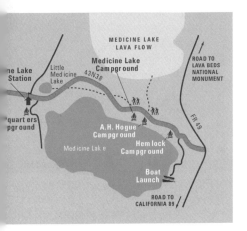

2.5 ▲   SO   Little Medicine Lake on left; then hiking trail crosses.

GPS: N41°35.30′ W121°36.58′

▼ 1.9   SO   Hiking trail on right goes to Little Medicine Lake. Track on left goes to Medicine Lake Guard Station and Headquarters USFS Campground.

2.3 ▲   SO   Hiking trail on left goes to Little Medicine Lake. Track on right goes to Medicine Lake Guard Station and Headquarters USFS Campground.

▼ 2.0   SO   Graded road on right goes to Schonchin Spring. Follow sign to Little Mount Hoffman.

2.2 ▲   SO   Graded road on left goes to Schonchin Spring.

GPS: N41°35.21′ W121°36.88′

▼ 2.6   SO   Track on left.

1.6 ▲   SO   Track on right.

▼ 4.0   SO   Track on right.

0.2 ▲   SO   Track on left.

GPS: N41°34.86′ W121°38.96′

3.4 ▲   SO   Medicine Lake USFS Campground on right. Hiking trail on left goes 0.8 miles to Little Medicine Lake. Road is now paved.

GPS: N41°35.29′ W121°35.74′

▼ 1.1   SO   Hiking trail crosses.

3.1 ▲   SO   Hiking trail crosses.

▼ 1.7   SO   Hiking trail crosses; then Little Medicine Lake on right.

Little Medicine Lake

▼ 4.2 TR Track straight ahead goes 0.6 miles to Little Mount Hoffman Fire Lookout. Zero trip meter and follow the sign for Little Glass Mountain.

0.0 ▲ Continue to the northeast.

GPS: N41°34.80' W121°39.14'

▼ 0.0 Continue to the northwest.

3.4 ▲ TL T-intersection. To the right goes 0.6 miles to Little Mount Hoffman Fire Lookout. Zero trip meter and follow the sign to Medicine Lake.

▼ 1.4 SO Track on left is 43N32. Trail now follows alongside Little Glass Mountain Lava Flow.

2.0 ▲ SO Track on right is 43N32. Trail leaves Little Glass Mountain Lava Flow.

GPS: N41°34.77' W121°40.39'

▼ 1.7 SO Passing alongside Little Glass Mountain.

1.7 ▲ SO Passing alongside Little Glass Mountain.

▼ 2.8 SO Track on left. Leaving Little Glass Mountain Lava Flow.

0.6 ▲ SO Track on right. Trail follows alongside Little Glass Mountain Lava Flow.

▼ 3.4 Trail ends on paved Davis Road (FR 15) at Junction 37. Turn right for Macdoel; turn left for California 89.

0.0 ▲ Trail starts on paved Davis Road (FR 15) at Junction 37. The turn is 2.1 miles south of the intersection with FR 77 and 5 miles south of the Corners Snowmobile Trailhead. Zero trip meter and turn northeast on graded dirt road 43N48.

GPS: N41°34.33' W121°42.46'

NORTH COAST #39

Tule Lake National Wildlife Refuge Trail

STARTING POINT Hill Road, 4.7 miles south of the Tule Lake Visitor Center
FINISHING POINT California 139 on the southern edge of Newell
TOTAL MILEAGE 15.4 miles

UNPAVED MILEAGE 10.6 miles
DRIVING TIME 1 hour
ELEVATION RANGE 4,000–4,200 feet
USUALLY OPEN Year-round
BEST TIME TO TRAVEL Year-round
DIFFICULTY RATING 1
SCENIC RATING 10
REMOTENESS RATING +0

Special Attractions

- Petroglyphs at Petroglyph Point in Lava Beds National Monument.
- Excellent waterfowl viewing in Tule Lake National Wildlife Refuge.
- Historic sites of Captain Jacks Stronghold, Canby Cross, and the Japanese internment camp at Newell.

History

The Tule Lake Basin has been occupied by humans possibly as early as 11,000 years ago. At an elevation close to 4,000 feet, winter conditions here were more favorable than those in neighboring mountain ranges.

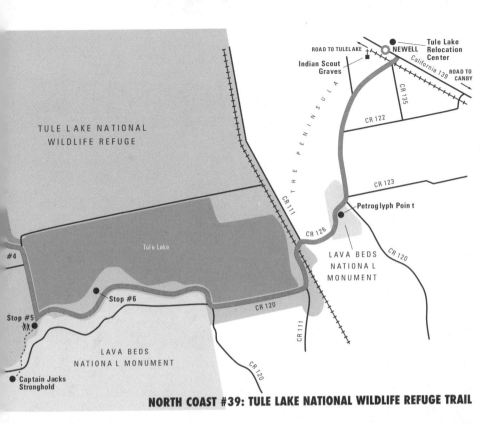

ROAD TO TULELAKE

Indian Scout
Graves

NEWELL

Tule Lake
Relocation
Center

California 139

ROAD TO
CANBY

CR 135

CR 122

THE PENINSULA

TULE LAKE NATIONAL
WILDLIFE REFUGE

CR 111

CR 123

CR 126

Petroglyph Point

#4

Tule Lake

LAVA BEDS
NATIONAL
MONUMENT

CR 120

Stop #6

CR 120

CR 111

Stop #5

LAVA BEDS
NATIONAL MONUMENT

CR 120

Captain Jacks
Stronghold

NORTH COAST #39: TULE LAKE NATIONAL WILDLIFE REFUGE TRAIL

Migratory birds at the Tule Lake National Wildlife Refuge

The volcanic formations on the shores of Tule Lake—Captain Jacks Stronghold

The Modoc have lived in the region for generations, and evidence of their habitation includes rock rings, developed depressions, middens, and broken and chipped tools. Tules, or reeds, were used to build shelters and boats.

Settlers and miners arrived in the region by the 1850s. Initially, relations were peaceful, but conflicts inevitably arose. The Modoc were eventually removed to a reservation in Oregon, which led to the Modoc War in 1872–73.

The Tule Lake National Wildlife Refuge Trail passes Petroglyph Point, once surrounded by Tule Lake. The people who created symbols here may predate the Modoc. Most of the petroglyphs are geometric shapes; there are very few animal and human figures. The exact date of the petroglyphs is not known, but many are thought to be between 2,500 and 4,500 years old. Many of the petroglyphs have suffered from wind and rain eroding the friable rock surface. The high outcrop is also known as Prisoner Rock, because Japanese detainees from the Tule Lake Relocation Center at Newell left inscriptions, too. More than 19,000 persons of Japanese ancestry were incarcerated here during World War II.

John C. Frémont passed this way in the spring of 1846, on his third western expedition. He named the lake Rhett in honor of his friend Barnwell Rhett of South Carolina. The name Rhett Lake remained until the late 1870s. In 1900, the nearby post office registered the name Tulelake.

The original shallow lake once covered almost 100,000 acres before the land was "reclaimed" and drained from 1912 to 1958. The reclamation effort created a more reliable water source and a massive expanse of fertile land for homesteads and large-scale agriculture. Prior to reclamation, the western edge of the lake was called High Rim, and its northern boundary stretched just over the Oregon state line; to the south, the lake extended to the northern boundary of today's Lava Beds National Monument. Tule Lake today is approximately one sixth its former size. In 1926, the Tule Lake National Wildlife Refuge was established. It is one of six wildlife refuges comprising the Klamath Basin National Refuges Complex.

Description

This easy trail travels a mix of paved and gravel roads past a variety of interesting features in the Tule Lake region. The first section runs along the gravel roads of Tule Lake National Wildlife Refuge. It passes along the south side of Sump 1-A before swinging alongside Sump 1-B. The bird life is prolific; thousands of birds inhabit or migrate through these wetlands. Pheasants live in the grasslands, and mule deer are often spotted near the lake. Photographers may like to take advantage of blinds on the water's edge. Hundreds of species of wildlife have been observed in the Klamath Basin. Fall and spring are excellent times to visit, as migratory flocks of ducks, geese, and other waterfowl pass through the refuge.

The trail exits the refuge at a 4-way intersection. To the right goes to the historical sites of Captain Jacks Stronghold and Canby Cross. There are two hikes at Captain Jacks Stronghold: A 0.5-mile trail loops around the inner stronghold, and a 1.5-mile trail loops to the outer line of defenses. Hikers can reach Captain Jacks Stronghold through the wildlife refuge by following an old vehicle trail that intersects the paved road opposite the trailhead. Please note that tracks mentioned in the refuge are not necessarily open to vehicles; they are mentioned for navigation purposes only.

The main trail turns east and follows a paved road for a short distance before turning off to enter a small section of Lava Beds National Monument. Here, the promontory of Petroglyph Point rises abruptly from the bed of what was once Lake Modoc. More than 5,000 symbols have been carved into the rock, making this one of the largest concentrations of petroglyphs in North America. Petroglyph Point is also an important nesting site for many species of birds. Sixteen raptor species have been sighted here, including red-tailed hawks, prairie falcons, and kestrels.

The trail ends on California 139 in Newell, a short distance south of the internment camp site.

Kientopoos

Indians in California suffered greatly from the white intrusion into their traditional homelands. Despite this, the Golden State had few of the conflicts that characterized Indian relations elsewhere in the west. An exception lasted over a short period when bands of Modoc in Northern California resisted U.S. Army troops in the 1870s.

Disagreements between the Modoc Indians and American settlers began as early as 1852, when a group of Modoc warriors who were accused of slaughtering a small party of whites were invited to a peace parley and then massacred. In response, the tribe ambushed a wagon train at Bloody Point and killed 65 settlers. Hostilities continued until 1864, when the Modoc agreed to move to a reservation in Oregon shared with their traditional enemies, the Klamath. However, the tribe found it impossible to coexist there.

During this tumultuous period, Chief Kientopoos (known to whites as Captain Jack) led the Modoc tribe. Kientopoos, also known as Kintpuash, was a Modoc born around 1839 near the village of Wa'chamshwash, situated on Lost River on the California-Oregon border. During his adolescence, his village and tribe faced increased encroachments by American settlers into their homeland. Kientopoos's father, a village chief, advocated retaliation against the settlers, but his young son spoke out against this. Kientopoos got on well with some of the local miners. One gave him a military jacket that he often wore. Settlers took to calling the friendly Indian Captain Jack.

In 1864, Kientopoos, who succeeded as chief after settlers killed his father, was leader of a Modoc band when the tribe was forced by treaty to move to a reservation shared with their traditional enemies, the Klamath, in Oregon. The Modoc left the reservation in 1865, partly because of the Klamath's hostility toward them. They returned for a short time in 1869, but some 300 fled permanently, returning to the vicinity of Lost River in 1870. Camping along Lost River, his small band caused inconvenience to whites who grazed cattle in the area. The settlers persuaded the government to force Kientopoos and his people back to the reservation.

In November 1872, U.S. cavalry troops confronted the Indians at their camps. Eight Modoc and seven soldiers were killed in the gunfights that ensued. The retreating Modoc killed several settlers as they fled to their traditional sanctuary called "The Stronghold"

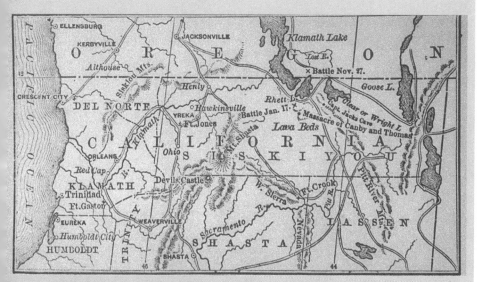

The Modoc War—The Region of the Lava Beds

among the lava beds south of Tule Lake, an area now encompassed by national forests and Lava Beds National Monument.

Kientopoos's band included just 50 to 90 warriors, and the group resisted repeated attacks by regular army and volunteer troops. Kientopoos wanted to negotiate a settlement with the army, but a majority of warriors rejected this approach. Kientopoos met with General Edward Canby, the leader of the American peace party, and other white men over a period of months. Finally, warriors, in a direct challenge to his leadership, persuaded Kientopoos to kill Canby, who had continued to bring reinforcements to the field throughout the negotiations. Within days, in April 1873, the army besieged the Modoc, who fled south.

As conditions worsened, Indians began to defect from Kientopoos's band. One leader, Hooker Jim, who had been the most eager to kill General Canby, surrendered to U.S. forces. He then guided the troops to Kientopoos, now deeply entangled in a conflict that he had never wanted and that he had resisted escalating. He proved adept at eluding the superior forces; he was now outnumbered by more than 20 to 1, and his position was untenable. Knowing that his surrender would mean death, Kientopoos laid down his arms on June 1, 1873.

Kientopoos and five other Indians were put on trial for the murder of General Canby. Hooker Jim, an instigator in the killing, testified against them. The trial was a farce—none of the Indians were fluent in English and no counsel was assigned to their defense. All six were sentenced to death, but President Ulysses S. Grant reduced two sentences to life in prison. On October 3, 1873, Kientopoos and three others were hanged for murder. The chief's body was interred at Fort Klamath, but it was dug up and sent to Washington, D.C., where it was displayed for a dime a view. Eventually, the skeleton was given to the Surgeon General's office, where it was kept as a specimen of Indian anatomy. The few remaining Modocs were sent to Indian Territory, as Oklahoma was called. There diseases virtually eradicated the band. To preserve space to graze cattle, settlers and the army had wiped out a culture that had existed in Northern California for centuries.

Tule Lake Relocation Center, a WW II Japanese Internment camp

Current Road Information

Tule Lake National Wildlife Refuge
4009 Hill Road
Tulelake, CA 26134
(530) 667-2231

Map References

BLM   Cedarville
USFS Modoc National Forest
USGS 1:24,000   Hatfield, Captain Jacks
        Stronghold, The Panhandle, Newell
        1:100,000 Cedarville
Maptech CD-ROM: Shasta-Trinity/Modoc
Northern California Atlas & Gazetteer, p. 28
California Road & Recreation Atlas, p. 47
Other: Modoc Country USFS/BLM Map

Route Directions

▼ 0.0   From paved Hill Road, 4.7 miles south of
         the Tule Lake Visitor Center and Refuge
         Headquarters, zero trip meter and turn
         east on gravel road, following the sign
         for the auto tour. The visitor center is 5

miles east of the town of Tulelake along
East West Road. The trail follows the
south side of Sump 1-A.

4.7 ▲   Trail ends at T-intersection with paved
         Hill Road. Turn right and proceed 4.7
         miles for the Tule Lake Visitor Center
         and Refuge Headquarters.
         GPS: N41°52.73′ W121°33.39′

▼ 0.1   SO Fee station on right. Pay daily fee here
4.6 ▲   SO Fee station on left. Pay daily fee here.
▼ 0.6   SO Auto tour stop #1.
4.1 ▲   SO Auto tour stop #1.
         GPS: N41°52.73′ W121°32.63′

▼ 1.0   TL Track straight ahead.
3.7 ▲   TR Track on left.
▼ 1.4   SO Auto tour stop #2.
3.3 ▲   SO Auto tour stop #2.
▼ 2.4   SO Track on right.
2.3 ▲   SO Track on left.
▼ 2.6   SO Track on right.
2.1 ▲   SO Track on left.
▼ 3.2   SO Auto tour stop #3.

.5 ▲ SO Auto tour stop #3.
  GPS: N41°52.31' W121°29.88'

▼ 4.4 SO Auto tour stop #4.
.3 ▲ SO Auto tour stop #4.
▼ 4.7 TR T-intersection in front of Sump 1-B. Zero trip meter.
.0 ▲ Continue to the west.
  GPS: N41°51.17' W121°29.50'

▼ 0.0 Continue to the south.
.6 ▲ TL Gravel road continues ahead. Zero trip meter.

▼ 0.3 SO Graded road on right.
.3 ▲ SO Graded road on left.
1.1 TL Auto tour stop #5. Turn left at T-intersection. Captain Jacks Stronghold is 0.8 miles southwest of this intersection (on foot) along a disused vehicle trail.
.5 ▲ TR Track continues straight ahead. Auto tour stop #5.
  GPS: N41°50.15' W121°29.48'

▼ 2.5 SO Auto tour stop #6.
.1 ▲ SO Auto tour stop #6.
▼ 2.6 SO Track on left is for authorized vehicles only.
.0 ▲ SO Track on right is for authorized vehicles only.
▼ 2.9 SO Track on left is for authorized vehicles only.
.7 ▲ SO Track on right is for authorized vehicles only.
▼ 3.4 SO Boardwalk on left to blind.
.2 ▲ SO Boardwalk on right to blind.
  GPS: N41°50.22' W121°27.20'

▼ 4.6 TL 4-way intersection. CR 120 is straight ahead and to the left. Paved road on right goes 3.5 miles to Captain Jacks Stronghold. Zero trip meter.
.0 ▲ Continue to the northwest on gravel road.
  GPS: N41°49.84' W121°26.11'

▼ 0.0 Continue to the east on paved CR 120.
.1 ▲ TR 4-way intersection. CR 120 continues to the left. Paved road straight ahead. Zero trip meter.
▼ 1.5 TL T-intersection with paved road. Remain on CR 120. Road on right is CR 111.

4.6 ▲ TR Paved road ahead is CR 111. Turn right, remaining on CR 120, following sign to Lava Beds National Monument Visitors Center.
  GPS: N41°49.87' W121°24.25'

▼ 2.2 TR Cross over railroad; then turn right onto CR 126. Road is now graded dirt.
3.9 ▲ TL Turn left onto CR 120 at T-intersection; then cross over railroad. Road is now paved.
  GPS: N41°50.50' W121°24.26'

▼ 2.8 SO Entering Lava Beds National Monument.
3.3 ▲ SO Leaving Lava Beds National Monument.
▼ 3.1 SO Petroglyph Point on right.
3.0 ▲ SO Petroglyph Point on left.
  GPS: N41°50.73' W121°23.41'

▼ 3.4 SO Petroglyph Bluff Hiking Trail on right. Trailhead parking on left.
2.7 ▲ SO Petroglyph Bluff Hiking Trail on left. Trailhead parking on right.
  GPS: N41°50.90' W121°23.30'

▼ 3.5 BL CR 120 on right. Road becomes paved. Leaving Lava Beds National Monument.
2.6 ▲ BR CR 120 continues to the left. Bear right onto CR 126. Road turns to graded dirt. Entering Lava Beds National Monument.
▼ 3.6 SO CR 123 on right.
2.5 ▲ SO CR 123 on left.
▼ 4.6 SO CR 122 on right.
1.5 ▲ SO CR 122 on left.
▼ 5.2 SO Track on left.
0.9 ▲ SO Track on right.
▼ 6.1 CR 135 on right; then cross over railroad; then trail ends at intersection with California 139 on the southern edge of Newell.
0.0 ▲ Trail commences on California 139 on the southern edge of Newell. Zero trip meter and turn south on paved CR 120, following sign to Captain Jacks Stronghold. Cross over railroad; then CR 135 on left.
  GPS: N41°52.74' W121°21.79'

Sand Buttes Trail

STARTING POINT California 139, 13.7 miles south of Newell

FINISHING POINT FR 10, 8.6 miles northwest of Tionesta

TOTAL MILEAGE 11.7 miles

UNPAVED MILEAGE 10.7 miles

DRIVING TIME 1.5 hours

ELEVATION RANGE 4,200–4,500 feet

USUALLY OPEN May to November

BEST TIME TO TRAVEL Dry weather

DIFFICULTY RATING 3

SCENIC RATING 8

REMOTENESS RATING +0

Special Attractions

- Trail passes historic sites from the Modoc War.
- Cinder pits at East Sand Butte.
- Wide-ranging views from an optional 4-rated spur to the top of East Sand Butte.

History

Skirmishes and battles of the Modoc War of 1872–73 (see page 192) took place in the vicinity of Sand Buttes Trail. The trail passes the Battle of Dry Lake site, where a group of Modoc attacked a unit led by Captain Henry Hasbrouck just before dawn on May 10, 1873. Horses stampeded in all directions at the first volley of shots and loud Indian yells. Men arose from sleep and took up arms. Within minutes, they were charging the nearby bluff where the Modoc had positioned themselves during the night. The troops flanked their assailants on three sides. However, the Modoc retreat was so fast that they had escaped to the next volcanic bluff before the troops and Warm River Indian scouts could cut them off. This flank and retreat battle continued all day and crossed nearly 4 miles before the exhausted troops abandoned pursuit.

Twelve of Hasbrouck's men were wounded during this engagement, and one Modoc was found dead at the battle scene. Two Indian scouts working for the U.S. Army were killed in the battle. There is a memorial to them on California 139 at Newell, at the end of North Coast #39: Tule Lake National Wildlife Refuge Trail.

Description

Sand Buttes Trail travels along the south side of a lava field, east of Lava Beds National Monument. The trail is predominantly smooth, with sections of embedded rock. The surface can be uneven, with some deep, fine sand traps in dry weather. In wet weather the trail is likely to be impassable and should not be attempted.

The turnoff for the trail from California 139 is not marked, but it is opposite Modoc County Road 136, so it is easy to find. The rest of the trail is sketchily marked, so pay close attention to the route directions and GPS coordinates to avoid taking a wrong turn. Right away, the trail enters Modoc National Forest; the entrance is unmarked. The site of the old Dry Lake Guard Station is immediately on the left—the new station is located approximately a mile south of the start of the trail on California 139.

The formed sandy trail passes around the northern edge of Dry Lake, which is littered with volcanic rock and covered with sagebrush. This was the site of the Battle of Dry Lake, one of the final battles in the Modoc War. There is no marker for the lakebed battle site.

The trail continues through open country to join an old railroad grade toward the prominent East Sand Butte. A cinder pit has removed much of the material from the south side of the butte. From the pit, a 4-rated side trail winds around the back of the butte and climbs a rough, narrow shelf road to the top. Hardy curl-leaf mahoganies and windblown junipers grow on top of the butte. The plateau of Devils Garden can be seen to the east.

The main trail turns sharply south and briefly joins the paved road before turning north and heading directly toward Big Sand Butte. Some ruins of stone military fortifications from the Modoc War are at the base of the butte. From here, the trail heads west to rejoin the paved road.

NORTH COAST #40: SAND BUTTES TRAIL

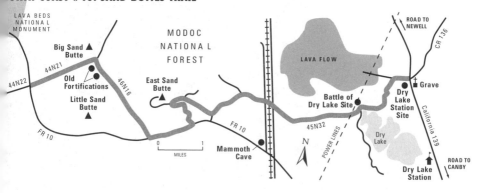

Current Road Information

Modoc National Forest
Double Head Ranger District
PO Box 369
Tulelake, CA 96134
(530) 233-2246

Map References

BLM   Tule Lake

USFS   Modoc National Forest
USGS   1:24,000   Perez, Caldwell Butte
1:100,000   Tule Lake
Maptech CD-ROM: Shasta-Trinity/Modoc
Northern California Atlas & Gazetteer,
pp. 29, 28
California Road & Recreation Atlas, p. 47
Other: Modoc Country USFS/BLM Map

Shelf road climbs along East Sand Butte

East Sand Butte

Route Directions

▼ 0.0   From California 139 opposite CR 136, 13.7 miles south of Newell and 0.1 miles south of Modoc County mile marker 30.5, zero trip meter and turn southwest on unmarked formed dirt trail. There is a grave on the southeast corner of the intersection.

3.9 ▲   Trail finishes at intersection of California 139 opposite CR 136. Turn left for Newell; turn right for Canby. There is a grave on the southeast corner of the intersection.

GPS: N41°42.15' W121°16.79'

▼ 0.1   SO   Pass site of old Dry Lake Guard Station on left.

3.8 ▲   SO   Pass site of old Dry Lake Guard Station on right.

▼ 0.2   SO   Wire gate.

3.7 ▲   SO   Wire gate.

▼ 0.3   TL   Track continues straight ahead along fence line. Turn left onto unmarked trail.

3.6 ▲   TR   T-intersection with track along fence line.

▼ 0.4   BR   Track on left.

3.5 ▲   BL   Track on right.

▼ 1.0   SO   Track on left.

2.9 ▲   SO   Track on right.

GPS: N41°41.62' W121°17.26'

▼ 1.6   TL   Track on right in front of power lines. This is the site of the Battle of Dry Lake (on the northwest corner of Dry Lake). Immediately track on right.

2.3 ▲   TR   Track on left; then turn right. Trail continues straight ahead. This is the site of the Battle of Dry Lake (on the northwest corner of Dry Lake).

GPS: N41°41.48' W121°17.87'

▼ 1.7 BR Track continues straight ahead.
.2 ▲ BL Track on right.
▼ 1.9 SO Pass under power lines.
.0 ▲ SO Pass under power lines.
▼ 2.0 SO Track on left and track on right along power lines.
.9 ▲ SO Track on left and track on right along power lines.
GPS: N41°41.28′ W121°18.14′

▼ 3.9 SO Track on left and track on right. Zero trip meter and cross over railroad.
.0 ▲ Continue to the east. Track on left and track on right.
GPS: N41°41.19′ W121°20.20′

▼ 0.0 Continue to the west. Track on left goes 1.1 miles to Mammoth Cave. Also track on right.
.4 ▲ SO Track on left. Track on right goes 1.1 miles to Mammoth Cave. Cross over railroad and zero trip meter.
▼ 0.7 SO Track on right.
.7 ▲ SO Track on left.
GPS: N41°41.26′ W121°20.97′

▼ 1.4 TR Track continues straight ahead. Turn right onto raised track of the old railroad grade and pass under power lines.
.0 ▲ TL Pass under power lines; then turn left at T-intersection, leaving the old railroad grade.
GPS: N41°40.79′ W121°21.59′

▼ 2.1 SO Track on right.
.3 ▲ SO Track on left.
▼ 2.4 TL Track straight ahead goes into cinder pit of East Sand Butte and continues for 1 mile to the top of the butte. Zero trip meter.
.0 ▲ Continue to the northeast.
GPS: N41°40.83′ W121°22.69′

▼ 0.0 Continue to the east.
.9 s TR Track straight ahead goes into cinder pit of East Sand Butte and continues for 1 mile to the top of the butte. Zero trip meter.

▼ 0.1 SO Track on right.
1.8 ▲ SO Track on left.
▼ 0.4 SO Track on right.
1.5 ▲ SO Track on left.
GPS: N41°40.82′ W121°22.29′

▼ 0.9 TR T-intersection with paved road.
1.0 ▲ TL Turn left onto formed trail at sign for East Sand Butte.
GPS: N41°40.53′ W121°22.02′

▼ 1.9 TR Turn right onto formed trail 46N16 and zero trip meter.
0.0 ▲ Continue to the northeast.
GPS: N41°40.12′ W121°23.08′

▼ 0.0 Continue to the northwest.
3.5 ▲ TL T-intersection with paved road. Zero trip meter.
▼ 1.8 SO Modoc War fortifications on left.
1.7 ▲ SO Modoc War fortifications on right.
▼ 2.0 TL Track on right. Turn left at the base of Big Sand Butte. On the left is the oblong shape of some military fortifications.
1.5 ▲ TR Track on left. Turn right at the base of Big Sand Butte. On the right is the oblong shape of some military fortifications.
GPS: N41°41.34′ W121°24.85′

▼ 2.1 SO Rock structure on left is military fortification ruin.
1.4 ▲ SO Rock structure on right is military fortification ruin.
GPS: N41°41.32′ W121°24.92′

▼ 2.5 SO Track on right.
1.0 ▲ SO Track on left.
▼ 3.5 Trail ends at intersection with paved Lava Beds National Monument Road (FR 10). Turn right for Lava Beds National Monument; turn left for Tionesta and California 139.
0.0 ▲ Trail commences on Lava Beds National Monument Road (FR 10) opposite 44N22, 8.6 miles northwest of Tionesta. Zero trip meter and turn east on formed trail marked 44N21.
GPS: N41°40.68′ W121°26.37′

Fairchild Swamp Trail

STARTING POINT California 299, 3.5 miles west of the intersection with US 395 at Alturas

FINISHING POINT California 139, 7 miles northwest of intersection with California 299 at Canby

TOTAL MILEAGE 36.1 miles

UNPAVED MILEAGE 36.1 miles

DRIVING TIME 4 hours

ELEVATION RANGE 4,400–5,200 feet

USUALLY OPEN June to November

BEST TIME TO TRAVEL June to November

DIFFICULTY RATING 1

SCENIC RATING 8

REMOTENESS RATING +0

Special Attractions

- Excellent birding opportunities for waterfowl and migratory birds.
- Chance to see pronghorn and wild horses.
- Fairchild Swamp petroglyphs.
- Peaceful fishing and camping at the four reservoirs along the trail.

History

Fairchild Swamp Trail begins in the region known as Devils Garden. This territory was occupied by the Modoc and Northern Paiute; Paleo-Indians may have lived here as much as 6,000 years ago. The Modoc and Northern Paiute had seasonal camps at Devils Garden to take advantage of the area's resources. They also had camps at Fairchild Swamp and Goose Lake, where they would hunt antelope and deer and collect edible roots.

The Modoc established temporary camps across the region during spring and would set up hunting blinds. Occasionally, chips of obsidian and basalt can be found at these campsites; such areas of lithic scatter should be left undisturbed. The Modoc built more permanent villages consisting of pit houses in the vicinity of Clear Lake.

Settlers raised sheep and cattle in this region, but attempts at crop production were seldom successful. The Triangle Ranch holdings were quite extensive, and there are ruin of ranch buildings midway along the trail.

Description

This easy graded road is suitable for passenger vehicles in dry weather. Sections of it follow a Back Country Byways Discovery Trail.

The trail begins a short distance west of Alturas and gradually climbs into the Devils Garden area. This high-elevation volcanic plateau is made up of predominantly flat swamps and plains, littered with volcanic boulders. Vegetation includes junipers, conifers, and, around old homestead sites, white poplars. There are many small reservoirs on the plateau; most have a boat launch, campsites, and picnic areas. The reservoirs may dry up during summer.

A herd of wild horses lives at Devils Garden. The forest service manages the herd of about 300. The area is also a prime spot for birders. The region is part of the Pacific Flyway, and the wetlands provide great opportunities to see migratory birds and waterfowl. Birders can look for Canadian geese, mallards, pintails, teals, shorebirds, sandhill cranes, ospreys, and bald eagles. The plains are also habitat for pronghorn; in particular, the Antelope Plains is a wonderful spot for observing these graceful animals.

The graded road passes part of the old Triangle Ranch. A short distance farther, near the man-made wetlands area of Joe Sweet Pond, is an abandoned wooden cabin. Dr. Joe G. Sweet was an enthusiastic supporter of wetlands habitat. The Triangle Ranch Headquarters are 0.6 miles north of the main trail in Round Valley. A wooden cabin remains in a dense stand of white poplars; two cabins built of local stone near a flowing spring also remain. The site is shown on topographical maps as Round Valley Ranch.

The main trail passes near Reservoir C, which has a boat ramp and a pleasant campground with juniper-shaded sites on the shore. Fairchild Swamp is being restored as a wetlands, however, because farmers in Oregon still own the water rights, the project is taking a long time to complete. The forest service is purchasing water rights. This restoration project shows the classic dichoto-

Bleached juniper trunks on the shoreline of Reservoir F

my between water for humans and water for wildlife. Restoration includes seeding and building a rock nesting island. The rocky cliffs on the western side of Fairchild Swamp have some petroglyphs high up near the rim. Other faint markings can be found on large boulders near the bottom. The petroglyphs are hard to locate; binoculars will help you find the ones high on the cliff. If you walk up for a closer look, be aware that the scrubby vegetation supports a large population of ticks.

The trail continues past Reservoir F, which also has a shady camping area on its shores, before coming to an end on California 139 west of Canby. Duncan Reservoir, which often dries up after dry seasons, is located a short distance from the trail's end. You can fish for trout and bass on Reservoir C, Reservoir F, and Duncan Reservoir, all of which are stocked by the forest service.

Current Road Information

Modoc National Forest
Devils Garden Ranger District
800 West 12th Street
Alturas, CA 96101
(530) 233-5811

Map References

BLM   Cedarville, Alturas
USFS   Modoc National Forest
USGS   1:24,000   Alturas, Big Sage
Reservoir, Whittemore Ridge, Boles
    Meadow East, Jacks Butte,
    Ambrose
    1:100,000 Cedarville, Alturas
Maptech CD-ROM: Shasta-Trinity/Modoc
Northern California Atlas & Gazetteer,
    pp. 40, 30, 29
California Road & Recreation Atlas, p. 48

NORTH COAST #41: FAIRCHILD SWAMP TRAIL

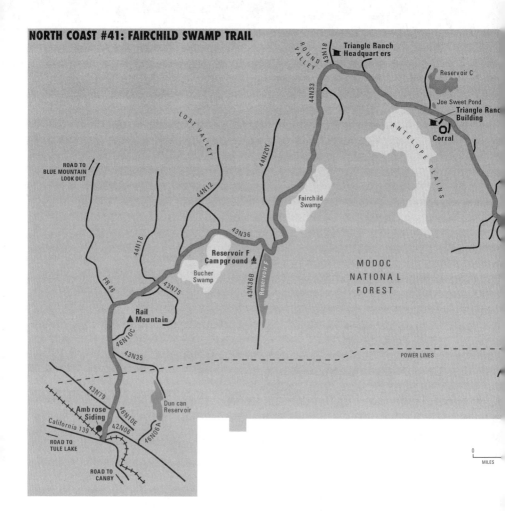

Route Directions

▼ 0.0   From California 299, 3.5 miles west of the intersection with US 395 in Alturas, zero trip meter and turn northwest on graded dirt CR/FR 73, following the sign to Devils Garden CCC.

5.9 ▲   Trail ends at T-intersection with California 299. Turn left for Alturas; turn right for Canby.
         GPS: N41°29.78' W120°36.48'

▼ 0.3   SO Cattle guard.
5.6 ▲   SO Cattle guard.

▼ 1.6   SO Track on right; then track on left; then track on right.
4.3 ▲   SO Track on left; then track on right; then track on left.

▼ 1.9   SO Track on right and track on left.
4.0 ▲   SO Track on right and track on left.

▼ 2.0   SO Graded road on left goes 2 miles to Devils Garden Camp, now a prison.
3.9 ▲   SO Graded road on right goes 2 miles to Devils Garden Camp, now a prison.
         GPS: N41°30.51' W120°38.04'

▼ 2.4   SO Graded road on right.
3.5 ▲   SO Graded road on left.

▼ 2.6   SO Cattle guard. Entering Modoc National Forest. Track on right.
3.3 ▲   SO Track on left. Leaving Modoc National Forest. Cattle guard.
         GPS: N41°30.95' W120°38.37'

▼ 2.7   SO Track on left.
3.2 ▲   SO Track on right.

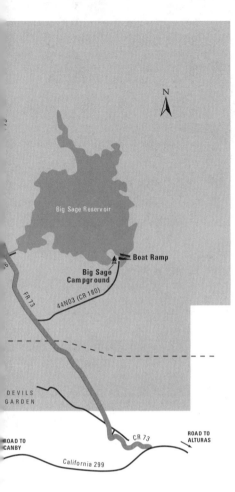

sign to California 299.

▼ 1.9   SO   Track on right.

1.6 ▲   SO   Track on left.

▼ 2.2   SO   Track on left is 43N06. Track on right goes 0.5 miles to the edge of Big Sage Reservoir. Cross over wash.

1.3 ▲   SO   Cross over wash. Track on right is 43N06. Track on left goes 0.5 miles to the edge of Big Sage Reservoir.
     GPS: N41°34.95' W120°41.87'

▼ 2.8   SO   Track on left to stock tanks.

0.7 ▲   SO   Track on right to stock tanks.

▼ 3.5   TL   Graded road on right is FR 73. Zero trip meter and turn left onto 43N18, following sign to Fairchild Swamp.

0.0 ▲   Continue to the south on FR 73.
     GPS: N41°36.11' W120°42.32'

▼ 0.0   Continue to the west.

5.8 ▲   TR   T-intersection. Graded road on left is FR 73. Zero trip meter and follow sign to California 299.

▼ 1.3   SO   Track on right.

4.5 ▲   SO   Track on left.

▼ 1.4   SO   Track on left.

4.4 ▲   SO   Track on right.

▼ 1.6   SO   Track on left.

4.2 ▲   SO   Track on right.

▼ 1.7   SO   Track on left.

4.1 ▲   SO   Track on right.

▼ 2.4   SO   Track on right.

3.4 ▲   SO   Track on left.

▼ 3.8   SO   Track on right.

2.0 ▲   SO   Track on left.

▼ 4.3   SO   Track on right.

1.5 ▲   SO   Track on left.

▼ 5.1   SO   Track on left to corral on the edge of the Antelope Plains.

0.7 ▲   SO   Track on right to corral on the edge of the Antelope Plains.
     GPS: N41°38.79' W120°45.88'

▼ 5.2   SO   Track on right.

0.6 ▲   SO   Track on left.

▼ 5.3   SO   Track on left through gate goes to an old cabin of the Triangle Ranch.

0.5 ▲   SO   Track on right through gate goes to an old cabin of the Triangle Ranch.
     GPS: N41°38.88' W120°46.08'

▼ 3.0   SO   Track on left.

2.9 ▲   SO   Track on right.

▼ 5.1   SO   Track on right and track on left under power lines.

0.8 ▲   SO   Track on right and track on left under power lines.

▼ 5.9   SO   Graded road on right is CR 180 (44N03), which goes 4 miles to Big Sage Reservoir, boat ramp, and USFS campground. Zero trip meter and follow the sign to Crowder Flat Station.

0.0 ▲   Continue to the southeast.
     GPS: N41°33.24' W120°40.84'

▼ 0.0   Continue to the northwest.

3.5 ▲   SO   Graded road on left is CR 180 (44N03), which goes 4 miles to Big Sage Reservoir, boat ramp, and USFS campground. Zero trip meter and follow the

Fishing on the remote Reservoir C

▼ 5.4 SO Cattle guard.
0.4 ▲ SO Cattle guard.
▼ 5.7 SO Joe Sweet Pond on right.
0.1 ▲ SO Joe Sweet Pond on left.
      GPS: N41°39.01' W120°46.43'

▼ 5.8 SO Graded road on right goes 1.3 miles to
          Reservoir C. Zero trip meter and follow
          the sign to Triangle Ranch.
0.0 ▲   Continue to the east.
      GPS: N41°39.05' W120°46.57'

▼ 0.0   Continue to the west.
3.5 ▲ SO Graded road on left goes 1.3 miles to
          Reservoir C. Zero trip meter and follow
          the sign to Alturas.

▼ 0.6 SO Track on left through gate; then track
          on right.
2.9 ▲ SO Track on left; then track on right
          through gate.
t 1.3 SO Track on left.

2.2 ▲ SO Track on right.
▼ 2.3 SO Track on right.
1.2 ▲ SO Track on left.
▼ 2.5 SO Track on right.
1.0 ▲ SO Track on left.
▼ 3.1 SO Track on right.
0.4 ▲ SO Track on left.
▼ 3.4 SO Cattle guard.
0.1 ▲ SO Cattle guard.
▼ 3.5 TL Round Valley. Straight ahead, 43N18
          goes 0.6 miles through Round Valley to
          the wooden cabin, stone ruins, and
          spring at Triangle Ranch. Zero trip
          meter and turn left on 44N33, follow-
          ing the sign to Fairchild Swamp. Spring
          at the intersection.
0.0 ▲   Continue to the east.
      GPS: N41°40.25' W120°50.23'

▼ 0.0   Continue to the south and cross cattle
          guard.

5.2 ▲	TR	Round Valley. Cattle guard. Straight ahead, 43N18 goes 0.6 miles through Round Valley to the wooden cabin, stone ruins, and spring at Triangle Ranch. Zero trip meter and turn right onto 43N18, following the sign for Alturas. Spring at the intersection.
▼ 0.2	SO	Track on right through gate.
5.0 ▲	SO	Track on left through gate.
▼ 0.9	SO	Track on left.
5.3 ▲	SO	Track on right.
▼ 1.6	SO	Cattle guard.
4.6 ▲	SO	Cattle guard.
▼ 1.8	SO	Cross over canal and start to run alongside Fairchild Swamp.
4.4 ▲	SO	Trail leaves Fairchild Swamp. Cross over canal.
▼ 3.1	SO	Cattle guard; then track on left. Cliffs on right.
3.1 ▲	SO	Track on right; then cattle guard. Cliffs on left.

GPS: N41°37.77′ W120°50.97′

▼ 4.1	SO	Track on left.
2.1 ▲	SO	Track on right.
▼ 6.2	BR	Three tracks on left across swamp. Follow the sign to Reservoir F and zero trip meter.
0.0 ▲		Continue to the northwest around Fairchild Swamp.

GPS: N41°35.54′ W120°51.95′

▼ 0.0		Continue to the southwest away from Fairchild Swamp. Track on left.
7.0 ▲	BL	Track on right; then three tracks on right across Fairchild Swamp. Follow the sign to Reservoir C and zero trip meter.
▼ 0.4	BL	Track on right is 44N20Y.
6.6 ▲	BR	Track on left is 44N20Y.
▼ 0.7	TR	Track on left goes to Reservoir F. Turn right onto 43N36, following the sign to California 139.
6.3 ▲	TL	Track on right goes to Reservoir F. Turn left onto 44N33, following the sign to Fairchild Swamp

GPS: N41°35.11′ W120°52.45′

▼ 1.0	SO	Cattle guard.
6.0 ▲	SO	Cattle guard.
▼ 1.1	SO	Track on left is 44N36B, which goes 0.2 miles to Reservoir F, campground, and boat launch.
5.9 ▲	SO	Track on right is 44N36B, which goes 0.2 miles to Reservoir F, campground, and boat launch.

GPS: N41°35.31′ W120°52.74′

▼ 1.2	SO	Track on right.
5.8 ▲	SO	Track on left.
▼ 2.1	SO	Cattle guard. Bucher Swamp on left.
4.9 ▲	SO	Cattle guard. Bucher Swamp on right.
▼ 2.8	SO	Track on right.
4.2 ▲	SO	Track on left.
▼ 4.4	SO	Graded road on right is 44N12 to Lost Valley. Follow the sign to California 139, remaining on 43N36.
2.6 ▲	SO	Graded road on left is 44N12 to Lost Valley. Follow the sign to Reservoir F, remaining on 43N36.

GPS: N41°34.87′ W120°55.95′

▼ 4.6	SO	Track on left to remains of log cabin beside Bucher Swamp.
2.4 ▲	SO	Track on right to remains of log cabin beside Bucher Swamp.
▼ 4.7	SO	Cattle guard; then track on left.
2.3 ▲	SO	Track on right; then cattle guard.
▼ 5.4	SO	Track on left is 43N75 and track on right is 44N16; then cattle guard.
1.6 ▲	SO	Cattle guard; then track on right is 43N75 and track on left is 44N16.

GPS: N41°34.29′ W120°56.79′

▼ 6.3	SO	Track on left.
0.7 ▲	SO	Track on right.
▼ 6.8	SO	Track on left.
0.2 ▲	SO	Track on right.
▼ 7.0	TL	T-intersection with FR 46. To the right goes to Blue Mountain Lookout. Zero trip meter and follow the sign to California 139.
0.0 ▲		Continue to the northeast.

GPS: N41°33.67′ W120°58.37′

▼ 0.0		Continue to the south.
4.2 ▲	TR	FR 46 continues straight ahead to Blue Mountain Lookout. Zero trip meter and turn right onto 43N36, following the sign to Fairchild Swamp.
▼ 1.0	SO	Track on left is 46N10C.
3.2 ▲	SO	Track on right is 46N10C.

GPS: N41°32.77′ W120°58.53′

Freshwater mussel shells on the caked swamp surface

▼ 1.1   SO Track on right.
3.1 ▲   SO Track on left.
▼ 1.4   SO Graded road on left is 43N35 to
            Duncan Reservoir.
2.8 ▲   SO Graded road on right is 43N35 to
            Duncan Reservoir.
▼ 2.0   SO Track on right and track on left under
            power lines.
2.2 ▲   SO Track on left and track on right under
            power lines.
▼ 3.3   SO Track on left is 46N10E.
0.9 ▲   SO Track on right is 46N10E.
▼ 3.4   SO Track on right is 43N79.
0.8 ▲   SO Track on left is 43N79.
▼ 4.1   SO Track on right; then track on left is
            42N06, which goes 2.4 miles to
            Duncan Reservoir (via a second left
            turn onto 46N06A after 1.3 miles).
0.1 ▲   SO Track on right is 42N06, which goes
            2.4 miles to Duncan Reservoir (via a
            left turn onto 46N06A after 1.3 miles);
            then track on left.
▼ 4.2   Ambrose Siding. Cross over railroad;
            then cattle guard. Road is now paved.
            Trail finishes at T-intersection with
            California 139. Turn left for Canby and
            Alturas; turn right for Tule Lake.

0.0 ▲   Trail commences on California 139 at
            Ambrose Siding, 7 miles northwest of
            Canby and California 299, 0.2 miles
            east of Modoc County mile marker 7.5.
            Zero trip meter and turn north on
            paved FR 46 at the sign for Loveness
            Road. Cross cattle guard; then cross
            over railroad. Road turns to graded dirt.
            GPS: N41°30.01′ W120°58.72′

NORTH COAST #42

Surprise Valley Trail

STARTING POINT CR 1, 5 miles north of
Cedarville
FINISHING POINT CR 8A in Nevada, 2.7 miles
east of the California-Nevada state line
TOTAL MILEAGE 11.5 miles, plus 3.1-mile spur
to Salt Creek
UNPAVED MILEAGE 11.5 miles, plus 3.1-mile spur
DRIVING TIME 2 hours
ELEVATION RANGE 4,500–5,500 feet
USUALLY OPEN Year-round
BEST TIME TO TRAVEL Dry weather

DIFFICULTY RATING 4
SCENIC RATING 8
REMOTENESS RATING +0

Special Attractions

■ Hot springs and a warm hot spring creek.
■ Chance to see herds of wild horses in Surprise Valley.
■ Trail follows a section of the historic Applegate Trail.

History

Surprise Valley, as the name suggests, was just that—a surprise to westbound emigrants who had survived the harsh Black Rock Desert of Nevada. The unexpected sight of this impressive north-south valley was a welcome relief to emigrants. They were in fact looking at the remains of ancient Lake Surprise, which covered the full length of the valley approximately 10,000 years ago.

Archaeologists have detected evidence of Paleo-Indians in this valley. After the last ice age, vegetation was lush and the region supported large mammals such as bison. Excavations indicate that these people lived in communal dwellings by the lakeshore. As the climate became more arid, Lake Surprise receded. The inhabitants adapted and settled by the marshy shores. Climatic conditions changed over 3,000 years, and the fauna changed, too. People and animals that survived the changing conditions continued to live in this great valley.

The Northern Paiute occupied the valley when settlers arrived in the mid-nineteenth century. The Paiute moved to higher elevations during spring and summer to gather enough seeds, roots, and game to last through the winter, which was spent at lower elevations on the valley floor.

Description

Surprise Valley is a long, arid valley in the northeasternmost corner of California, between the Warner Mountains to the west and the Hayes Range to the east. The valley is known for its dry lakebeds and proliferation of hot springs. Surprise Valley Trail passes a few undeveloped hot springs and follows a section of the Applegate Trail.

The trail leaves Surprise Valley Road (CR 1) north of Cedarville. For the first few miles, it follows a graded county road called Fortynine Lane across the flat Surprise Valley. The trail crosses a small flowing creek, fed by some unnamed hot springs a short distance to the north. The entire creek is warm, and by following an unmarked vehicle trail along the creek to the north, you will come to some informal, undeveloped soaking areas. The farther up the creek you go, the hotter the water. These areas are shallow and lightly used. This side trip crosses land shown on maps as private, but there are no signs posting the property, so access seems to be okay. However, be considerate and should no trespassing signs be posted, respect them. There is an alternate, lesser used trail to the east that accesses the springs by traveling across public lands.

Farther to the east, a spur travels past buttes and abundant sagebrush to a pretty stop along

NORTH COAST #42: SURPRISE VALLEY TRAIL

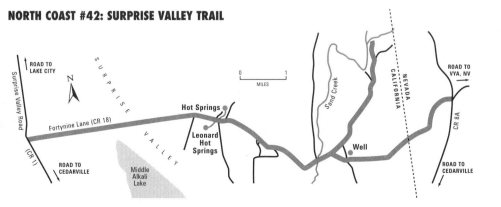

Hot spring soaking area beside Warm Creek

a tributary of Sand Creek. One of the side trails, which leads east to the Nevada state line, offers the best chance to see a wild horse herd. The horses are called Sand Creek duns for their predominant coloring. Many are descended from a quarter horse stallion turned out by a local rancher. The horses carry his color as well as quarter horse confirmation.

The main route diverges from the graded road to follow a section of the Applegate Trail. The California Trail Association has placed several markers along the trail, but these can blend into the background and may be hard to spot. This section gives the trail its difficulty rating of 4. It climbs up and over a rocky ridge, with large embedded boulders that must be negotiated. The smooth valley sections of the trail are impassable in wet weather. These sections break up the slow rocky crawls over the ridges. The trail ends on CR 8A in Nevada, 2.7 miles east of the California state line.

Current Road Information

Bureau of Land Management
Surprise Field Office
602 Cressler Street
Cedarville, CA 96104
(530) 279-6101

Map References

BLM   Cedarville, Vya (NV)
USFS   Modoc National Forest
USGS   1:24,000   Cedarville, Leonards
    Hot Springs, Fortynine Mtn.
    1:100,000 Cedarville, Vya (NV)
Maptech CD-ROM: Shasta-Trinity/Modoc;
    Northwest Nevada/Winnemucca/
    Sheldon Wildlife Refuge (NV)
Northern California Atlas & Gazetteer, p. 31
Nevada Atlas & Gazetteer, p. 18
California Road & Recreation Atlas, p. 49
Other: Modoc Country USFS/BLM Map
    (incomplete)

Route Directions

▼ 0.0   From Surprise Valley Road (CR 1), 5 miles north of Cedarville, 0.2 miles north of Modoc County mile marker 34, zero trip meter and turn east on small paved Fortynine Lane (CR 18).

7.8 ▲   Trail ends at intersection with Surprise Valley Road (CR 1). Turn left for Cedarville; turn right for Lake City.
     GPS: N41°36.15′ W120°10.84′

▼ 0.8 SO Road turns to graded dirt.
7.0 ▲ SO Road becomes paved.
▼ 1.2 SO Cattle guard.
6.6 ▲ SO Cattle guard.
▼ 1.9 SO Track on left.
5.9 ▲ SO Track on right.
▼ 4.1 SO Track on right. Graded road on left is the Applegate-Lassen Trail. Trail now follows this route.
3.7 ▲ SO Track on left. Graded road on right is the Applegate-Lassen Trail. Trail now leaves that route.
     GPS: N41°36.11′ W120°05.92′

▼ 4.5 SO Leonard Hot Springs on private property beside the road on right.

3.3 ▲ SO Leonard Hot Springs on private property beside the road on left.
▼ 4.6 SO Track on left; then cross over warm water creek; then track on right. Follow the track on left, west of the crossing, alongside the warm creek to the hot spring soaking areas.
3.2 ▲ SO Track on left; then cross over warm water creek; then track on right. Follow the track on right, west of the crossing, alongside the warm creek to the hot spring soaking areas.
     GPS: N41°35.89′ W120°05.31′

▼ 4.8 SO Track on left.
3.0 ▲ SO Track on right.
▼ 5.0 SO Small track on left goes to the same hot springs by way of BLM land. Track on right.
2.8 ▲ SO Small track on right goes to the same hot springs by way of BLM land. Track on left.
▼ 5.8 SO Track on right.
2.0 ▲ SO Track on left.
▼ 6.1 SO Track on right.
1.7 ▲ SO Track on left.
▼ 7.1 SO Track on right.
0.7 ▲ SO Track on left.

Mustang herd in Surprise Valley

▼ 7.3	SO	Track on right.
0.5 ▲	SO	Track on left.
▼ 7.5	SO	Track on left; then cross through Sand Creek.
0.3 ▲	SO	Cross through Sand Creek; then track on right.

GPS: N41°34.74' W120°02.59'

▼ 7.8	BR	Unmarked well-used track on left is the spur to Sand Creek. Bear right, remaining on graded road. Zero trip meter.
0.0 ▲		Continue to the southwest.

GPS: N41°34.82' W120°02.17'

Spur to Sand Creek

▼ 0.0		Proceed to the northeast.
▼ 0.2	SO	Track on left.
▼ 0.3	SO	Track on right opposite butte.
▼ 0.5	SO	Track on left.
▼ 1.2	SO	Track on left.
▼ 2.0	BR	Track on left.

GPS: N41°36.16' W120°00.68'

▼ 2.6	BL	Track on right goes 0.6 miles to the Nevada state line.

GPS: N41°36.61' W120°00.54'

▼ 3.0	SO	Track on left.
▼ 3.1		Trail ends at a turnaround beside a tributary of Sand Creek.

GPS: N41°37.06' W120°00.53'

Continuation of Main Trail

▼ 0.0		Continue to the southeast.
3.7 ▲	BL	Unmarked, well-used track on right is the spur to Sand Creek. Bear left, remaining on graded road. Zero trip meter.

GPS: N41°34.82' W120°02.17'

▼ 0.4	TL	Track on left; then well on left; then immediately turn left.
3.3 ▲	TR	Well on right; then T-intersection with graded road.

GPS: N41°34.62' W120°01.77'

▼ 0.8	SO	Applegate Trail marker on right.
2.9 ▲	SO	Applegate Trail marker on left.

▼ 2.1	SO	Posts and cairn on either side of the trail mark Nevada state line.
1.6 ▲	SO	Post and cairn on either side of the trail marks California state line.

GPS: N41°34.89' W120°00.00'

▼ 3.4	SO	Applegate Trail marker on left.
0.3 ▲	SO	Applegate Trail marker on right.
▼ 3.7		Trail finishes at T-intersection with CR 8A. Fortynine Mountain is southeast of the trail. Turn right for Cedarville.
0.0 ▲		Trail commences on CR 8A, 2.7 miles east of California-Nevada state line. Zero trip meter and turn west on formed dirt trail. There is an Applegate Trail maker at the intersection, but otherwise the intersection is unmarked. A second track leads north from the same point.

GPS: N41°35.55' W119°58.42'

Obsidian Needles Trail

STARTING POINT Surprise Valley Road (CR 1) in Lake City
FINISHING POINT US 395 at Davis Creek
TOTAL MILEAGE 22.9 miles
UNPAVED MILEAGE 21.7 miles
DRIVING TIME 3.5 hours
ELEVATION RANGE 4,500–7,700 feet
USUALLY OPEN June to December
BEST TIME TO TRAVEL Dry weather
DIFFICULTY RATING 3
SCENIC RATING 9
REMOTENESS RATING +0

Special Attractions

- Rockhounding for obsidian.
- Historic Lake City Flour Mill at the start of trail.
- Long, pretty trail through the Warner Mountains.

History

Obsidian Needles Trail begins in the Surprise Valley town of Lake City, founded in 1857.

The town, just east of the Warner Mountains, is near several playa, or dry lakes in this basin. Water was essential for at least two of the town's businesses: a sawmill built in 1866, and the Lake City Flouring Mill, built in 1867. The flour mill consists of hand-hewn timbers with wooden wedged joinery. The mill's owner, John Bucher, produced a variety of desirable flours: wheatgerm, stoneground and graham flour, cornmeal, and unbleached flour. Lake City Flouring Mill closed in 1935, swung back into action the following year, and continued to supply surrounding communities until the 1960s. Sadly the innards of the mill have been removed

The obsidian needles that can be found along this trail were highly sought after by the Northern Paiute. Such fine needles could be used as a tool to penetrate animal skin or as arrowheads and spear points for hunting. They could be chipped from the larger pieces of obsidian that are plentiful across this part of the range.

The end of the trail, in Davis Creek, marks the start of the Lassen Trail (see page 212). In 1848, Danish emigrant Peter Lassen left from here to blaze a trail south, leading a group of 12 wagons into the Sacramento Valley. The difficult route took them through the future site of Alturas, southeast along the Pit River, and eventually to the Sacramento Valley. Lassen's route veers off the Applegate Trail at this point, which crossed the lower reaches of Goose Lake and went through Devils Garden toward Tule Lake.

Description

This trail travels from Lake City, on the east side of the Warner Mountains, over to Davis Creek on the west side of the range. It leaves Lake City up South Water Street, passing the old Lake City Flouring Mill. The privately owned building is currently in a state of disrepair.

The route travels up Lake City Canyon—a tight, rocky passage along Mill Creek. It is a sin-

Lake City Flour Mill, built in 1870

THE LASSEN AND NOBLES TRAILS

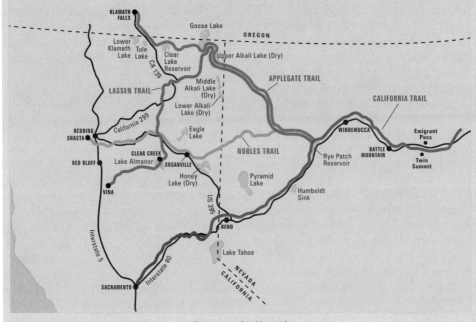

The Lassen and Nobles Trails

A native of Denmark, Peter Lassen emigrated to America in 1829, first blacksmithing in Boston until 1839 and then moving to the Oregon frontier. When he reached the Sacramento Valley in 1844, John Sutter helped him obtain a land grant in what is now Tehama County, where he cultivated wheat and grapes. To promote Benton City, a proposed town on his property, Lassen traveled to Missouri in 1847 to recruit settlers. On his return in

gle-vehicle width shelf road for much of the way, but with plenty of passing places. There are a few scattered campsites sheltered below pine trees beside the creek. The route climbs out of the canyon and across open slopes at the top. There are excellent views east over Surprise Valley toward Nevada. The trail improves slightly when it joins wide, graded FR 30, part of the network of California Back Country Discovery Trails. These trails are marked by distinctive route markers. Obsidian Needles Trail intersects the Discovery trail several times.

A narrow trail leaves FR 30 to travel a smaller, rougher loop that diverges near the edge of the range. There are views here back down to the Surprise Valley. Those not wanting to travel this section can remain on FR 30;

the two routes rejoin after a couple of miles.

One of the major features of this part of Modoc National Forest are the rockhounding sites where it is possible to view and collect different types of obsidian. Non-commercial users must obtain a free permit from the forest service to rockhound here. The first of these sites, Pink Lady, is 0.1 miles from the main trail. The collecting area is littered with obsidian. Simply step out of your vehicle and start collecting. The site has a lot of black obsidian and some smoky gray obsidian, lightly tinged with pink. Obsidian of all types is scattered along much of this trail. Note that collecting outside designated areas is not permitted.

The second obsidian collecting area, Obsidian Needles, offers easy rockhound-

1848 he convinced the wagon train to use the Applegate Trail to Goose Lake and then led them southwest through Devil's Garden to the Pit River, 4 miles west of the future site of Alturas. Lassen and his party followed the Pit River, crossing it for the first time just south of Canby, and made their way west through Stone Coal Valley where they met up again with the Pit River. Led south by the river, Lassen forded the rocky waterway several times before finally crossing it 10 miles north of Lookout. They reached Lassen's ranch in the Sacramento Valley after wandering for two months. Prospectors from Oregon rescued the party and put them on the right route to the Sacramento Valley.

Although the trail was arduous, as many as 8,000 emigrants followed the Lassen Trail into gold country in 1849. The trail was referred to as "Lassen's Death Route," among other nicknames, because it took a month longer to travel than other emigrant trails, the terrain was rough, and there were hostile Indians along the way. Portions of the trail are still evident today in Pit River Canyon. From the intersection of California 299 and California 139 in Canby, take 299 southwest to the Canby Bridge. Travel 4 miles west on Forest Road 84 to where the Pit River turns south; a trail marker is located here. From the primitive campsite just up a short dirt road, follow the trail heading south along the banks of the Pit River to a site along the original Lassen Trail.

Supported by businessmen from the town of Shasta, William H. Noble raised $2,000 to find an alternative to the Lassen Trail in 1851. Nobles' cutoff left the Humboldt River at Rabbit Springs, Nevada, and entered California near Honey Lake. The trail passed through present-day Susanville and crossed the Cascade Range north of Lassen Peak through Nobles Pass, now on California 89 near the Manzanita Lake entrance station to Lassen Volcanic National Park. From Viola to Redding, California 44 parallels Nobles Trail. The trail is marked at Honey Lake, Shaffer Station, Willow Creek Crossing, Roop's Fort, the Susanville County Park, Feather Lake (intersection of Lassen and Nobles Trails), Poison Lake, and Butte Creek. Emigrants frequently used the trail in the early 1850s, but it became obsolete when other Sierra passes and wagon roads opened and the subsequent railroad was constructed. In one period, from August 2, 1857, to October 4, 1857, a record keeper at Roop's trading post near Susanville counted 99 wagon trains, with 306 wagons and carriages, and a total of 1,479 men, women, and children.

ing for the super-fine obsidian needles that give the trail its name. Specimens here are black, clear, and mahogany, found in large pieces as well as the distinctive fine rock needles. This site is right beside the main trail, and once again, specimens are very easy to find. A few minutes of hunting will yield many fine pieces. Remember, recreational collectors must not enter zones reserved for commercial use.

Past Obsidian Needles, the trail winds down the western side of the Warner Mountains on easier graded forest roads. It finishes on US 395 in Davis Creek, where the Applegate and Lassen Trails diverge.

Current Road Information
Modoc National Forest
Warner Mountain Ranger District
PO Box 220
Cedarville, CA 96104
(530) 279-6116

Map References
BLM Cedarville
USFS Modoc National Forest
USGS 1:24,000 Lake City, Sugar Hill, Davis Creek
    1:100,000 Cedarville
Maptech CD-ROM: Shasta-Trinity/Modoc
Northern California Atlas & Gazetteer, p. 31
California Road & Recreation Atlas, p. 49
Other: Modoc Country USFS/BLM Map

NORTH COAST #43: OBSIDIAN NEEDLES TRAIL

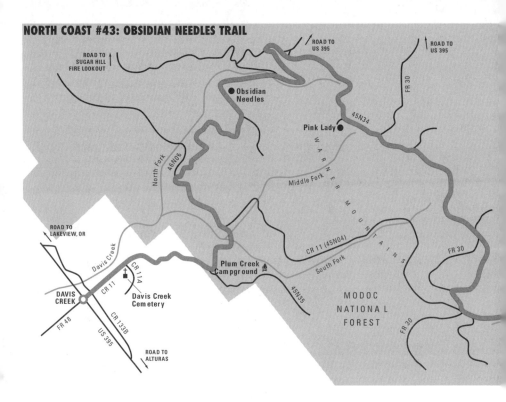

Route Directions

▼ 0.0   From Surprise Valley Road (CR 1) at Lake City, zero trip meter and turn west on CR 17, following the sign for Benton Meadows and Plum Creek Campground.

0.4 ▲   Trail ends at intersection with Surprise Valley Road (CR 1) in Lake City. Turn left for Fort Bidwell; turn right for Cedarville.
         GPS: N41°38.72′ W120°12.72′

▼ 0.2   TL Turn left onto Main Street.
0.2 ▲   TR Turn right onto CR 17.
▼ 0.4   TR Turn right onto formed dirt South Water Street, following the sign for Benton Meadows. Zero trip meter.
0.0 ▲   Continue to the northwest.
         GPS: N41°38.49′ W120°12.91′

▼ 0.0   Continue to the southwest.
5.8 ▲   TL Turn left onto paved Main Street. Zero trip meter.
▼ 0.1   SO Lake City Flour Mill on left; then cross through creek; then track on left.

5.7 ▲   SO Track on right; then cross through creek; then Lake City Flour Mill on right.
▼ 0.2   SO Cattle guard.
5.6 ▲   SO Cattle guard.
▼ 0.3   SO Cross over Mill Creek. Start of shelf road.
5.5 ▲   SO End of shelf road. Cross over Mill Creek.
▼ 0.8   SO Entering Modoc National Forest at sign.
5.0 ▲   SO Leaving Modoc National Forest at sign.
         GPS: N41°38.53′ W120°13.77′

▼ 0.9   SO Cattle guard.
4.9 ▲   SO Cattle guard.
▼ 3.5   SO Cross over Mill Creek.
2.3 ▲   SO Cross over Mill Creek.
         GPS: N41°39°19′ W120°16.38′

▼ 4.9   SO End of shelf road. Cross through creek.
0.9 ▲   SO Cross through creek. Start of shelf road.
▼ 5.3   SO Track on left.
0.5 ▲   SO Track on right.
▼ 5.7   SO Track on left; then cattle guard.
0.1 ▲   SO Cattle guard; then track on right.
▼ 5.8   TR 4-way intersection. FR 30 goes left to Joseph Creek Basin. Straight ahead is

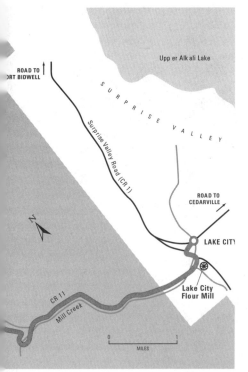

		45N04 (CR 11) to Davis Creek. Zero trip meter and turn right onto FR 30, following the sign to Sugar Hill Lookout.
0.0 ▲		Continue to the southeast.
		GPS: N41°40.55' W120°17.23'
▼ 0.0		Continue to the northeast.
4.2 ▲	TL	4-way intersection. FR 30 continues straight ahead to Joseph Creek Basin. Road on right is 45N04 (CR 11) to Davis Creek. Zero trip meter and turn left onto on 45N34 (CR 11), following the sign to Lake City.
▼ 0.4	TR	Graded road continues straight ahead. Turn right onto small, unmarked trail.
3.8 ▲	TL	T-intersection with graded FR 30.
		GPS: N41°40.87' W120°17.14'
▼ 1.0	SO	Track on right.
3.2 ▲	SO	Track on left.
▼ 1.4	SO	Track on right.
2.8 ▲	SO	Track on left.
▼ 1.5	SO	Track on right.
2.7 ▲	SO	Track on left.

Obsidian needles discovered along the trail

Pink Lady obsidian collecting area

▼ 1.7 TR T-intersection with FR 30. Turn right and rejoin this road; then track on right.

2.5 ▲ TL Track on left; then graded road continues straight ahead. Turn left onto small unmarked trail.
   GPS: N41°41.22′ W120°16.15′

▼ 2.8 SO Track on right; then track on left.
1.4 ▲ SO Track on right; then track on left.
▼ 3.5 SO Track on left.
0.7 ▲ SO Track on right.
▼ 3.6 SO Track on right.
0.6 ▲ SO Track on left.
▼ 4.2 TL Graded road continues straight ahead to Harris Flat and US 395. Zero trip meter and turn left onto 45N34, following the sign to Sugar Hill Lookout.
0.0 ▲ Continue to the southwest.
   GPS: N41°43.12′ W120°16.39′

▼ 0.0 Continue to the northwest.
0.6 ▲ TR T-intersection with graded dirt FR 30. To the left goes to Harris Flat and US 395. Zero trip meter and follow the sign to Lake City.
▼ 0.1 SO Track on right.
0.5 ▲ SO Track on left.
▼ 0.6 SO Unmarked track on left goes 0.1 miles to the Pink Lady obsidian collecting site. Zero trip meter.
0.0 ▲ Continue to the southeast.
   GPS: N41°43.58′ W120°16.76′

▼ 0.0 Continue to the northeast.
3.7 ▲ SO Unmarked track on right goes 0.1 miles to the Pink Lady obsidian collecting site. Zero trip meter.
▼ 0.9 SO Track on right.
2.8 ▲ BR Track on left.
   GPS: N41°43.99′ W120°16.27′

▼ 1.2 SO Track on right.
2.5 ▲ SO Track on left.
▼ 1.9 SO Track on right.
1.8 ▲ SO Track on left.
▼ 2.0 SO Track on right.
1.7 ▲ SO Track on left.
▼ 2.4 SO Track on right.
1.3 ▲ SO Track on left.

▼ 3.7 TL Track straight ahead goes to the Sugar Hill Fire Lookout. Zero trip meter.
0.0 ▲ Continue to the southeast.
   GPS: N41°44.71′ W120°17.23′

▼ 0.0 Cross over North Fork Davis Creek; then track on left is dead end. Continue to the northwest.
3.6 ▲ TR Track straight ahead is a dead end; then cross over North Fork Davis Creek; then T-intersection. To the left goes to the Sugar Hill Fire Lookout. Zero trip meter and turn right, following sign to Buck Mountain.
▼ 0.9 SO Obsidian Needles collecting area on left, marked by a sign.
2.7 ▲ SO Obsidian Needles collecting area on right, marked by a sign.
   GPS: N41°44.86′ W120°18.16′
▼ 1.5 BR Track on left.
2.1 ▲ BL Track on right.
▼ 3.6 TL T-intersection with 46N06. Zero trip meter.
0.0 ▲ Continue to the east.
   GPS: N41°44.46′ W120°19.81′

▼ 0.0 Continue to the south.
4.6 ▲ TR Graded road continues ahead. Zero trip meter and turn right onto 45N34 for 4WDs, ATVs, and motorbikes.
▼ 1.2 SO Graded road on left is 45N04 (CR 11) to Davis Creek obsidian collecting area and Lake City.
3.4 ▲ SO Graded road on right is 45N04 (CR 11) to Davis Creek obsidian collecting area and Lake City. Join 45N04, following sign to Buck Mountain.
   GPS: N41°43.51′ W120°19.67′

▼ 1.4 SO Cross over Middle Fork Davis Creek.
3.2 ▲ SO Cross over Middle Fork Davis Creek.
▼ 1.6 SO Cross over South Fork Davis Creek.
3.0 ▲ SO Cross over South Fork Davis Creek.
▼ 2.4 SO Graded road on left is 45N35, which goes 1 mile to Plum Creek USFS Campground. Follow sign to Davis Creek.
2.2 ▲ BL Graded road on right is 45N35, which goes 1 mile to Plum Creek USFS Campground. Follow sign to Buck Mountain.

▼ 2.5	SO	Cattle guard. Leaving Modoc National Forest.
2.1 ▲	SO	Cattle guard. Entering Modoc National Forest.
▼ 2.8	SO	Cattle guard.
1.8 ▲	SO	Cattle guard.
▼ 3.0	SO	Track on right.
1.6 ▲	SO	Track on left.
▼ 3.5	SO	Track on right.
1.1 ▲	SO	Track on left.
▼ 3.8	SO	Paved CR 11A on left. Join this road. Davis Creek Cemetery is 0.1 miles to the left.
0.8 ▲	BL	Paved CR 11A continues straight ahead and goes 0.1 miles to Davis Creek Cemetery. Bear left onto FR 11, following sign to Plum Creek Campground.

GPS: N41°44.00' W120°21.53'

▼ 3.9	SO	Davis Creek Cemetery on left; then cattle guard.
0.7 ▲	SO	Cattle guard; then Davis Creek Cemetery on right.
▼ 4.5	SO	Cross over CR 133B.
0.1 ▲	SO	Cross over CR 133B.
▼ 4.6		Trail ends on US 395 at Davis Creek, opposite FR 48. Turn right for Lakeview, OR; turn left for Alturas.
0.0 ▲		Trail commences on US 395 at Davis Creek, opposite FR 48. Zero trip meter and turn east on CR 11, following sign to Plum Creek Campground and the Needle Mines.

GPS: N41°44.01' W120°22.45'

Fandango Pass Trail

STARTING POINT Surprise Valley Road (CR 1), 10.5 miles north of Lake City

FINISHING POINT US 395, 7.5 miles south of New Pine Creek

TOTAL MILEAGE 14.7 miles, plus 2.3-mile spur to Rainbow Mine

UNPAVED MILEAGE 14 miles, plus 2.3-mile spur

DRIVING TIME 1.5 hours

ELEVATION RANGE 4,600–6,200 feet

USUALLY OPEN May to November

BEST TIME TO TRAVEL Dry weather

DIFFICULTY RATING 1

SCENIC RATING 9

REMOTENESS RATING +0

Special Attractions

- Fandango Pass—an important point on the historic Applegate Trail.
- Rockhounding for obsidian at the Rainbow Mine.
- Good trail to see fall colors.

History

Fandango Pass (6,332 feet) is a memorable spot, not only for its beauty and significance as an historic pass, but also for the settlers and miners who lost their lives while traveling this passage through the Warner Mountains.

The Applegate Trail (see page 212), an emigrant trail blazed through this pass in 1846, was an alternative to a difficult section of the Oregon Trail, west of Fort Hall in present-day Idaho. Lindsey Applegate found the route.

Stories behind Fandango Pass's name vary. One explanation is that emigrants believed the pass was their last major climb—that they had crossed to the Pacific slope and were now on their final downhill run. The celebrations as they crested the pass often included dancing the fandango. Another explanation is that forty-niners spent a cold night on the pass and danced around to keep warm. Either way, cresting this ridge, which rises 1,800 feet above Surprise Valley, was a major achievement for emigrants and the oxen pulling their heavy wagons.

Description

Fandango Pass Trail winds up the grade from CR 1 in Surprise Valley to Fandango Pass in approximately 20 minutes. There are great views east as you climb over Upper Alkali Lake, Surprise Valley, and into Nevada.

The top of the pass has an historical marker that describes where the Lassen and Applegate Trails diverged, which is at Davis Creek (at the end of North Coast #43: Obsidian Needles Trail). Those with high-clearance 4WDs might like to take a short, narrow formed side trail that runs 0.6 miles to a viewpoint over Surprise Valley, Fandango Valley, and Goose Lake. The spur travels a side slope that reaches a tilt of 25 degrees in places and there is limited room for turning. This spur is rated 5 for difficulty.

The main trail descends to Fandango Valley, now private property, and a possible site of the Fandango Massacre; there is no marker. Remain on the county road and please respect property owners' rights. A short distance past the Buck Creek Guard Station, the trail turns southwest. A spur leads to the Rainbow Mine—an obsidian collecting area open to the public. Collectors must have a permit in hand (free) issued at any Modoc National Forest office. The site mainly has black obsidian, which is easy to find. Lassen Creek USFS Campground is a short distance past the collecting site, and has mainly undeveloped sites in a pretty spot beside Lassen Creek. Lassen Creek is habitat for the rare redband trout, which also live in Goose Lake. Catch and release rules apply.

The entire trail follows graded dirt county roads and in dry weather, it is suitable for passenger vehicles. Much of the trail passes through private property, so campers will find Lassen Creek USFS Campground the best option.

Current Road Information

Modoc National Forest
Warner Mountain Ranger District
PO Box 220
Cedarville, CA 96104
(530) 279-6116

Map References

BLM   Cedarville
USFS   Modoc National Forest
USGS   1:24,000   Fort Bidwell, Sugar Hill,
Willow Ranch
      1:100,000 Cedarville
Maptech CD-ROM: Shasta-Trinity/Modoc
Northern California Atlas & Gazetteer, p. 31
California Road & Recreation Atlas, p. 49
Other: Modoc Country USFS/BLM Map

Fandango Pass

Route Directions

▼ 0.0   From Surprise Valley Road (CR 1), 10.5 miles north of Lake City, zero trip meter and turn northwest on graded dirt CR 9 at the sign for FR 9, forest access.

3.6 ▲   Trail ends at T-intersection with paved CR 1. Turn left for Fort Bidwell; turn right for Cedarville.

GPS: N41°47.49' W120°10.36'

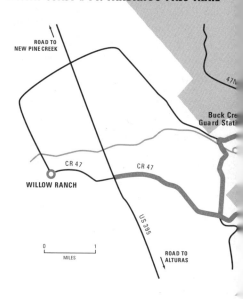

▼ 0.2   SO   Cattle guard.
3.4 ▲   SO   Cattle guard.
▼ 2.2   SO   Look to the right to see a section of the hand-built military road.
1.4 ▲   SO   Look to the left to see a section of the hand-built military road.
▼ 2.3   SO   Entering Modoc National Forest at sign.
1.3 ▲   SO   Leaving Modoc National Forest at sign.

GPS: N41°47.78' W120°12.00'

▼ 2.9   SO   Track on right.
0.7 ▲   SO   Track on left.
▼ 3.6   SO   Fandango Pass. Historical marker at the pass. Zero trip meter.
0.0 ▲   Continue to the east.

GPS: N41°48.11' W120°12.27'

▼ 0.0   Continue to the west. Track on left—there is an Applegate Trail marker a short distance down this trail on the right—goes 0.6 miles to an excellent viewpoint over Surprise Valley and Goose Lake. This side trail is rated 5.
6.6 ▲   SO   Track on right—there is an Applegate Trail marker a short distance down this trail on the right—goes 0.6 miles to an excellent viewpoint over Surprise Valley and Goose Lake. This side trail is rated 5. Fandango Pass. Historical marker at the pass. Zero trip meter.
▼ 0.8   SO   Track on right goes to Shinn Spring.
5.8 s   SO   Track on left goes to Shinn Spring.
▼ 2.5   SO   Track on left along fence line. Entering Fandango Valley.
4.1 ▲   SO   Track on right along fence line. Leaving Fandango Valley.
▼ 2.7   SO   Track on right; then cattle guard.
3.9 ▲   SO   Cattle guard; then track on left.
▼ 4.8   SO   Track on left to corral.

1.8 ▲   SO   Track on right to corral.
▼ 6.1   SO   Track on left to heliport.
0.5 ▲   SO   Track on right to heliport.

GPS: N41°51.87' W120°17.02'

▼ 6.6   SO   Paved road on right is 47N72 to Del Pratt Spring. Zero trip meter.
0.0 ▲   Continue to the southeast on FR 9, following the sign to Fandango Pass. Road is now graded dirt.

GPS: N41°52.19' W120°17.41'

▼ 0.0   Continue to the northwest on FR 9, following sign to Buck Creek Guard Station. Road is now paved. Cattle guard.
2.3 ▲   SO   Cattle guard. Paved road on left is 47N72 to Del Pratt Spring. Zero trip meter.
▼ 0.1   SO   Buck Creek USFS Guard Station on right and left.
2.2 ▲   SO   Buck Creek USFS Guard Station on right and left.
▼ 0.7   TL   Paved road continues straight ahead to US 395. Turn left onto graded dirt road, following sign to Lassen Creek.
1.6 ▲   TR   T-intersection with paved FR 9 (CR 133C). Follow sign to Fandango Pass.

GPS: N41°52.61' W120°18.04'

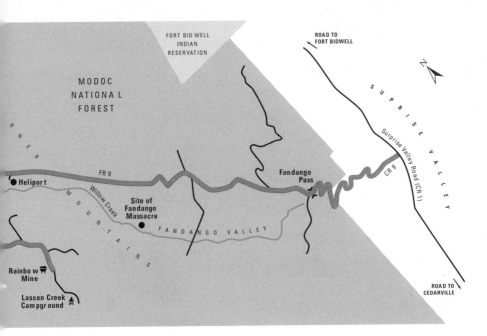

▼ 0.9	SO	Cross over Willow Creek on bridge.
1.4 ▲	SO	Cross over Willow Creek on bridge.
▼ 2.3	TR	4-way intersection. Track on left is the spur to Rainbow Mine. Zero trip meter and follow sign to US 395.
0.0 ▲		Continue to the northeast.
		GPS: N41°51.65′ W120°19.17′

Spur to Rainbow Mine

▼ 0.0		Proceed to the south.
▼ 0.7	SO	Track on right.
▼ 1.3	SO	Track on left.
▼ 1.7	SO	Track on left.
▼ 2.0	SO	Track on left.
▼ 2.3		Rainbow Mine—obsidian collecting site—on right, marked by a sign. Two tracks on left. Lassen Creek USFS Campground is 0.5 miles farther along this road.
		GPS: N41°50.13′ W120°17.75′

Continuation of Main Trail

▼ 0.0		Continue to the northwest and cross cattle guard.
2.2 ▲	TL	Cattle guard; then 4-way intersection.

Track straight ahead is the spur to the Rainbow Mine. Zero trip meter and turn left onto FR 30.

GPS: N41°51.65′ W120°19.17′

▼ 0.8	SO	Track on left.
1.4 ▲	SO	Track on right.
▼ 1.3	SO	Track on left; then cattle guard.
0.9 ▲	SO	Cattle guard; then track on right.
▼ 1.9	SO	Track on left.
0.3 ▲	SO	Track on right.
▼ 2.0	SO	Track on left to transfer station.
0.2 ▲	SO	Track on right to transfer station.
▼ 2.2		Trail ends at US 395. Turn right for New Pine Creek and Oregon; turn left for Alturas. CR 47 continues straight ahead and travels 1.4 miles to the site of the lumber mills and the settlement of Willow Ranch.
0.0 ▲		From US 395 at Modoc County mile marker 54, 7.5 miles south of New Pine Creek, zero trip meter and turn east on graded dirt FR 30 (CR 47). To the west, CR 47 continues 1.4 miles to the site of lumber mills and the settlement of Willow Ranch.
		GPS: N41°53.33′ W120°20.39′

New Pine Creek to Fort Bidwell Trail

STARTING POINT US 395 at New Pine Creek
FINISHING POINT Intersection of CR 1 and CR 6 at Fort Bidwell
TOTAL MILEAGE 16.5 miles
UNPAVED MILEAGE 15.4 miles
DRIVING TIME 1.5 hours
ELEVATION RANGE 5,600–7,500 feet
USUALLY OPEN June to December
BEST TIME TO TRAVEL June to December
DIFFICULTY RATING 2
SCENIC RATING 8
REMOTENESS RATING +0

Special Attractions

- Easy picturesque trail provides access to other 4WD trails in the Warner Mountains.
- Camping and picnicking at Lily Lake.
- Aspen viewing in the fall.

History

New Pine Creek enjoyed a boom period after the 1905 discovery of gold in the nearby Highgrade Mining District. New Pine Creek had a population of about 100 when the initial discovery was made, and by 1911, the population had shot up to nearly 1,000. The stagecoach service changed its route to facilitate the booming mountaintop mining community. The stages had previously crossed the Warner Mountains via the well-formed Fandango Pass route; now they traveled a longer and rougher route. The twisting grade to the settlement of Highgrade was an additional 1,300 feet higher than the more straightforward Fandango Pass. Our trail follows close to the original stagecoach trail.

Stages passed a mill just before the crest of the mountain. The mill was on the south side of the wagon road beside the old Bonanza Mine, only a few hundred yards before the turn for Dismal Swamp. The Big Four, Consolidated, and Custom Mines also operated large stamp mills in the area. The stages stopped off at the Highgrade hotel and continued down the east side of the range to Fort Bidwell.

The fort had been established back in 1866 to protect settlers in Surprise Valley and assure the safe passage of freight wagons to and from Idaho. John Bidwell (see page 226) of the Chico region had vested interests in wagon roads to Idaho and pushed for appropriate military protection in this region. Fort Bidwell, named for the then Congressman, reflected his success. Troops at the new fort were involved in major engagements throughout the late 1860s, lesser so in the 1870s except for the Modoc War of 1872–73. By the late 1870s, Fort Bidwell consisted of an imposing number of buildings on a quadrangle. The officers' quarters were of splendid construction, with front verandas and excellent views of the valley. The impressive general store in the growing town, which still stands, was built in 1874. The fort was abandoned in 1893 and became a non-reservation boarding school for Native Americans until 1930.

The community at Fort Bidwell pursued agriculture and logging industries, and enjoyed the increased trade brought by the gold rush at Highgrade. The Fort Bidwell Hotel and restaurant were constructed during this period. Though mining continued into the 1930s, the boom times of New Pine Creek and Fort Bidwell dwindled after 1913. The stone schoolhouse at the eastern end of the trail was built in 1917.

Description

This trail travels a roughly graded county road from New Pine Creek, up and over the Warner Mountains, to Fort Bidwell in Surprise Valley. The road is rough enough that a high-clearance vehicle is preferable.

Two miles from the start of the trail, you will see a rock house on the left that was built in the early 1900s by a man wanting to please his wife. The house is built in the style of her home country of Ireland, and is listed in Modoc County's historical houses tour. It is privately owned; please respect the occupants' privacy and remain on the road.

Lily Lake, a small natural lake in a basin surrounded by aspens and conifers, is especially picturesque. There is a forest service picnic ground at the lake, which is particularly lovely in fall when the aspens are golden. The best time to see fall colors along this trail is mid-September to mid-October. The Cave Lake USFS Campground is a short way past the lake, and a hiking trail circles the lake and connects the picnic area and the campground.

Two more difficult 4WD trails intersect at the high point of this trail. To the north is North Coast #46: Dismal Swamp Trail; to the south is North Coast #47: Highgrade Trail. Both require high-clearance 4WDs. The old mining shanty town of Highgrade was on the northwest corner of this intersection. Little remains at the privately owned site.

The trail descends the eastern side of the Warner Mountains, passing the remains of the Klondike Mine, and crosses open country with sagebrush and stands of aspens. There are views west to Mount Vida and southeast to the Surprise Valley. The trail ends in the quiet hamlet of Fort Bidwell. Look for the stone schoolhouse on a rise at the end of the trail. Built of local stone by a mason from Scotland, it is one of the few stone buildings to remain, most have been razed. The schoolhouse is privately owned.

Current Road Information

Modoc National Forest
Warner Mountain Ranger District
PO Box 220
Cedarville, CA 96104
(530) 279-6116

Map References

BLM   Cedarville
USFS Modoc National Forest
USGS 1:24,000   Willow Ranch, Mt.
        Bidwell, Fort Bidwell
        1:100,000 Cedarville
Maptech CD-ROM: Shasta-Trinity/Modoc
Northern California Atlas & Gazetteer, p. 31
California Road & Recreation Atlas, p. 49
Other: Modoc Country USFS/BLM Map

Historic Fort Bidwell schoolhouse

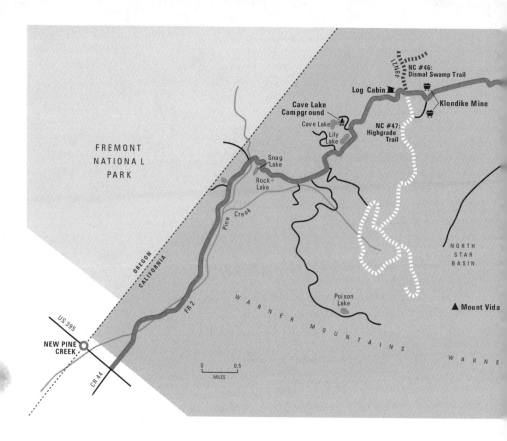

Route Directions

▼ 0.0   From US 395 at New Pine Creek, 0.5
          miles south of the Oregon state line,
          zero trip meter and turn east on paved
          FR 2, following the sign for Lily Lake
          and Cave Lake Campground. Remain
          on paved road for 0.6 miles.

4.8 ▲   Trail ends at intersection with US 395
          at New Pine Creek, opposite CR 44.
          Turn right for Oregon; turn left for
          Alturas.
          GPS: N41°59.16′ W120°17.82′

▼ 0.6   SO Track on left. Road turns to graded dirt.
4.2 ▲   SO Track on right. Road is now paved.
▼ 0.9   SO Cross over Pine Creek.
3.9 ▲   SO Cross over Pine Creek.
▼ 1.5   SO Track on right; then cross over Pine Creek.
3.3 ▲   SO Cross over Pine Creek; then track
          on left.
▼ 1.7   SO Stone house on left is private property.
3.1 ▲   SO Stone house on right is private property.

▼ 2.6   SO Track on right.
2.2 ▲   SO Track on left.
▼ 2.7   SO Track on right.
2.1 ▲   SO Track on left.
▼ 2.8   SO Track on left.
2.0 ▲   SO Track on right.
▼ 3.1   SO Track on left; then small lake on left.
1.7 ▲   SO Small lake on right; then track on right.
          GPS: N41°59.39′ W120°14.34′

▼ 3.7   SO Track on left; then cross over creek.
1.1 ▲   SO Cross over creek; then track on right.
▼ 3.8   SO Cross over creek.
1.0 ▲   SO Cross over creek.
▼ 3.9   SO Track on right; then Snag Lake on right
          (privately owned).
0.9 ▲   SO Snag Lake on left (privately owned);
          then track on left.
▼ 4.4   SO Track on right; then Rock Lake on right
          (privately owned); then track on right.
0.4 ▲   SO Track on left; then Rock Lake on left
          (privately owned); then track on left.
▼ 4.6   SO Track on right is a dead end.

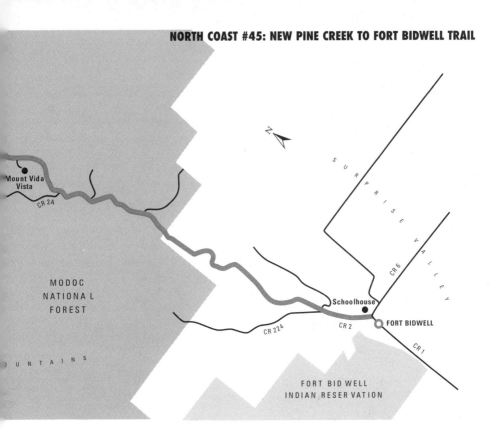

.2 ▲   SO Track on left is a dead end.
GPS: N41°58.82′ W120°13.61′

▼ 4.8   SO Graded road on right goes to Poison Lake. Follow sign to Cave Lake Campground. Zero trip meter.

.0 ▲   Continue to the northwest.
GPS: N41°58.70′ W120°13.46′

▼ 0.0   Continue to the southeast.

.2 ▲   SO Graded road on left goes to Poison Lake. Zero trip meter.

▼ 0.1   SO Track on left.

.1 ▲   SO Track on right.

▼ 0.2   SO Track on left.

.0 ▲   SO Track on right.

▼ 0.4   SO Graded road on right.

.8 ▲   SO Graded road on left.
GPS: N41°58.57′ W120°13.10′

▼ 0.7   BR Graded road on left.

.5 ▲   BL Graded road on right.
GPS: N41°58.62′ W120°12.80′

▼ 0.9   SO Graded road on left goes a short distance to Lily Lake Picnic Area.

0.3 ▲   SO Graded road on right goes a short distance to Lily Lake Picnic Area.
GPS: N41°58.55′ W120°12.63′

▼ 1.2   BR Graded road on left goes into Cave Lake USFS Campground and continues 0.3 miles to the lake. Zero trip meter.

0.0 ▲   Continue to the south.
GPS: N41°58.64′ W120°12.40′

▼ 0.0   Continue to the northeast.

1.2 ▲   BL Graded road on right goes into Cave Lake USFS Campground and continues 0.3 miles to the lake. Zero trip meter.

▼ 0.7   SO Two tracks on right.

0.5 ▲   SO Two tracks on left.

▼ 1.0   SO Small track on left; then remains of a log cabin on left; then two tracks on right.

0.2 ▲   SO Two tracks on left; then remains of a

JOHN BIDWELL

John Bidwell

John Bidwell, born in 1819 in New York, was raised in Pennsylvania and Ohio. After a brief stint as a teacher, he moved to Missouri where he claimed land for a farm, but lost it to a claim jumper in 1840. Bidwell helped organize the Western Emigration Society, and he spent the winter of 1840-41 preparing for an expedition to California. In May 1841, a group of 77 people, including Jesuit missionary Pierre-Jean De Smet, led by mountain man Thomas Fitzpatrick, set out from St. Louis. Half of the party followed Fitzpatrick into Oregon, but 32 people completed the journey to California.

The Bartleson-Bidwell party (John Bartleson was the nominal leader) was the first emigrant party to traverse overland from the Missouri River to South Pass in what is now Wyoming, north of the Great Salt Lake, and through the Sierra Nevada. No one in the group was an experienced trailsman and they only knew to head west. They negotiated numerous rivers, crossed stretches of desert, and endured rain, dust, and wind, and had little success hunting. They decided to abandon their wagons after passing the Great Salt Lake and had to resort to eating their livestock. It was not until November 1841 that the exhausted pioneers completed their journey. Their route came to be known as the California Trail.

Once in California, Bidwell worked for John Sutter. In 1844, he became a Mexican citizen and gained a large land grant at today's Rio Vista. He joined in the Bear Flag Revolt of 1846 and marched with John C. Frémont's volunteers from Sonoma to Monterey, eventually returning to work again for Sutter in 1847.

The gold discovery in 1848 led Bidwell to prospect successfully for gold at Bidwell's Bar on the North Fork of the Feather River. By 1849, he was able to purchase a 28,000-acre ranch in the vicinity of Chico. Bidwell established himself as one of the state's finest agriculturists and his 26-room mansion in Chico is now a state historic park. He embarked on a political career and served in the House of Representatives, from 1865 to 1867; he made an unsuccessful bid for the Presidency on the Prohibition Party ticket in 1892.

Bidwell recounted his pioneer experiences in a series of articles titled "Echoes of the Past" in the popular *Century Magazine* in 1890 and 1891; he died in 1900.

---

log cabin on right; then small track on right.
GPS: N41°58.41' W120°11.50'

▼ 1.2 SO 4-way intersection on saddle. To the right is North Coast #47: Highgrade Trail. To the left is North Coast #46: Dismal Swamp Trail (48N21). Zero trip meter and follow the sign to Fort Bidwell.

0.0 ▲ Continue to the northwest.
GPS: N41°58.38' W120°11.37'

▼ 0.0 Continue to the southeast.

4.0 ▲ SO 4-way intersection on saddle. To the left is North Coast #47: Highgrade Trail. To the right is North Coast #46: Dismal Swamp Trail (48N21). Zero trip meter and follow the sign to Lily Lake and US 395.

▼ 0.2 SO Track on right.

3.8 ▲ SO Track on left.

▼ 0.4 SO Klondike Mine on left, track on right, and log cabin on right.

3.6 ▲ SO Log cabin on left, track on left, and Klondike Mine on right.

Small lake near the beginning of the trail

▼ 0.9 SO Track on left.
3.1 ▲ SO Track on right.
▼ 1.6 SO Track on left.
2.4 ▲ SO Track on right.
▼ 3.1 SO Track on right goes 0.1 miles to Mount Vida Vista.
0.9 ▲ SO Track on left goes 0.1 miles to Mount Vida Vista.
GPS: N41°56.44′ W120°10.65′

▼ 3.6 SO Track on left.
0.4 ▲ SO Track on right.
▼ 3.8 SO Cross over ditch; then track on right.
0.2 ▲ SO Track on left; then cross over ditch.
▼ 4.0 SO Graded road on right is CR 2A to North Star Basin. Zero trip meter.
0.0 ▲ Continue to the northwest.
GPS: N41°55.80′ W120°10.62′

▼ 0.0 Continue to the southeast.
5.3 ▲ SO Graded road on left is CR 2A to North Star Basin. Zero trip meter and follow the sign to Cave and Lily Lakes.
▼ 0.1 SO Cattle guard.
5.2 ▲ SO Cattle guard.
▼ 0.5 SO Track on left.
4.8 ▲ SO Track on right.
▼ 1.3 SO Track on left.
4.0 ▲ SO Track on right.
▼ 1.9 SO Cattle guard. Leaving Modoc National Forest.
3.4 ▲ SO Cattle guard. Entering Modoc National Forest.
GPS: N41°54.44′ W120°10.07′

▼ 2.3 SO Track on right.
3.0 ▲ SO Track on left.
▼ 3.1 SO Cattle guard.
2.2 ▲ SO Cattle guard.
▼ 4.7 SO Graded road on left.
0.6 ▲ SO Graded road on right.
▼ 4.8 SO Paved road on right is CR 224, which goes to Bidwell Canyon Trail and Mill Creek Access. Road is now paved. Remain on paved road, following sign to Fort Bidwell. Cattle guard.
0.5 ▲ SO Cattle guard; then paved road on left is CR 224, which goes to Bidwell Canyon

Trail and Mill Creek Access. Road is now graded dirt. Continue straight ahead on CR 2 (FR 2), following sign to Cave and Lily Lakes.
GPS: N41°52.22′ W120°09.36′

▼ 5.3 Trail ends at T-intersection with paved CR 1 and CR 6 in Fort Bidwell. Turn right for Cedarville. The old stone Fort Bidwell Schoolhouse is up on the hill to the left at the intersection.
0.0 ▲ Trail commences on the north side of Fort Bidwell where CR 1 meets CR 6. Zero trip meter and turn northwest on paved CR 2, following the sign for Mill Creek and US 395. The old stone Fort Bidwell Schoolhouse is up on the hill to the right at the intersection.
GPS: N41°51.84′ W120°09.05′

NORTH COAST #46

Dismal Swamp Trail

STARTING POINT North Coast #45: New Pine Creek to Fort Bidwell Trail, 7.2 miles east of New Pine Creek
FINISHING POINT Moonlight Mine at the end of the loop, 0.4 miles east of North Coast #45: New Pine Creek to Fort Bidwell Trail
TOTAL MILEAGE 11.4 miles
UNPAVED MILEAGE 11.4 miles
DRIVING TIME 2.5 hours
ELEVATION RANGE 7,000–8,200 feet
USUALLY OPEN June to December
BEST TIME TO TRAVEL Dry weather
DIFFICULTY RATING 6
SCENIC RATING 10
REMOTENESS RATING +1

Special Attractions
■ Open expanse of the very pretty Dismal Swamp.
■ Aspen viewing in the fall.
■ Views into three states from Bidwell Mountain.

View of Oregon from Bidwell Mountain

History

'Dismal" is a misnomer for this picturesque high mountain region, but it probably describes the way settlers felt when their land was appropriated for an army post. Initially, the site for a post was selected just south of Lake City in 1865, but it was changed to the vicinity of what is now Fort Bidwell. Major Robert S. Williamson's choice meant that the government usurped the land held by three settlers. Though letters were written to appropriate authorities, their cries of injustice went unanswered. One settler, a Mr. Disabell, moved north to the wetlands that took on his name. Over the years, however, the name changed from Disabell to Dismal.

Dismal Swamp Trail leaves the old New Pine to Fort Bidwell wagon road at the crest of the Warner Mountains near the site of Highgrade, a mining camp that enjoyed a boom period until 1912.

Description

Don't be fooled by the name of this trail. Dismal Swamp is anything but dismal. The trail leaves North Coast #45: New Pine Creek to Fort Bidwell Trail opposite the start of North Coast #47: Highgrade Trail. The well-used road leads through the forest, passing the site of the still-active Moonlight Mine to enter the Dismal Swamp–Twelvemile Creek Area. This is a sensitive wildlife and vegetation area. Dismal Swamp is an open area, dissected by small creeks and surrounded by conifers and aspens. In fall, the area is a popular base camp for deer hunters. The trail wraps around the edge of the open area and crosses briefly into Fremont National Forest in Oregon. It follows unmarked small formed trails that traverse the open sagebrush areas to Bidwell Mountain. In fall the area is bright with golden aspens.

A short but worthwhile side trail leads 0.4 miles to the top of Bidwell Mountain. From

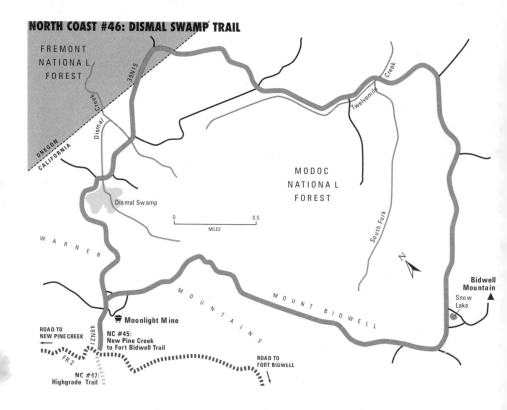

the rocky open summit, there are excellent views toward Oregon and Nevada. To the southeast is small Lake Annie at the foot of Lake Annie Mountain, the seasonal Cow Head Lake, and north end of Surprise Valley. To the west are the Warner Mountains.

The main trail immediately passes small Snow Lake. When dry, large boulders of obsidian can be seen on the lakebed. The trail continues along the ridge top to Mount Bidwell (not to be confused with Bidwell Mountain), and travels across the open top. Mount Vida is to the south, Goose Lake to the west, and North Coast #45: New Pine Creek to Fort Bidwell Trail is below.

The trail becomes more difficult at the descent from Mount Bidwell. As far as the top of the mountain, it is rated a 4 for difficulty. As you descend, the rating increases to a 5. The final section of the trail descends a very steep pinch to exit back to the start of the trail. This final descent is rated 6. Continuing straight ahead past the top of the final descent may enable you to exit via an easier trail

that travels through the workings of the Moonlight Mine. This is an active mine, and the owners may impose travel restrictions. Should this happen, please respect their rights and use only the more difficult route to exit.

This trail is lightly used, and you are unlikely to see other travelers except in hunting season. Mountain bikers know the trail as the North Star Basin Trail, rated for novices. Campers will find many suitable backcountry sites along this trail. Some of the best are on the edge of Dismal Swamp, but there are other more exposed sites on top of Mount Bidwell. The trail is best traveled in the direction described below.

Current Road Information

Modoc National Forest
Warner Mountain Ranger District
PO Box 220
Cedarville, CA 96104
(530) 279-6116

A view from Mount Bidwell

Map References

BLM Cedarville
USFS Modoc National Forest
USGS 1:24,000 Mt. Bidwell, Lake Annie
      1:100,000 Cedarville
Maptech CD-ROM: Shasta-Trinity/Modoc
Northern California Atlas & Gazetteer, p. 31
California Road & Recreation Atlas, p. 49
      (incomplete)
Other: Modoc Country USFS/BLM Map

Route Directions

▼ 0.0   From North Coast #45: New Pine Creek to Fort Bidwell Trail, 7.2 miles east of New Pine Creek, zero trip meter and turn northeast on formed dirt trail 48N21, following the sign to Dismal Swamp. North Coast #47: Highgrade Trail is opposite.
        GPS: N41°58.38′ W120°11.37′

▼ 0.3 SO Track on left; then Moonlight Mine on right. This is the alternate end of the loop.
        GPS: N41°58.56′ W120°11.07′

▼ 0.4 SO Track on right. This is the end of the loop. Continue straight ahead. Trail is best traveled in the direction described.
        GPS: N41°58.63′ W120°11.00′

▼ 0.5 SO Track on right.
▼ 0.7 SO Track on right.
▼ 0.8 SO Entering Dismal Swamp–Twelvemile Creek Area.
        GPS: N41°58.78′ W120°10.72′

▼ 1.7 TR Track on left; then cross over Dismal Creek. This is the old dam.
        GPS: N41°59.32′ W120°10.34′

▼ 1.8 SO Track on right.
▼ 2.1 SO Cross through wash.
▼ 2.2 BL Track on right.
        GPS: N41°59.40′ W120°09.83′

▼ 2.6 SO Cattle guard at Oregon state line. Cross into Oregon and enter Fremont National Forest. Road is now designated 39N15. Zero trip meter.
        GPS: N41°59.67′ W120°09.48′

▼ 0.0   Continue to the northeast.
▼ 0.4 TR Turn right onto unmarked track and cross through wash.
        GPS: N41°59.80′ W120°09.17′

▼ 0.6 SO Track on left; then pass through gate. Re-entering California and Modoc National Forest.
        GPS: N41°59.70′ W120°09.06′

▼ 1.0 TR Track on left.
        GPS: N41°59.49′ W120°08.65′

▼ 1.2 SO Tank on left.
▼ 1.5 SO Unmarked 4-way intersection. Continue to the south.
        GPS: N41°59.12′ W120°08.63′

▼ 2.3 SO Track on right.
▼ 2.6 SO Cross through South Fork Twelvemile Creek.
        GPS: N41°58.64′ W120°07.65′

▼ 2.7 BL Track on right.
▼ 3.2 SO Track on left.
        GPS: N41°58.34′ W120°07.17′

▼ 3.9 SO Cattle guard; then track on left.
▼ 4.2 SO Cross through wash.
▼ 4.8 SO Track on left.
▼ 5.2 TR Short climb; then T-intersection. Track on left goes 0.4 miles past Snow Lake to Bidwell Mountain. Zero trip meter. Intersection is unmarked.
        GPS: N41°57.01′ W120°08.43′

▼ 0.0   Continue to the west.
▼ 0.1 SO Snow Lake on left.
▼ 0.2 SO Track on left.
▼ 0.4 SO Track on left.
▼ 0.6 BR Track on left.
▼ 1.2 BL Track on right.
▼ 2.0 SO Track on left.
▼ 2.4 SO Wire gate.
        GPS: N41°58.31′ W120°09.98′

▼ 2.8 SO Cross through creek.

▼ 2.9 SO Trail becomes rockier and looser as it descends toward the Moonlight Mine.
GPS: N41°58.45′ W120°10.43′

▼ 3.3 TR Turn right onto lesser used trail and descend short steep slope. Track ahead and is an easier alternate exit through the Moonlight Mine.
GPS: N41°58.54′ W120°10.81′

▼ 3.5 Track on right. Bear left; then end of loop. Turn left to exit back to North Coast #45: New Pine Creek to Fort Bidwell Trail
GPS: N41°58.63′ W120°11.00′

NORTH COAST #47

Highgrade Trail

STARTING POINT North Coast #45: New Pine Creek to Fort Bidwell Trail, 7.2 miles east of New Pine Creek
FINISHING POINT Mount Vida
TOTAL MILEAGE 5.3 miles (one-way), plus 1.4-mile spur to Mount Vida
UNPAVED MILEAGE 5.3 miles, plus 1.4-mile spur
DRIVING TIME 1 hour (one-way)
ELEVATION RANGE 6,800–8,000 feet
USUALLY OPEN June to December
BEST TIME TO TRAVEL Dry weather
DIFFICULTY RATING 7
SCENIC RATING 9
REMOTENESS RATING +0

Special Attractions

■ Remains of Highgrade Mining District.
■ Views from Mount Vida over Surprise Valley and Goose Lake.
■ Challenging steep climb at the end of the trail.

History

Prior to its designation as a mining district, the Northern Paiute knew the Highgrade Mining District, immediately south of the Oregon border, as a source of obsidian for spear points and arrowheads.

In 1905, a shepherd discovered the rumored Hoags gold site, named for Daniel Hoag, a scout from Fort Bidwell who found the site in the 1860s but was killed before he could map his find. A rush to the area ensued and by 1910, New Pine Creek's population neared 1,000. Fort Bidwell also enjoyed the boom. The camp at Highgrade could not meet all of the miners' needs. Branley sprouted up south of the main east-west wagon road, just uphill from Mineral Spring.

More than 70 mines were in operation at the Highgrade district's peak in 1911. Some of the mines you'll pass along the trail, roughly in order as you head south along Alturas Ridge, are Evening Star, White Quartz, Mountain Sheep, Klondike, Alturas, Mineral Spring, and Alturas Fraction before you enter the old site of Branley. Beyond Yellow Mountain, mine claims start again: Crown Point, then another Klondike claim, Diamond Fraction, Old Glory, Valley View, Leland, and Uncle Joe, which is close to the spur toward Mount Vida, just below the rise called Discovery Hill.

After the ore played out in the late 1910s, the Highgrade district began to fade away, though mining activity continued into the 1930s, and still continues on a very small scale. The whole area still has the ghostly feel of a mountain community swept up by a gold rush and long abandoned.

Description

This short spur trail partly follows the Highgrade National Recreation Trail through the remains of Highgrade. A very difficult spur also runs 1.4 miles toward Mount Vida, where it turns into a hiking trail. Initially, the trail is lightly graded as it winds through the forest. Many tracks lead off through the forest, some the remains of mine sites. There are shafts and some old log cabins scattered among the trees.

After a short distance, Mineral Spring bubbles up alongside the trail. The trail then passes the remains of the Warlock Mine. Old cabins, two stamp mills, and several old vehicles remain at the site. A spur leads away from the trail and skirts the north side of North Star

Remains of Warlock Mine stamp mill

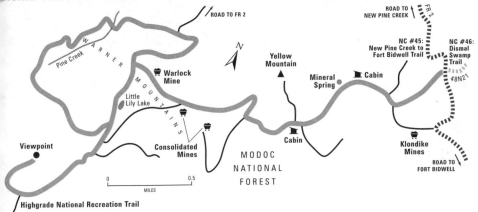

Basin toward Mount Vida. This spur is rated a 7 for difficulty and should not be underestimated. The rating comes from a 0.3-mile section with a side slope that tilts vehicles toward the drop. The track is also steep and loose, with some sharp, awkward turns. Once on the difficult section, there is nowhere safe to turn until the top of the ridge, visible at the end of the climb. You can see the difficult section ahead, twisting down into a gully and climbing steeply to the ridge. The final climb to the ridge is extremely steep, with a loose, low traction surface. Drivers should be very sure of their ability to make the climb before attempting the stretch. It is not an option to reverse and should be considered a highly dangerous manuever.

The spur continues along the ridge to a high point with views over Goose Lake, north into Oregon, east into Nevada, and of Mount Vida and the bald top of Mount Bidwell.

Drivers who do not wish to tackle the 7-rated section should turn at the hiking trail mentioned in the route directions. A short hike west to the top of the ridge will yield the same views. The trail to this point is rated a 4 for difficulty, as is the main loop.

The main loop travels back on small forest roads crossing over Pine Creek and returning to the Warlock Mine. Mule deer are here, and the area is popular with hunters in season. Sections of the 4WD trail are also used by mountain bikers, who can continue along the national recreation trail to the south of Mount Vida. The mountain bike route is rated moderate.

Current Road Information

Modoc National Forest
Warner Mountain Ranger District
PO Box 220
Cedarville, CA 96104
(530) 279-6116

Map References

BLM   Cedarville
USFS   Modoc National Forest
USGS   1:24,000   Mt. Bidwell
      1:100,000   Cedarville
Maptech CD-ROM: Shasta-Trinity/Modoc
Northern California Atlas & Gazetteer, p. 31
California Road & Recreation Atlas, p. 49
Other: Modoc Country USFS/BLM Map

Route Directions

▼ 0.0   From North Coast #45: New Pine Creek to Fort Bidwell Trail, 7.2 miles east of New Pine Creek, zero trip meter and turn south on formed dirt trail marked Highgrade Trail, National Recreation Trail, following sign to Mineral Spring. North Coast #46: Dismal Swamp Trail is opposite the start.

      GPS: N41°58.38' W120°11.37'

Highgrade trail signpost

▼ 0.4 TR Track on left goes to the Klondike Mines. Track straight ahead. Follow sign to Mineral Spring, remaining on the national recreation trail.
GPS: N41°58.09′ W120°11.57′

▼ 0.5 SO Track on right.
▼ 0.6 SO Mine tailings on right; then track on right.
GPS: N41°58.14′ W102°11.73′

▼ 0.7 SO Collapsed log cabin on right.
▼ 0.8 BL Mineral Spring on right; then track on left.
GPS: N41°58.06′ W120°11.95′

▼ 1.1 SO Track on left; then log cabin on left in the trees; then track on right.
GPS: N41°57.78′ W120°12.12′

▼ 1.5 TR Track on left into the Consolidated Mines.
GPS: N41°57.68′ W120°12.52′

▼ 2.1 SO Track left goes 0.1 miles to the Consolidated Mines. National recreation trail goes left at this point.
GPS: N41°57.58′ W120°12.95′

▼ 2.3 SO Track on right goes through the Warlock Mine workings.
GPS: N41°57.58′ W120°13.14′

▼ 2.4 SO Second entrance to Warlock Mine.
▼ 2.5 TL T-intersection. Turn left and start the loop. Track on right is end of the loop.
GPS: N41°57.63′ W120°13.35′

▼ 2.7 SO Track on left to Little Lily Lake.
▼ 2.9 TR Track straight ahead is the spur to Mount Vida. Zero trip meter and turn right, following sign to the Sunset Mine.
GPS: N41°57.30′ W120°13.31′

Spur to Mount Vida

▼ 0.0 Continue to the southeast.
GPS: N41°57.30′ W120°13.31′

▼ 0.1 SO Track on left.
GPS: N41°57.21′ W120°13.29′

▼ 0.7 SO Track on left with viewpoint over North Star Basin. Track on right.
GPS: N41°57.12′ W120°13.26′

▼ 0.9 SO Marker for the national recreation trail on right. Drivers not wishing to do the difficult 7-rated section should turn here.
GPS: N41°57.03′ W120°13.44′

▼ 1.0 SO Start of off-camber section with a difficult twist.
GPS: N41°56.91′ W120°13.52′

▼ 1.2 TR T-intersection. Track on left.
GPS: N41°56.75′ W120°13.70

▼ 1.4 Spur trail finishes at a high viewpoint.
GPS: N41°56.93′ W120°13.73′

Continuation of Main Trail

▼ 0.0 Continue to the southwest.
GPS: N41°57.30′ W120°13.31′

▼ 1.4 BR Track on left; then track on right; then cross over Pine Creek.
GPS: N41°57.75′ W120°13.63′

▼ 1.8 TR T-intersection.
GPS: N41°57.86′ W120°13.20′

▼ 2.0 SO Track on left.
▼ 2.4 End of loop. Turn left to exit back the way you came.
GPS: N41°57.63′ W120°13.35′

Selected Further Reading

AAA California, Nevada Tour Book, 2001.

Alt, David D., and Donald W. Hyndman. *Roadside Geology of Northern California.* Missoula, Mont.: Mountain Press Publishing Co., 1996.

—. *Roadside Geology of Northern and Central California.* Missoula, Mont.: Mountain Press Publishing Co., 2000.

Bauer, Helen. *California Mission Days.* New York: Doubleday & Company, Inc., 1951.

Beck, Warren A., and Ynez D. Haase. *Historical Atlas of California.* Norman, Okla.: University of Oklahoma Press, 1974.

Bischoff, Matt C. *Touring California & Nevada Hot Springs.* Helena, Mont.: Falcon Publishing, Inc., 1997.

Boessenecker, John. *Gold Dust and Gunsmoke.* New York: John Wiley & Sons, Inc., 1999.

Braasch, Barbara. *California's Gold Rush.* Medina, Wash.: Johnston Associates International, 1996.

Bright, William. *1500 California Place Names, Their Origin and Meaning.* Berkeley, Calif.: University of California Press, 1998.

Broman, Mickey, and Russ Leadabrand. *California Ghost Town Trails.* Baldwin Park, Calif.: Gem Guides Book Company, 1981.

Brown, Ann Marie. *California Waterfalls.* San Francisco: Foghorn Press, 1997.

Brown, Vinson. *The Californian Wildlife Region.* Happy Camp, Calif.: Naturegraph Publishers, Inc., 1999.

Browning, Peter. *Place Names of the Sierra Nevada.* Berkeley, Calif.: Wilderness Press, 1992.

—. Day Trips: *Roaming the Backroads of Northern California.* San Francisco: Chronicle Books, 1979.

California Historical Landmarks. Sacramento, Calif.: State of California—The Resource Agency, 1996.

Clark, Carol. *Explorers of the West.* Salt Lake City, Utah: Great Mountain West Supply, 1997.

Clark, Lew, and Ginny Lew. *High Mountains & Deep Valleys, The Gold Bonanza Days.* San Luis Obispo, Calif.: Western Trails Publications, 1978.

Crutchfield, James A. *Mountain Men of the American West.* Boise, Idaho: Tamarack Books, Inc., 1997.

Deverell, William. *Railroad Crossing: Californians and the Railroad, 1850-1910.* Los Angeles: University of California Press, 1996.

Dunn, Jerry Camarillo, Jr. *National Geographic's Driving Guides to America: California and Nevada and Hawaii.* Washington, D.C.: The Book Division National Geographic Society. 1996.

Durham, David L. *Place Names of California's North Coast.* Clovis, Calif.: Word Dancer Press, 2000.

—. *Place-Names of Northeastern California.* Clovis, Calif.: Word Dancer Press, 2000.

—. *Place-Names of California's North Sacramento Valley.* Clovis, Calif.: Word Dancer Press, 2000.

—. *Place-Names of California's North San Joaquin Valley.* Clovis, Calif.: Word Dancer Press, 2000.

—. *Place-Names of California's North Sacramento Valley.* Clovis, Calif.: Word Dancer Press, 2000.

—. *Place-Names of Central California.* Clovis, Calif.: Word Dancer Press, 2000.

—. *Place-Names of the San Francisco Bay Area.* Clovis, Calif.: Word Dancer Press, 2000.

Egan, Ferol. *Frémont.* Reno, Nevada: University of Nevada Press, 1985.

Florin, Lambert. *Ghost Towns of The West.* New York: Promontory Press, 1993.

Fujimoto, I., and D. Sunada, "Tule Lake Relocation Center, 1942-1946." Colorado Statue University, Fort Collins, CO

Gersch-Young, Marjorie. *Hot Springs and Hot Pools of the Southwest.* Santa Cruz, Calif.: Aqua Thermal Access, 2001.

Gudde, Erwin G. *1000 California Place Names.* Berkeley, Calif.: University of California Press, 1959.

Harris, Edward D. *John Charles Frémont and the Great Western Reconnaissance.* New York: Chelsea House Publishers, 1990.

—. *California Place Names.* Berkeley, Calif.: University of California Press, 1998.

Hart, James D. *A Companion to California.* New York: Oxford University Press, 1978.

Heizer, Robert F., ed. *The Destruction of California Indians.* Lincoln, Nebraska: University of Nebraska Press, 1993.

Heizer, Robert F., and Albert B. Elasser. *The Natural World of the California Indians.* Berkeley, Calif.: University of California Press, 1980.

Helfrich, Devere, Helen Helfrich, and Thomas Hunt. *Emigrant Trails West.* Reno, Nevada: Trails West Inc., 1984.

Hirschfelder, Arlene. *Native Americans.* New York: Dorling Kindersley Publishing, Inc., 2000.

The Historical Guide to North American Railroads. Waukesha, Wisc.: Kalmbach Publishing, 2000.

Holliday, J.S. *Rush for Riches: Gold Fever and the Making of California.* Berkley, Calif.: University of California Press, 1999.

Holmes, Robert. *California's Best-Loved Driving Tours.* New York: Macmillan Travel, 1999.

Hoxie, Frederick E., ed. *Encyclopedia of North American Indians.* Boston: Houghton Mifflin Company, 1996.

Huegel, Tony. *California Coastal Byways.* Idaho Falls, Idaho: The Post Company, 1996.

—. *Sierra Nevada Byways.* Idaho Falls, Idaho: The Post Company, 1997.

Indians of California, The. Alexandria, Va.: Time-Life Books, 1994.

Jameson, E. W., Jr., and Hans J. Peeters. *California Mammals.* Berkeley and Los Angeles: University of California Press, 1988.

Jameson, W. C. *Buried Treasures of California.* Little Rock, Ark.: August House Publishers, Inc., 1995.

Johnson, William Weber. *The Old West: The Forty-niners.* New York: Time-Life Books, 1974.

Johnston, Verna R. *California Forests and Woodlands.* Berkeley, Calif.: University of California Press, 1994.

Kavanagh, James, ed. *The Nature of California.* Helena, Mont.: Waterford Press Ltd., 1997.

Keyworth, C.L. *California Indians.* New York: Checkmark Books, 1991.

Klein, James. *Where to Find Gold in Northern California.* Baldwin Park, Calif.: Gem Guides Book Company, 2000.

Kricher, John. *California and Pacific Northwest Forests.* New York: Houghton Mifflin Company, 1998.

Kroeber, A. L. *Handbook of the Indians of California.* New York: Dover Publications, Inc., 1976.

Kyle, Douglas E. *Historic Spots in California.* Stanford, Calif.: Stanford University Press, 1990.

Lamar, Howard R., ed. *The New Encyclopedia of the American West.* New Haven, Conn.: Yale University Press, 1998.

Lewellyn, Harry. *Backroad Trips and Tips.* Costa Mesa, Calif.: Glovebox Publications, 1993.

Lewis, Donovan. *Pioneers of California.* San Francisco: Scottwall Associates, Publishers, 1993.

Marinacci Barbara, and Rudy Marinacci.

California's Spanish Place. Houston, Texas: Gulf Publishing Company, 1997.

Martin, Don, and Betty Martin. *California-Nevada Roads Less Traveled.* Henderson, Nevada: Pine Cone Press, Inc. 1999.

May, Antoinette. *Haunted Houses of California.* San Carlos, Calif.: Wide World Publishing/Tetra, 1998.

McConnell, Doug. *Bay Area Backroads.* San Francisco: Chronicle Books, 1999.

McDannold, Thomas A. *California's Chinese Heritage: A Legacy of Places.* Stockton, Calif.: Heritage West Books, 2000.

McDermott, John D. *A Guide to the Indian Wars of the West.* Lincoln, Nebraska: University of Nebraska Press, 1998.

McFerrin, Linda Watanabe. *Best Places Northern California.* Seattle, Wash.: Sasquatch Books, 2001.

McGrath, Roger D. *Gunfighters Highwaymen & Vigilantes, Violence on the Frontier.* Berkeley, Calif.: University of California Press, 1987.

Milner, Clyde A., II, Carol A. O'Conner, and Martha A. Sandweiss, eds. *The Oxford History of the American West.* New York: Oxford University Press, 1996.

Mitchell, James R. *Gem Trails of Northern California.* Baldwin Park, Calif.: Gem Guides Book Company, 1995.

Mitchell, John D. *Lost Mines and Buried Treasures Along the Old Frontier.* Glorieta, N. Mex.: 1995.

Morgan, Dale L. *Jedediah Smith and the Opening of the West.* Lincoln, Nebraska: University of Nebraska Press, 1964.

Nadeau, Remi. *Ghost Towns & Mining Camps of California.* Santa Barbara, Calif.: Crest Publishers, 1999.

Nash, Jay Robert. *Encyclopedia of Western Lawmen and Outlaws.* New York: Da Capo Press, 1994.

National Audubon Society Field Guide to California. New York: Alfred A. Knopf, Inc., 1998.

National Audubon Society Field Guide to North American Mammals. New York: Alfred A. Knopf, Inc., 1996.

Norris, Robert M., and Robert W. Webb. *Geology of California.* Santa Barbara: John Wiley & Sons, Inc., 1976.

North American Wildlife. New York: Readers Digest Association, Inc., 1982.

Oakeshott, Gordon B. *California's Changing Landscapes.* San Francisco: McGraw-Hill Book Company, 1978.

O'Neal, Bill. *Encyclopedia of Western Gunfighters.* Norman, Okla.: University of Oklahoma Press, 1979.

Paher, Stanley W. *Early Mining Days – California Gold Country: The Story Behind the Scenery.* KC Publications, Inc., 1996.

Patterson, Richard. *Historical Atlas of the Outlaw West.* Boulder, Colo.: Johnson Publishing Company, 1985.

Pearson, David W. *This Was Mining in the West.* Atglen, Penn.: Schiffer Publishing, 1996.

Pierce, L. Kingston. *America's Historic Trails with Tom Bodett.* San Francisco: KQED Books, 1997.

Poshek, Lucy, and Roger Naylor, comps. *California Trivia.* Nashville, Tenn.: Rutledge Hill Press, 1998.

Powell, Jerry A., and Charles L. Hogue. *California Insects.* Berkeley, Calif.: University of California Press, 1979.

Powers, Stephen. *Tribes of California.* Berkeley and Los Angeles: University of California Press, 1976.

Prucha, Francis Paul. *American Indian Treaties.* Berkeley, Calif.: University of California Press, 1994.

Roberts, George, and Jan Roberts. *Discover Historic California.* Baldwin Park, Calif.: Gem Guides Book Co., 1999.

Robertson, Donald B. *Encyclopedia of Western Railroad History, Volume IV: California.* Caldwell, Idaho: The Caxton Printers, Ltd., 1998.

Rolle, Andrew. *California: A History.* Wheeling, Ill.: Harlan Davidson, Inc., 1998.

Sagstetter, Beth, and Bill Sagstetter. *The Mining Camps Speak.* Denver: Benchmark Publishing, 1998.

Seagraves, Anne. *Soiled Doves: Prostitution in the Early West.* Hayden, Idaho: Wesanne Publications, 1994.

Secrest, William B. *California Desperadoes.* Clovis, Calif.: World Dancer Press, 2000.

—. *Lawmen & Desperados.* Spokane, Wash.: The Arthur H. Clark Company, 1994.

Schaffer, Jeffery P., Ben Schifrin, Thomas Winnett, and Ruby Johnson Jenkins. *The Pacific Crest Trail, Volume 1: California.* Berkeley, Calif.: Wilderness Press, 2000.

Schoenherr, Allan A. *A Natural History of California.* Berkeley, Calif.: University of California Press, 1992.

Smith, Raymond M. *Ten Overnight Trips on the Backroads of Nevada & California.* Minden, Nevada: Mr. Raymond M. Smith, 1994.

Takaki, Ronald. *Journey to Gold Mountain: The Chinese in 19th Century America.* New York: Chelsea House Publishers, 1994.

Taylor, Colin F. *The Native Americans: The Indigenous People of North America.* London: Salamander Books Ltd., 2000.

Thollander, Earl. *Earl Thollander's Back Roads of California.* Seattle, Wash.: Sasquatch Books, 1994.

Thrap, Dan L. *Encyclopedia of Frontier Biography.* 3 vols. Lincoln, Nebr.: University of Nebraska Press, 1988.

Trafzer, Clifford E., and Joel R. Hyer, eds. *Exterminate Them!* East Lansing, Mich.: Michigan State University Press, 1999.

Twain, Mark. *Roughing It.* New York: New American Library, 1962.

Varney, Philip. *Ghost Towns of Northern California.* Stillwater, Minn.: Voyager Press, Inc., 2001.

Waldman, Carl. *Encyclopedia of Native American Tribes.* New York: Facts on File, 1988.

Wright, Ralph B., ed. *California's Missions.* Los Angeles: The Stirling Press, 1967.

Wyman, David M. *Backroads of Northern California.* Stillwater, Minn.: Voyager Press, Inc., 2000.

Zauner, Lou, and Phyllis Zauner. *California Gold: Story of the Rush to Riches.* Sonoma, Calif.: Zanel Publications, 1997.

Zauner, Phyllis. *Those Legendary Men of the Wild West.* Sonoma, Calif.: Zanel Publications, 1991.

Selected Web sources

Arcata, CA, http://www.arcata.com/

California Environmental Resources Evaluation System (CERES), http://ceres.ca.gov/geo_area/index.html

California Historical Society, http://californiahistoricalsociety.org

California Missions, http://www.californiamissions.com

California State Parks, http:www.parks.ca.gov/

Ghost Towns, http://www.ghosttowns.com

GORP.com, http://gorp.away.com

Hoopa Tribal Museum, http://bss.sfsu.edu/calstudies/hupa/Hoopa.HTM

Humboldt State University Library, Arcata, CA: Regional studies, http://library.humboldt.edu/infoservices/humboldt.htm

Langeller, John Phillip, and Daniel Bernard Rosen, "El Presidio de San Francisco: A History under Spain and Mexico, 1776-1846, August, 1992, http://www.nps.gov/prsf/history/hrs/elpresid/elresid.htm

McCloud, CA, http://www.mccloudchamber.com

Mount Shasta, CA,

http://www.mtshastachamber.com

Northern California Travel and Tourism
Information System,
http://www.shastacascade.org

Pacific Crest Trail Association, http://pcta.org

Trinity County, CA,
http://www.trinitycounty.com

U.S. Bureau of Land Management,
California, http://www.blm.gov/ca

U.S. Forest Service, Pacific Southwest
Region, http://www.fs.fed.us/r5/forests.html

U.S. National Park Service, http://nps.gov/

About the Authors

Peter Massey grew up in the outback of Australia, where he acquired a life-long love of the backcountry. After retiring from a career in investment banking in 1986 at the age of thirty-five, he served as a director for a number of companies in the United States, the United Kingdom, and Australia. He moved to Colorado in 1993.

Jeanne Wilson was born and grew up in Maryland. After moving to New York City in 1980, she worked in advertising and public relations before moving to Colorado in 1993.

After traveling extensively in Australia, Europe, Asia, and Africa, the authors covered more than 80,000 miles touring the United States and the Australian outback between 1993 and 1997. This experience became the basis for creating the Backcountry Adventures and Trails guidebook series.

As the research team grew, a newcomer became a dedicated member of the Swagman team.

Angela Titus was born in Missouri and grew up in Virginia, where she attended the University of Virginia. She moved to Alabama and worked for *Southern Living Magazine* traveling, photographing, and writing about southeastern U.S. She moved to Colorado in 2002.

Since research for the Backcountry Adventures and Trails guidebooks began, Peter, Jeanne, and Angela have traveled more than 75,000 miles throughout the western states.

Photo Credits

Unless otherwise indicated in the following list of acknowledgments (which is organized by page number), all photographs were taken by Bushducks—Maggie Pinder and Donald McGann.

37 California Historical Society, San Francisco; **59** The North American Indian, by Edward S. Curtis; **81** California Historical Society, San Francisco; **87** Corel; **126** California Historical Society, San Francisco; **158** Corel; **192** California Historical Society, San Francisco; **193** California Historical Society, San Francisco; **226** California Historical Society, San Francisco.

Cover photography: Bushducks—Maggie Pinder and Donald McGann

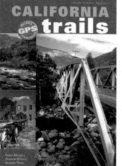
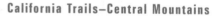

arizona trails
backroad guides

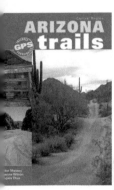

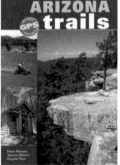

Arizona Trails–Northeast
This guidebook consists of meticulous details and directions for 47 trails located near the towns of Flagstaff, Williams, Prescott (northeast), Winslow, Fort Defiance and Window Rock. **ISBN-10, 1-930193-02-5; ISBN-13, 978-1-930193-02-4; Price $19.95**

Arizona Trails–West
This volume consists of comprehensive statistics and descriptions for 33 trails located near the towns of Bullhead City, Lake Havasu City, Parker, Kingman, Prescott (west), and Quartzsite (north). **ISBN-10, 1-930193-00-9; ISBN-13, 978-1-930193-00-0; Price $19.95**

Arizona Trails–Central
This field guide includes meticulous trail details for 44 off-road routes located near the towns of Phoenix, Wickenburg, Quartzsite (south), Payson, Superior, Globe and Yuma (north). **ISBN-10, 1-930193-01-7; ISBN-13, 978-1-930193-01-7; Price $19.95**

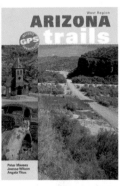

Arizona Trails–South
This handbook is composed of comprehensive statistics and descriptions for 33 trails located near the towns of Tucson, Douglas, Mammoth, Reddington, Stafford, Yuma (southeast), Ajo and Nogales. **ISBN-10, 1-930193-03-3; ISBN-13, 978-1-930193-03-1; Price $19.95**

to order
call 800-660-5107 or
visit 4WDbooks.com

utah trails
backroad guides

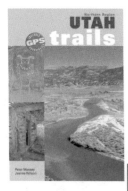

Utah Trails–Northern
This field guide includes meticulous trail details for 35 off-road routes near the towns of Vernal, Logan, Salt Lake City, Price, Wendover, Beaver, and Milford. **ISBN-10, 1-930139-30-0; ISBN-13, 978-1-930193-30-7; Price $16.95**

Utah Trails–Central
This volume is composed of comprehensive trail statistics for 34 trails near the towns of Green River, Richfield, Hanksville, Crescent Junction, and Castle Dale. **ISBN-10, 1-930193-31-9; ISBN-13, 978-1-930193-31-4; Price $16.95**

Utah Trails–Southeast
This guidebook contains detailed trail information for 57 trails in and around Moab, Monticello, Canyonlands National Park, Arches National Park, Green River, Mexican Hat, Bluff, and Blanding. **ISBN-10, 1-930193-09-2; ISBN-13, 978-1-930193-09-3; Price $19.95**

Utah Trails–Southwest
This travel guide outlines detailed trail information for 49 off-road routes in the Four Corners region and around the towns of Escalante, St. George, Kanab, Boulder, Bryce Canyon, Hurricane, and Ticaboo. **ISBN-10, 1-930193-10-6; ISBN-13, 978-1-930193-10-9; Price $19.95**

colorado trails
backroad guides

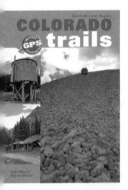

Colorado Trails—North-Central
This guidebook is composed of comprehensive statistics and descriptions of 28 trails, including 8 trails additional to those profiled in the Adventures Colorado book, around Breckenridge, Central City, Fraser, Dillon, Vail, Leadville, Georgetown, and Aspen. ISBN-10, 1-930193-11-4; ISBN-13, 978-1-930193-11-6; Price $16.95

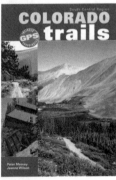

Colorado Trails—South-Central
This edition of our Trails series includes meticulous trail details for 30 off-road routes located near the towns of Gunnison, Salida, Crested Butte, Buena Vista, Aspen, and the Sand Dunes National Monument. ISBN-10, 1-930193-29-7; ISBN-13, 978-1-930193-29-1; Price $16.95

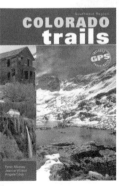

Colorado Trails—Southwest
This field guide is comprised of painstaking details and descriptions for 31 trails, including 15 trails additional to those described in the Adventures Colorado book. Routes are located around Silverton, Ouray, Telluride, Durango, Lake City, and Montrose. ISBN-10, 1-930193-32-7; ISBN-13, 978-1-930193-32-1; Price $19.95

to order
call 800-660-5107 or
visit 4WDbooks.com

backcountry adventures
guides

Each book in the award-winning *Adventures* series listed below is a beautifully crafted, high-quality, sewn, 4-color guidebook. In addition to meticulously detailed backcountry trail directions and maps of every trail and region, extensive information on the history of towns, ghost towns, and regional history is included. The guides provide wildlife information and photographs to help readers identify the great variety of native birds, plants, and animals they are likely to see. This series appeals to everyone who enjoys the backcountry: campers, anglers, four-wheelers, hikers, mountain bikers, snowmobilers, amateur prospectors, sightseers, and more...

Backcountry Adventures Northern California

Backcountry Adventures Northern California takes readers along 2,653 miles of back roads from the rugged peaks of the Sierra Nevada, through volcanic regions of the Modoc Plateau, to majestic coastal redwood forests. Trail history comes to life through accounts of outlaws like Black Bart; explorers like Ewing Young and James Beckwourth; and the biggest mass migration in America's history—the Gold Rush. Contains 152 trails, 640 pages, and 679 photos.
ISBN-10, 1-930193-25-4; ISBN-13, 978-1-930193-25-3
Price, $39.95.

Backcountry Adventures Southern California

Backcountry Adventures Southern California provides 2,970 miles of routes that travel through the beautiful mountain regions of Big Sur, across the arid Mojave Desert, and straight into the heart of the aptly named Death Valley. Trail history comes alive through the accounts of Spanish missionaries; eager prospectors looking to cash in during California's gold rush; and legends of lost mines. Contains 153 trails, 640 pages, and 645 photos.
ISBN-10, 1-930193-26-2; ISBN-13, 978-1-930193-26-0
Price, $39.95.

backcountry adventures
guides

Backcountry Adventures Utah

Backcountry Adventures Utah navigates 3,721 miles through the spectacular Canyonlands region, to the top of the Uinta Range, across vast salt flats, and along trails unchanged since the riders of the Pony Express sped from station to station and daring young outlaws wreaked havoc on newly established stage lines, railroads, and frontier towns. Trail history comes to life through the accounts of outlaws like Butch Cassidy; explorers and mountain men; and early Mormon settlers. Contains 175 trails, 544 pages, and 532 photos.
ISBN-10, 1-930193-27-0; ISBN-13, 978-1-930193-27-7
Price, $39.95.

Backcountry Adventures Arizona

Backcountry Adventures Arizona guides readers along 2,671 miles of the state's most remote and scenic back roads, from the lowlands of the Yuma Desert to the high plains of the Kaibab Plateau. Trail history is colorized through the accounts of Indian warriors like Cochise and Geronimo; trailblazers; and the famous lawman Wyatt Earp. Contains 157 trails, 576 pages, and 524 photos.
ISBN-10, 1-930193-28-9; ISBN-13, 978-1-930193-28-4
Price, $39.95.

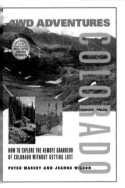

4WD Adventures Colorado

4WD Adventures Colorado takes readers to the Crystal River or over America's highest pass road, Mosquito Pass. This book identifies numerous lost ghost towns that speckle Colorado's mountains. Trail history is brought to life through the accounts of sheriffs and gunslingers like Bat Masterson and Doc Holliday; millionaires like Horace Tabor; and American Indian warriors like Chief Ouray. ains 71 trails, 232 pages, and 209 photos.
ISBN 0-9665675-5-2.
Price, $29.95.

to order
call 800-660-5107 or
visit 4WDbooks.com

other
colorado outdoors
guides

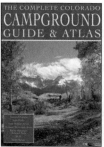

Fishing Close to Home

This book is for anglers who want to spend their time reeling in the big one rather than hours on the road. It provides directions, fishing information, lake size, and more for hot spots near metro Denver, Boulder and Clear Creek Counties. ISBN-10, 0-930657-51-9; ISBN-13, 978-0-930657-51-2; Price $9.95

Colorado Fishing Guide & Atlas

This top-selling guide is the ultimate for any angler looking for new fishing spots in Colorado. It is packed with extensive information on hot spots in Colorado's public lands. It includes directions, detailed maps, information about governing agencies, and insightful comments. ISBN 0-930657-41-1; Price $24.95

Colorado Biking Trails

From urban bike paths to scenic mountain roads, challenging single-track rides to manicured trails, this bike guide has something for everyone. It includes directions to trailheads, maps, trail length, elevation gain, and difficulty for more than 77 trails throughout Colorado. ISBN-10, 0-930657-52-7; ISBN-13, 978-0-930657-52-9; Price $14.95

The Complete Colorado Campground Guide & Atlas

This guide is packed with information about more than 500 campgrounds in Colorado's public lands. It includs directions, regulations and restrictions, fee information, detailed maps, and more. New fully revised eleventh edition. ISBN 0-930657-23-3; Price $19.95

The Best of Colorado 4-Wheel Drive Roads

Whether you are a novice out for the first time or an expert well-versed in off-road driving, there is something in this book for you. Full of detailed maps, directions, and vital information, this guide takes you off the paved roads and into Colorado's scenic backcountry. ISBN 1-930657-40-3; Price $15.95

to order
call 800-660-5107 or
visit 4WDbooks.com

other
colorado outdoors
guides

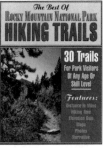

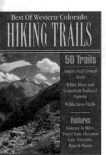

Colorado's Guide to Hunting

Colorado's backcountry is habitat for all sorts of game animals. The guide contains land regulations, permits needed, detailed directions and maps for the best places to hunt. **ISBN 0-930657-42-X; Price $14.95**

Best of Northern Colorado Hiking Trails

Contains 77 trails from short, easy day hikes to difficult backpacking adventures. The book covers Arapaho, Roosevelt, White River, and Routt National Forests. It includes directions, maps, trail length, elevation gains, and difficulty. **ISBN 0-930657-18-7; Price $12.95**

Best of Western Colorado Hiking Trails

Contains 50 trails from short, easy day hikes to difficult backpacking adventures. The book covers White River and Gunnison National Forests. It includes directions, maps, trail length, elevation gains, and difficulty. **ISBN 0-930657-17-9; Price $9.95**

Best of Rocky Mountain National Park Hiking Trails

Contains 30 trails for hikers of all skill levels from short, easy hikes to more difficult trails. It includes camping information, estimated hiking time, trail narratives, directions, maps, trail length, elevation gains, and difficulty. **ISBN 0-930657-39-X; Price $9.95**

Colorado Lakes & Reservoirs: Fishing and Boating Guide

Colorado is home to hundreds of natural and man-made lakes. This book provides information about 150 of them. Included are driving directions, maps, fishing regulations, lake size, fish species, boating ramps, camping facilities, and contact information. **ISBN 0-930657-00-4; Price $14.95**

to order

call 800-660-5107 or
visit 4WDbooks.com